The Holy Vote

The Holy Vote

*Inequality and Anxiety among
White Evangelicals*

Sarah Diefendorf

UNIVERSITY OF CALIFORNIA PRESS

University of California Press
Oakland, California

Library of Congress Cataloging-in-Publication Data

Names: Diefendorf, Sarah H., author.
Title: The holy vote : inequality and anxiety among white
    evangelicals / Sarah Diefendorf.
Description: Oakland, California : University of
    California Press, [2023] | Includes bibliographical
    references and index.
Identifiers: LCCN 2022020935 (print) | LCCN 2022020936
    (ebook) | ISBN 9780520355590 (cloth) |
    ISBN 9780520355606 (paperback) | ISBN
    9780520975958 (ebook)
Subjects: LCSH: Evangelicalism—United States—
    History—21st century. | Equality—United States. |
    Equality—Religious aspects—Christianity. | Anxiety—
    United States. | Anxiety—Religious aspects—
    Christianity. | Christians, White—United States—
    History—21st century. | Christianity and politics—
    United States—History—21st century.
Classification: LCC BR1642.U5 D54 2023 (print) |
    LCC BR1642.U5 (ebook) | DDC 277.308/3—dc23/
    eng/20220906
LC record available at https://lccn.loc.gov/2022020935
LC ebook record available at https://lccn.loc.gov/2022020936

32   31   30   29   28   27   26   25   24   23
10   9   8   7   6   5   4   3   2   1

Contents

Acknowledgments

I've read many book acknowledgments that begin with a similar senti-ment: book writing is anything but an individual process. I always thought this start was a bit trite, but then I tried to write a book. It turns out there is a very good reason why so many begin this process of thanks in a similar way. While we might have a cultural image of book writing as an isolating experience, perhaps locked in an office with a desk piled high with papers and a refusal to interact with the outside world, for me, at least, and indeed it seems many others, that was just not how this process played out. This was and is a gift. As an ethnographer in a career path dictated by research, and a form of research that can often feel quite isolating due to the sheer number of hours in the field and the ethical obligations that require many details of the realities of fieldwork to remain in the head of the researcher, writing this book brought me back into the community that makes me most animated about the profession of sociology. One of the greatest joys of writing this book was working with those whose presence in my life made it possible.

I would first like to thank Naomi Schneider, my editor, who reached out to me about this work in its infancy. Thank you, and the team at UC Press, including Summer Farah and Stephanie Summerhays, for see-ing its potential and ushering this process along so smoothly.

Material in this book appeared previously in 2019 as "Evangelical Responses to Feminism and the Imagined Secular" in *Signs: Journal of*

Women in Culture and Society 44 (4): 1003–26. Chapter 3 of this book is derivative of this original publication in *Signs*.

This book manuscript began as my doctoral dissertation research. I am deeply grateful to my dissertation committee for their support of this work from day one: Sarah Quinn, Julie Brines, Judy Howard, Shirley Yee, and CJ Pascoe. Thank you for your encouragement, humor, and deep commitment to supporting feminist scholarship.

The research that informs this book was generously supported with funding from the Herbert Costner Distinguished Graduate Student Paper Award, the American Sociological Association Martin P. Levine Memorial Dissertation Award, the Pepper Schwartz Endowed Fellowship in Sexuality and Relationships, and the University of Washington Presidential Dissertation Fellowship.

This funding, in part, allowed me the privilege of working with Danielle Nichols and Lilla King, who were remarkable research assistants while undergraduates at UW. Thank you for your contributions to this work.

I am grateful to the rest of my community at the University of Washington that supported this work. To Annie McGlynn-Wright, Patrick Denice, Marco Brydolf-Horwitz, Emily Gade, Victoria Sass, and Steve Karceski, thank you for your support, listening ears, and feedback, which ushered this project through its final dissertation stages; to my lovely cohort mates Ande Reisman, Jenni Branstad, Nicole Kravitz-Wirtz, Angela Bruns, and Kerice Doten; department encouragement from Heather Evans, Hedy Lee, Alexes Harris, Kate Stovel, Becky Pettit, Aimée Dechter, Susan Pitchford, Pepper Schwartz, Emily Knaphus-Soran, Erin Carll, and, last but not least, the UW Gender Group, particularly Christina Hughes, Annie, Angela, Daiki Hiramori, and Connor Gilroy. Cheers to making and sustaining the community we needed.

As I began the task of turning a dissertation into a book manuscript, I benefited greatly from the support of my writing group. Thank you to Melanie Heath, Caity Collins, and CJ Pascoe for your feedback on these chapters. I am so grateful for the online community we created and maintained as we wrote books in various stages at the same time. Your insights are all over these pages.

In addition, I am thankful to the organizers and those in attendance at the University of Utah Political Science Colloquium, the University of Texas at Austin Ethnography Lab, the UT Austin Inequality Working Group, and Fem(me) Sem. Special thanks to Jim Curry, Becky Pettit, and Jennifer Glass for your organizing, support, and feedback.

My postdoctoral fellowship with the Scholars Strategy Network provided me with the time and funding to think through much of this manuscript. And as it entered its first full drafts, I benefited tremendously from the thinking of some of my favorite scholars of religion: Lynne Gerber, Dawne Moon, Gerardo Marti, and Gail Murphy-Geiss.

To my wonderful family, given and chosen, that checked in and supported me throughout this entire process, from the early days of fieldwork to the final book edits: Bob Diefendorf, Anne Diefendorf, Jenn Bégon, Manny Bégon, Diane Adair McDonald, Megan Sheppard, Kristen Veiga McVaugh, Morissa Henn, Jamie Henn, Michael Staley, Brayden Jensen, Nicki Dunnavant, Amy Juneau, Alex Reisman, Erica Reisman, Robin Reisman, Howard Reisman, and Ahmmad Brown. Thank you all for your love. Bowman Dickson: thank you for the hours you spent, listening intently as I verbalized this entire book outline to you while we were deep in the Grand Teton wilderness. Your reflections and creativity meant the world, and this book title is all yours. Diane and Jenn: I am so glad I am not the only book writer in the family. Thank you for your time, edits, and advice on craft. To Spencer, Parker, and Emerson: thank you for the laughter, silliness, and our weekly trips to Hogwarts and Wildwood. You remind me daily what is important. CJ, we talked each other through the figurative up- and down-hills of fieldwork, writing, and life, as well the literal ones; grateful for those long runs, and for what we joke is near-constant communication but for us is just our friendship.

To my partner, Ande. Thank you for your patience, emotional support, commitment to read drafts or listen to my ideas after long days of work, your unwavering confidence in my ability to see this project through, and the countless ways you took care of us and our home so that I had the time to write.

Finally, I remain grateful to everyone at Lakeview Church who was willing to share their world, experiences, fears, and vulnerabilities with an outsider. I hope we can all grow and learn together for a more just world in the years ahead.

CHAPTER I

Good and Godly in Trump's America

On January 22, 2017, the Sunday morning after the inauguration of President Donald Trump, a pastor at a predominantly White evangelical megachurch in the Pacific Northwest looked out onto his congregation with weary eyes. Two large screens on either side of the stage displayed a close-up of his face as he began speaking. Pastor Dave started his sermon: "In the midst of this broken world, I keep envisioning one thing: our church is on the operating table."

Pastor Dave's words suggest a level of vulnerability that we do not often associate with White evangelicals in the United States, especially following the 2016 election of Donald Trump. The pastor's opening statement acknowledges a broken world, but also implies that perhaps the church is part of that brokenness and needs to be repaired too. Pastor Dave elaborated on his first thoughts with, "We are living in a broken world. Sometimes the corrupt is all we see. The election cycle did not help with that!" Some people in the room of 500 or so congregants at this place I call Lakeview Church laughed, and others nodded along. "Those presidential debates were messy . . . but the world is not divided into good and evil."

On this cold January day, the otherwise usually upbeat and smiley pastor seemed distracted and concerned. The 52-year-old White pastor continued his sermon and told his congregation that as a result of the brokenness of the world, he believes that Christians are suffering. Pastor Dave suggested to his congregation that they need to work through this suffering, and learn not to respond to it with ugliness, anger, bitterness, or madness, but "to react in a godly way." Pastor Dave bowed his head and exited the stage.

Pastor Amy replaced Pastor Dave on the large stage. Pastor Amy is an associate pastor at Lakeview church. This job title includes assisting Pastor Dave, as the lead pastor, in religious services and other daily operations of the church. Pastor Amy is a 35-year-old White woman and mother whose young children would often accompany her on stage. This morning, however, Pastor Amy walked slowly to the front of the stage with two heavy, large, green buckets. Pastor Amy lifted each of the two buckets up onto a stool, and the cameras zoomed in on the buckets, bringing them, along with the liquid in each of them, into focus on the screens at the back of the stage. Pastor Amy was wearing a wireless headset and microphone, barely visible under her blonde bob. Pastor Amy raised a large yellow sponge in the air and asked the congregation to identify the object in her hand. When they responded accordingly, Pastor Amy asked, "How do we find out what is inside the sponge?" Before the crowd responded again Pastor Amy excitedly yelled, "Squeeze it!"

Pastor Amy dunked the sponge in the bucket of dark-colored water and then removed it, squeezing it over the bucket for everyone to see. The camera zoomed in on her hands. Pastor Amy held the sponge as black liquid flowed from it. She said, "This is you. We don't like it. This is what the world does when it is hurt or pressed."

Pastor Amy then dipped the sponge in the bucket of clear water and held it up to the crowd before squeezing it again and said, "But here is our challenge. When you're pressed this is what happens. When you're pressed it is rivers of living water that come forth. It's not the suffering that gets us noticed, but how we *react*." Clear water dripped down Pastor Amy's arms as she continued to hold the sponge out above her. The worship team started to quietly play a new song on the stage behind her, and Pastor Amy joined in with the lyrics. She chanted, "I'm trading my sorrows. I'm trading my shame. I'm laying them down for the joy of the Lord . . . " as she vigorously squeezed the remaining clear, or "living," water out of the sponge for all in the room to see.

Pastor Dave returned to the stage to explain the meanings of the demonstrations to the congregation. Pastor Dave turned Pastor Amy's elaborate and metaphorical demonstration into a clearly translated lesson for all watching: that they all need to learn to respond to their suffering without letting any *ugliness* show.

During the two years I spent conducting research at Lakeview Church, it became quite clear that "ugly" was a stand-in for being marked as racist, sexist, or homophobic. Since the emergence of the culture wars in the United States in the 1970s, White evangelicals have come to political power and exuded great cultural influence through battles that privilege and protect the interests of White Christians, and most often White Christian men. Indeed, the lived experiences of White Christian men and women are often synonymous with, and the default category for, what is understood to be American (Marti 2020). Now, religious affiliation is declining across the United States. Younger generations feel more abstract and unknown than ever as the social landscape shifts dramatically with the legalization of same-sex marriage, the Black Lives Matter movement, and the #MeToo movement, to name a few. The suffering the church perceives is directly tied to the status loss around White Christian manhood, and what it might mean for their long-standing cultural projects if many in the United States are unwilling to accept these identities as a default experience and, perhaps even worse for the church, unwilling to support the organizations that continue to protect these identities as a top priority.

Three months prior to Pastor Dave's sermon, Donald Trump and Hillary Clinton engaged in three presidential candidate debates that quickly became known for their unprecedented hostility. The *New York Times* referred to the debates as a "90-minute spectacle of character attacks." Clinton referenced the leaked tape recorded in 2005 in which Trump referred to his ability to grope women because of his fame. Trump repeatedly brought up accusations that President Bill Clinton was abusive toward women, and that Hillary Clinton was also responsible for attacking those same women. Trump said, on air, that Hillary Clinton had "tremendous hate in her heart" and infamously referred to her as a "nasty woman," which became the rallying cry and self-identification for many who organized against Trump. In her book a year later, Hillary Clinton referred to the debates as experiences in which her "skin crawled." Pastor Dave and many at Lakeview Church acknowledge the "messiness" of those debates while appearing to avoid taking a side. For a group of people who believe quite strongly in the binaries of sinner/savior, and heaven/hell, they recognize that, at the intersections of their religious beliefs, their political beliefs, and their own perceived need for change and growth, thinking in binary terms, or, in this case, "good and evil," doesn't really work. Instead, Pastor Dave and Lakeview Church see themselves *in* the messiness of those debates.

How do White evangelicals reconcile a need to grow and retain members in a rapidly changing social environment in which their beliefs, and by extension their own sense of self, might be understood or labeled as "ugly"? What does it mean to react to this perceived suffering in a way that is, according to pastors Dave and Amy, godly and good, and what needs to happen on the metaphorical operating table for this to happen? How the church wrestles with these questions and navigates its responses is at the heart of this book.

This book documents the vulnerability, anxiety, and confusion that White evangelicals profess as they work to re-create themselves as good and godly, and to avoid being marked as ugly. I show how White evangelicals negotiate their personal beliefs around questions of gender, the family, race, and sexuality alongside the larger goals of the church of which they are a part. This book uncovers the ways in which a mega-church and its congregants seek to grow their membership and, by logical extension, hold on to their cultural status. I illustrate the ways in which these goals work in tandem with continued White evangelical support for conservative politics, a long-standing relationship that continues to shape the social, cultural, and political landscape of the United States.

. . .

I entered Lakeview Church for the first time in late fall 2015, with the goal of documenting the ways in which White evangelicals were debating questions related to gender and sexuality, especially after the federal legalization of same-sex marriage in June 2015. However, in the two years I spent at Lakeview Church, the political landscape shifted around me.

On November 8, 2016, a year into my fieldwork, I found myself among those who reportedly voted Donald Trump into office. I was already documenting the daily life, rituals, and debates of Lakeview Church, many of which were related to gender, sexuality, the family, and questions about the state of the church in a nation perceived to be in a cultural moment of great upheaval and change. The goals of my initial research project that brought me to Lakeview, then, are different, and smaller, than the goals of this book. But they are connected.

White evangelicals are willing to work to change with the times in an effort to uphold their cultural relevance, especially around questions and beliefs related to gender, sexuality, and the White family. However, these changes come with increased anxiety and feelings of confusion and resentment. And these changes often reflect the goals of the church instead of the concerns for the livelihood of others, as church members and the organizations of which they are a part work to reconcile an ugly past while appealing to younger generations for a more sustainable future as a church.

To both illustrate and complicate this idea of change among White evangelicals, this book is oriented around a concept I call the *imagined secular*. I find that evangelicals at Lakeview talk about a range of liberal projects: topics like feminism, trans rights, reproductive justice, "deviant" sexuality, and the Black Lives Matter movement. The imagined secular encapsulates what White evangelicals imagine these liberal projects to be and shapes their responses to them. Importantly, the imagined secular holds the feelings associated with these cultural changes in the United States as the church seeks to respond to and understand their own beliefs in relation to these topics. Conversations, debates, and concerns about the imagined secular occur among members in small groups within the church and are openly discussed by the pastoral team in Sunday sermons. These conversations encapsulate the very messiness to which Pastor Dave alludes, and they also show the church's proverbial hand, as the content of these debates identifies what the church thinks it needs to engage with to be understood as good. In order to not be understood, or marked, as sexist, the church needs to talk about feminism. To avoid the label of racist, they need to talk about Black Lives Matter. And to no longer be homophobes, the church needs to reconcile its position in response to the federal legalization of same-sex marriage.

The White evangelical church is facing dual projects: it needs to continue to grow its membership, and it needs to work to grow during a time in which rapid cultural shifts are illuminating the inequalities that form the pillars on which the church is built. In an effort to accomplish both of these intertwined goals—to appear welcoming and increase membership among younger generations—the church provides a space for the messy, varied responses to the components of the imagined secular world. However, I document the ways in which the church also engages in a *bounded welcoming* of components of the imagined secular: the church entertains conversations about feminism, Black Lives Matter, and same-sex marriage, but Lakeview Church is an organization governed by hierarchies of gender, race, and sexuality; as such, the church engages with the imagined secular as an organization in a way that allows for (and, really, encourages) inequalities to endure. *How* they respond to the imagined secular sheds light on the ways in which conservative politics endure even in the midst of engagement with these mass cultural movements and shifts.

This book documents how the church and its congregants claim feminism as part of the church's beliefs while upholding gendered inequalities, how they reconcile and also reinforce White nationalist tendencies with the need to now reach across racial lines, and how evangelicals retain a privileged position around reinforcements of a heterosexual Christian family while jettisoning some of their former associations with homophobia. The church is finding a way to respond to the "suffering" that it perceives, and it is doing so, in line with the advice of Pastor Amy, without letting its "ugliness" show. But the individual engagement with the imagined secular reflects what I call an instrumental acceptance (chapter 4) and forced excitement (chapter 6) of these cultural shifts, paying lip service to the ideas and ideals that challenge the foundations of the church while also simultaneously retaining power central to the intersections of whiteness, Christianity, masculinity, and heterosexuality.

In Trump, White evangelicals found a politician who could help them with this project, someone who could do the ugly work for them to maintain the status quo, halt progressive change, and defend their faith while they continue to wrestle with a host of questions about their collective identity. The evangelicals at Lakeview Church did not necessarily vote for Donald Trump because of what he stands for. Rather, in many ways, Trump symbolizes his own type of wall that can hold the imagined secular at bay while the church regroups during a period of time in which its feels as though it is quickly losing cultural sway, especially among younger generations. Indeed, to Make America Great Again is to uphold a history of white supremacy and Christian nationalism, and to Keep America Great is to ensure that no one else receives access to the privileges long afforded White Christian Americans. Trump and his policies can publicly enforce what many White evangelicals would rather support in private. Trump represented one politician ready to support and manifest a White evangelical political and cultural project, but he is not the first or the last.

Lakeview Church is located in the Pacific Northwest; as such, this research moves the focus on White evangelical support for Trump out of the geographic South—out of the working-class, disillusioned communities who voted for him, as Arlie Hochschild (2016a) documents, because they feel they have lost their spot in line for the American Dream. Instead, this research centers those who embody the American Dream, and also voted for Trump. I investigate the "coastal elites": the middle- and upper-middle-class suburban White evangelicals who live in one of the areas of the United States with the best quality of life, and who don't want to lose it. This work expands our understandings of the enduring relationship between White evangelism and conservative politics by asking these questions in an area of the country where such a relationship is often presumed irrelevant.

To explore the intersections of White evangelicals' fear of cultural loss and the ways in which they reconcile that fear with a need to expand and grow as an organization, I utilize sociological theories of religion and feminist theories of religion and agency. Many of the very mechanisms that allow White evangelicals to remain an active and thriving religious group in a country with declining religiosity help explain some of their support for Trump.

RELIGION IN THE UNITED STATES

A variety of measures document declines in US religiosity (Schnabel and Bock 2017, 2018; Voas and Chaves 2016). White protestants have declined from 37% of all US adults to 29% between 2009 and 2019. However, of this group, White, born-again evangelicals have experienced the slowest rate of decline, such that they now make up a larger share of those who are White protestants in the United States, totaling 56% in 2019 (Pew 2019). Although Americans are increasingly likely to *not* identify with a religious group, White evangelical Christians remain a prominent force in this changing landscape; the most intensely religious remain firm in their beliefs (Schnabel and Bock 2018). While White evangelicals are maintaining their base more successfully than other religious groups, a decline is a decline. Pastor Dave and the members of Lakeview Church might be experiencing exaggerated feelings about this decline, but it is the existence of those feelings themselves that matters for our understandings of their current beliefs, practices, and goals.

This religious decline is especially evident among younger populations. Recent data from the General Social Survey finds that for those under the age of 30 in the United States, 37% of men and 34% of women do not identify with a religious affiliation, which represents a consistent decline for men and an over 6% increase for the rate of decline for women in two years (Smith et al. 2019).[1] In 2019, the Pew Research Center found that 40% of Millennials are religiously unaffiliated, a 13-percentage-point decline between 2009 and 2019 (Pew 2019).

The continued monitoring of these shifts and years of research on these questions reflect larger theoretical debates in the sociology of religion: that is, just how "secular" or "religious" is the United States, and why does it matter?

Sociologists understand churches, synagogues, mosques—places of religious worship—in the United States to be examples of social organizations, bounded places wherein individuals learn certain norms and values that help them to navigate the world around them, to make sense of their surroundings, to provide meaning to their day-to-day experiences, and to feel a sense of belonging. The ways in which religious organizations help socialize individuals have been the subject of decades of work, ranging in topic from the relationship between religious affiliation and mental health, to the frequency of drinking, sexual activity, educational outcomes, and numerous others. For many in the United States, and across the world, religious spaces matter in helping to understand individual and collective social life.

However, there is quite a bit more debate regarding the bounds of the reach of the church as an influencing body. What happens when individuals walk out the door of their place of worship? And what happens when religious beliefs come into conflict with the tides of social upheaval and change?

Many scholars predicted that the remnants and results of the twin processes of industrialization and modernization, such as the vast social changes in the United States from the 1950s to 1970s, would result in a decline in the significance of religion in public life. This line of work theorizes that, in the wake of modernization, religion and religious life wane. For example, Peter Berger (1967) provides a conceptual model of a religious "sacred canopy" that sustains a distinct worldview and envelops and protects its members from "anomic chaos and terror" (Smith 1998:106). However, this protection fails during times of change; Berger argues that the sacred canopy is "torn apart" by modernity, providing his readers with a vivid image of the seemingly destructive forces that the ticking of time might have on religious life.

Religion has not disappeared from the United States, even in the wake of great social change. While the United States has experienced marked shifts in collective religious life throughout the history of the nation, it seems that Berger's work fails to encapsulate the idea that religion, religious life, and "modern" society can coexist.[2]

Other scholars have theorized the continued presence of religion in public life in the United States. Some suggest that religious groups, such as evangelicals, continue to flourish by many measures in the United States because they thrive on *distinction*. Evangelicals might hold on to certain beliefs precisely because they are one of the few markers that distinguish them from nonevangelicals (see both Gallagher 2003 and Smith 1998 for overviews of this theoretical perspective). This distinction can provide meaning for the group and sustain it during times of change.

This language of distinction might be misleading, though. Craig Calhoun (Calhoun, Juergensmeyer, and VanAntwerpen 2011) argues that thinking about the religious and the secular as distinct assumes a false dichotomy. Calhoun suggests we think of the process of increased secularization as a presence that affects religion, religious life, and American culture broadly (2011:335). And Lynne Gerber (2011) argues that American [secular] culture is also a locus of evangelical identity formation, and even aspiration. Secularization is not something that is left behind when religion declines, and religion is not merely reactionary to the ways of the secular world.

The ways in which both religious and secular communities mutually influence and constitute each other is especially clear when we look at empirical work on understandings of sexuality and gender. A variety of scholarship finds that White evangelical identity is often constructed in relation to perceptions of secular ideals. For example, John Bartkowski studied evangelical men involved in the Promise Keepers movement, a movement known for its efforts to reclaim and put forth a new definition and practice of masculinity for evangelical men. Bartkowski (2004) documents the ways in which men involved with the Promise Keepers work to create a "godly masculinity" that is understood in relation to a secular masculinity. Bartkowski analyzes Promise Keepers advice manuals from the 1980s and early 1990s to show that leaders within the Promise Keepers movement worked to promote an array of godly masculinities that did not advance a singular notion of manhood, but rather contained four archetypes that allowed the group to understand and define themselves in relation to changing notions of gender in the United States at the time.

In her research on Christian sexuality websites, Kelsy Burke (2016) documents the ways in which evangelicals construct a new sexual logic around "godly sex." Burke illustrates the ways in which evangelical Christians debate and support one another in their questions, concerns, and commitments to various sexual practices, and how they do so while both maintaining their evangelical faith and demonstrating their knowledge of, and interactions with, contemporary secular values about sex.

In my previous work on evangelical men who pledge sexual abstinence until marriage, I show how young men construct a sacred sexuality against what they understand to be a beastly sexuality of the secular world (Diefendorf 2015). And in her research on evangelical Christians and their beliefs about gay marriage, Dawne Moon finds that the "church was not separate from secular life, but a place where people went, in part, to learn how to be better persons in the secular world" (2004:4). When studying evangelicals, we must account for this interplay between religious and secular beliefs, the malleability, and the moments of tension and compromise. Religious groups may thrive, not because of their distance from, or even accommodations to, processes of secularization, but rather because of a direct engagement with the world outside of the church.

In foundational work on contemporary evangelical life, Christian Smith (1998) suggests that a religious movement that unites both clear cultural distinction *and* intense social engagement will be capable of thriving in the modern world. Smith argues that religious groups have always found ways to reformulate their orthodoxies to best engage with the changing social landscape they face. As such, groups that are better at constructing these distinct identities, and doing so in times of change, will grow in size and strength, whereas those who have difficulty will grow relatively weaker.

One of the ways that social groups, and indeed religious groups, provide their members with these distinct identities and meaning is by supplying them with a "moral orientation" to understand their own lives and the world in which they live (Smith 1998:90). Oftentimes, the construction of this moral orientation is done against a selected referent out-group. Another way of saying this is that social groups know who they are in large measure by knowing who they are not (Smith 1998).

Religious groups can continue to grow and fortify their strength through the tensions and conflicts between them and other groups (Smith 1998). These groups, whether real or imagined, can be understood as *external threats* that help build internal solidarity. Through engagement with these groups, these perceived threats, and identity-building in relation to them, evangelicals can thrive (Smith 1998).

White evangelicals might thrive because they are quite good at creating these in- and out-group boundaries and because, as a collective, they have the ability to "sustain the articulation of the tradition's essential orthodoxy in a reformulated way appropriate for their given context" (Smith 1998:101). However, as our contemporary theoretical and empirical work on religion shows, we must critically interrogate the presumed divides between religious and secular life in the United States today. That is, how "external" is this threat off of which evangelicals understand and maintain their own group identity? If there is considerable overlap, or at least engagement, with the secular world "outside" of evangelical communities, what is established as an external threat, and how do evangelicals debate values and ideals that require engagement on the part of the church? If we pay attention to both what gets defined as an external other and what elements of secular life require intense engagement and debate, we can better uncover and complicate the larger meanings associated with what Smith calls this identity work.

Smith suggests that it is precisely this engagement with external threats—indeed, what he calls an "embattlement" with these external threats—that results in continued solidarity for the religious group. As Smith states, "There is nothing quite like an outside threat or enemy to bring people together, make them set aside their internal differences, and increase their dedication and loyalty to the group" (1998:114). I suggest, however, that there are many steps between an identification of an external threat and group cohesion. If evangelical and secular worlds are not separate, but rather mutually influence each other while remaining somewhat distinct, we can picture them in a somewhat constant dance around questions of culture and society crucial to our contemporary moment. And we can imagine that this constant dance, of engaging with the world to remain relevant and grow, requires quite a bit of work. This work is not necessarily linear or uniform, and as Pastor Dave alluded to in his Sunday sermon following the presidential inauguration of 2017, this work can cause quite a bit of anxiety and tension and feelings of vulnerability. If we are able to capture both what is defined as an external threat and how these threats are engaged with on a day-to-day basis, we can uncover a much more nuanced picture of how White evangelicals understand their place in the social world, and how this understanding has larger implications for their continued support for conservative politics.

The concept of the imagined secular world helps to capture the ways in which the evangelicals at Lakeview internalize these external threats. It captures the messy process through which they discuss these threats and the debates, rearticulations, and decisions around what requires engagement and what does not. I approach this work with the theoretical assumption that White evangelical Christians have held their place in the modern social landscape of the United States by interacting with, and reformulating their orthodoxies in (at least partial) accordance with, the secular landscape of which they are a part, but I argue that this process of reformulation includes many steps before reaching the goal of group solidarity. And this work of internalizing external threats might maintain not only group solidarity and perseverance but inequality as well.

The imagined secular, this bundle of external threats, represents the fights and ideas that challenge the lives and privileges of white, middle- and upper-middle-class straight evangelicals. This work shows how this group of individuals endeavors to construct and maintain their status as *not ugly*—as good and, in many ways, even as unseen, as normal. The changing terrain of life in the United States threatens to mark this group as intolerant at best, and the organization to which they belong as racist, sexist, and homophobic at worst. And many in the United States have long thought of White evangelicals in this way. White evangelicals are not neutral or passive subjects in this equation, beholden without power to the labels they increasingly receive. But I write about their *own* feelings and perceptions of their cultural position as increasingly under threat, as these beliefs are fundamental to their continued alignment with conservative politics.

White evangelicals want to retain the authority and privileges that have always come hand in hand with being members of a dominant racialized, classed, and religious organization in the United States, and this work centers both the everyday practices and beliefs of members of Lakeview Church, and the organization (and organization's goals) of which they are a part.

WHAT IT MEANS TO BE AN EVANGELICAL

The term "evangelical" is a contested one. Its meaning has adapted throughout its history in the United States, and the people who identify with the term change, too. Evangelical does not represent one denomination or a single tradition. There is no pope who reinforces a single definition or set of beliefs. There is not a website full of resources or a unified governing body that articulates an overarching mission statement. Rather, it is a movement that has found its home in a variety of denominations across the United States and globally, with a central focus on the renewal of Christianity. There is, however, a commonality and shared sense of understanding in the use of the term that leaves many invigorated by it and others wanting to disassociate from the term altogether, especially following the 2016 presidential election.

In October 2017, the Princeton Evangelical Fellowship, a student organization that had, at that point, existed for over eighty years, officially changed its name to the Princeton Christian Fellowship. The group director cited concerns about "baggage" about what evangelical means. In an interview for *Christianity Today,* Kara Powell, the executive director of the Fuller Youth Institute,[3] commented that she did not see this title change as a negative move, and, instead, would "be more concerned if organizations who were moving away from the term evangelical were moving away from what it means to *be* evangelical" (Shellnut 2017, emphasis mine).

What it means in practice to be an evangelical varies, but I use the definition relied on by many other scholars to give clarity to the group in focus in this book. Following Bebbington's (1989), Noll's (2001), and Wellman's (2008) articulations, I use evangelical in this text as the umbrella term for conservative Christians in the United States. I focus on evangelical Protestants in this book, those who represent a fairly homogenous political bloc (Wellman 2008). This broad group shares four core tenets of faith: (1) a belief in the importance of Christ's sacrifice on the cross as atonement for human sin; (2) a belief that the Bible is the literal word of God; (3) the importance of individual decision-making to convert to follow Jesus Christ; and (4) missionary activity centered on the importance of such conversion, in other words, getting other people to follow Jesus Christ, too (Bebbington 1989; Noll 2001; Wellman 2008). In more succinct terms, Thomas Kidd (2019) defines evangelicals as "born-again Protestants who cherish the Bible as the Word of God and who emphasize a personal relationship with Jesus Christ through the Holy Spirit."

Writer Jonathan Merritt (2015) quipped of the meaning of evangelical, "To the pollster, it is a sociological term. To the pastor, it is a denominational or doctrinal term. And to the politician, it is a synonym for a White Christian Republican." For our purposes, it is indeed a combination of all three: a term that means something specific to members of Lakeview Church in their beliefs and practices, a term that carries with it sociological significance as many White evangelicals occupy organizations and institutions that carry and enforce cultural sway in the larger social landscape, and a term that symbolizes, reflects, and continues to uphold a very specific political history in the United States.

LAKEVIEW CHURCH

I documented this anxiety, the negotiations about what it currently means to be an evangelical (and, really, a White evangelical), and what

Pastor Dave perhaps nicely encapsulated as the "messiness" of this current moment, during two years of fieldwork at a place I call Lakeview Church.

Inside Lakeview, the two main foyers of the church bustle before Sunday services. In one area, congregants gather in front of tables where small groups advertise their meetings and mission trips display photographs as part of their fundraising efforts. Others skip these tables entirely and head straight for the donut wall, where about 100 wooden pegs protrude from a wall and hold three to four donuts each. Individuals grab donuts just as fast as the high school volunteers can replace them on the pegs, and then many often head into the second foyer and stand in line for a latte at International Java. Volunteers work behind the counters at the registers and as baristas, moving quickly below large banners that hang from the ceiling with photos that depict smiling children of color outside of the United States. All proceeds from International Java go directly to Lakeview's international mission trips. For those who just want coffee, there are multiple stands set up at all entrances to Lakeview, where individuals can fill Styrofoam cups before entering the sanctuary.

The sanctuary at Lakeview seats 1000 individuals. There are seven separate entrances to the sanctuary, and an individual greeter is stationed at each set of doors to pass out Lakeview's weekly bulletin to all of its members. The weekly bulletin advertises many facets of Lakeview's community life, including upcoming church events, small groups that are accepting new members, community service opportunities, youth groups, volunteer opportunities in the church, ways to contribute financially to the church, mission trips, Lakeview's social media presence, and information about children's summer camps. On the back page of the weekly bulletin, Lakeview provides space to take notes on the Sunday sermons. Sometimes, this space includes an outline of the sermon to come. The weekly bulletin and church's social media presence reflect the highly curated and hip brand of the church, with identical fonts, consistent color schemes, and graphic icons that depict and distinguish small groups by types.

Lakeview was founded in the 1970s and still exists in the same building today. Lakeview Church is a member of the Foursquare denomination. Harvard Chaplain Janelle Ibaven describes Foursquare evangelicals, jokingly, as "Pentecostals with a seat-belt on" (Harvard University 2018).[4] In the spectrum of evangelical denominations, we might understand those who belong to Foursquare as among the more conservative, but not quite as socially and politically conservative as most Pentecostals. Lakeview is one of 1600 Foursquare churches in the United States and one of 66,000 Foursquare churches worldwide. Lakeview's membership in this denominational network makes it a bit more representative of a more "typical" megachurch than other stand-alone nondenominational churches across the country.

The church's campus is sprawling, with massive parking lots, and a multistoried structure that is the compilation of many additions over the building's 50-year history. In the spring, cherry trees bloom and cover the building's boundaries in blankets of pink. Children often play tag outside in the mornings, running through the trees as their parents encourage them to come indoors. Teenagers congregate by the northern entrance to the building, and a group of young men usually toss around a football in the parking lot to the dismay of incoming drivers. Police officers are present on Sundays to ensure the easy flow of exit traffic at the end of each service, of which there are three every Sunday. Small buses crowd the roundabout at the entrance for ease in dropping off local senior citizens for the services.

A particular rhythm guides Sunday services: for the first twenty minutes, the worship team, a band of individual musicians that varies in size each week, leads the congregation in song and prayer. The pastoral team usually stands with their families in the front rows to worship during this part of the service. The lyrics to each song are projected onto a large screen behind the stage. A series of church announcements follows the worship songs before the lead pastor comes up onto the stage and the Sunday sermon begins. The lead pastor wears a wireless headset and microphone and uses a tablet to refer to notes for their sermon. A group of people operates a sound board at the back of the room, and another group of people operates cameras that project the lead pastor onto large screens behind the stage. Often, the images on the screen toggle between live views of the pastor, slides that include bullet points, Bible verses,[5] phrases from the Sunday sermon, and graphic designs that in some way relate to the theme of the sermon for the day. For example, during a sermon series titled "Jonah" an image appeared on the screen of a man on a wooden boat, floating on bright teal water above the outline of a massive whale just below.

Lakeview Church is located in a suburban city in the Pacific Northwest. Lakeview is home to a majority White, economically and generationally diverse congregation of about 1500 members, qualifying it as a megachurch.[6] About 15% of the congregants at Lakeview Church do not identify as White,[7] which makes Lakeview Church about as diverse as the evangelical community that makes up the state of Washington. Evangelicals in Washington state are 84% White, 5% Black, 5% Latino and 1% Asian, and 5% Other/Mixed according to Pew's Religious Landscape Survey from 2014. A note about race: I identify the racial and ethnic identification of each person described in this book; but, when I use the term "White evangelical" frequently in my analysis in this text, it is to reflect the goals of an organization defined by Whiteness that seeks to promote the needs and concerns of White people over others, a key reason why inequalities endure in this space. This is the subject matter of chapter 4.

Evangelicals in Washington State are more highly educated than evangelicals across the country (Pew 2015a), and Lakeview Church reflects these higher rates of education. Every person interviewed in this work completed at least some college. In comparison, this is true for only 35% of evangelicals across the United States (Pew 2015a). These levels of education, combined with the types of employment reported by those I spoke with at Lakeview, suggest that Lakeview's congregation reflects a highly educated, majority middle- and upper-middle-class population typical of the Coastal Pacific Northwest. Members of the Lakeview community work in the technology industry, in software and graphic design, in human resources, in the military, in engineering, and as nurses, social workers, and lawyers, and some work for Lakeview Church itself.

With its Sunday morning routines, bustling halls, and full weekly schedules, Lakeview represents one of many majority-White evangelical churches in the United States today. And the demographic makeup of the church body, as reflected in their racial and socioeconomic composition, makes notions of an unmarked identity both plausible and attainable. That is, this church body reflects the mythical substance of the American Dream: White, well-off suburbanites who are good people who work hard, own their homes, and go to church on Sundays—an existence that has been rendered normal, moral, and right for so many years by the most powerful in the United States that they are just for the first time questioning how any part of their beliefs or worldview could be ugly.

Capturing Agency, Malleability, and Qualifying Change

I conducted just over two years of ethnographic fieldwork at Lakeview Church between late fall 2015 and early winter 2018. I began my data collection by attending Sunday services and attending a small group for adults within the church that I call Disciples' Journey. Disciples' Journey was founded in 2014, just the year before I began fieldwork at Lakeview. Disciples' Journey was broadly defined as an adult support group, and what I came to realize during my time with them was that this was a group in which adults worked together to understand their multifaceted lives as evangelicals: as family members, husbands and wives, followers of Jesus, church members, parents, coworkers, and friends. Four of the group members spent three years developing a curriculum, titled "Pathways," that they wanted to implement in all general small groups at Lakeview. If successful at Lakeview, they hoped to then sell the curriculum to other churches. Disciples' Journey members became the beta testers for this curriculum.

Disciples' Journey as a group, along with its individual members, represents a *data outcropping* (Luker 2010), a case or set of cases that is reasonably representative of the larger phenomenon I sought to investigate. A small group in which men and women engaged in dialogue and debate and support over issues, concerns, and questions related to evangelical life was a methodologically appropriate venue through which to investigate how evangelicals work to shift their beliefs in light of larger cultural shifts.

In addition, I follow other feminist religious scholarship that questions a gendered assumption of agency in religious spaces. As John Bartkowksi states, academics have often assumed that "women who join conservative religious groups are unwitting accomplices in their own oppression" (2004:17). Instead, Orit Avishai (2008) suggests that we frame women's participation in religious organizations as an agentic "doing" of religion. I situate and represent the voices, experiences, and actions of both women and men equally in this work, and a group setting in which men and women are actively debating each other is a good place to begin such an empirical endeavor.

Small groups become an interactional space through which new ideas and debates emerge, and through which a sense of community is forged within the larger organization. However, small groups are not always reflective of the content and messages of larger Sunday sermons, or of the beliefs of the institution and all of the people who belong to it. For this reason and many others, sociologists differentiate analyses between individual agency and the larger organizations and institutions within which individuals operate. Many social theorists have found ways to account for both the importance of individual action and the power of larger social organizations, in this case the church (see Bourdieu 1977, 1991; Giddens 1984; and Habermas 1987). This distinction becomes especially important when we look to measure or ask questions about social change. That is, while I started this research with Disciples' Journey intentionally, I cannot assume that the debates occurring in that space are either unique *or* a result of the larger space in which they occur. I follow the work of sociologists of gender (Pascoe 2011; Schippers 2007), sexuality (Carpenter and DeLamater 2012; Luker 2007), religion (Smith 1998), and race (Ray 2019) that suggest that we must capture individual, interactional, and organizational and institutional aspects in our methodological design in order to adequately address this interplay between individual life and the larger social structures of which we are all a part, and indeed, often constrained by. To understand the bounds of the external threats that White evangelicals currently face, and their relationship to this political and religious moment, we must pay attention to the many arenas in which these external threats are created, contested, and maintained. I expanded my research outside of Disciples' Journey to attend to these multiple levels of analysis.

Levels of Analysis

Interactional

Disciples' Journey often devoted meetings to issues of gender, sexuality, and the family, so observations of this group provided insight into the ways in which church members debated these issues outside of Sunday sermons. I conducted participant observation at Disciples' Journey to better understand the ways in which meanings were produced interactionally in this space. As Dawne Moon reflected in her work on evangelical debates around sexuality, "In church debates I found people committed to articulating their beliefs, to seeking shared moral ground— much more so than in many secular debates. By articulating to one another their logics, members reveal their grounding assumptions, allowing us to refine our understanding of what is at stake in such debates" (2004:5). Further, and importantly, religious beliefs depend on individual religious believers to reproduce them (Berger 1967; Moon 2004), and in only focusing on the content of Sunday sermons, researchers potentially deny "that members are thinking and communicating people who learn from a variety of sources, including one another" (Moon 2004:13; Dillon 1999). My interactional observations at Disciples' Journey largely formed my understanding of White evangelical debates today, and provided greater nuance and detail to the content of

Lakeview's Sunday sermons. At times, these observations also contradicted the content of the Sunday sermons. The time I spent with Disciples' Journey helped inform the rest of my methodological approach to the church. And while these small-group observations provided rich interactional data for this work, I also wanted to capture both the individual beliefs of congregants and the organizational messages put forth by the church leadership.

Individual

I spent over a year attending both Disciples' Journey and Sunday sermons before I asked congregants attending the small group for individual interviews. After 16 months of fieldwork, Lakeview offered to put my interview request on the weekly bulletin, which is distributed at Sunday sermons. This interview request ran for three months over summer 2017. These interviews introduced me to the larger church community, where I was otherwise just another body attending a large Sunday sermon. I conducted individual, semistructured interviews with 36 members of Lakeview Church, with attention to the sample regarding the representation of gender, age, marital status, and race/ethnicity. I recruited additional members of the church for interviews via snowball sampling. These interviews lasted between one hour and two hours and 20 minutes and were recorded for transcription and analysis.

I also interviewed 10 evangelical dating and married couples to investigate the ways in which men and women bring gendered messages from the small group and the church to a heterosexual partnership. Five of these individuals were also members of Disciples' Journey, so I conducted interviews with 41 different people in total. Couples were recruited for interviews from Disciples' Journey and via the announcement that went out in the weekly bulletin. These interviews typically lasted longer than the individual interviews and ranged in duration between two hours and two hours and 50 minutes.

As Nancy Ammerman puts it, "People use words in all sorts of ways to trace the contours of their social worlds and make the links to spiritual life" (2016:88). These interviews allowed me to learn more about individuals' sense of their own social worlds and their individual voices and beliefs outside of group settings. As such, I was able to hold space in this work for the "lived religion sensibilities" of everyday life outside of the church (Ammerman 2016). The lived religion practiced on a given day can often stand in contrast to the prescribed beliefs and practices of the religious institution (Ammerman 2006, 2016; Hall 1997; McGuire 2008).

This interview data, combined with the data collected by observing Disciples' Journey, also helps to account for concerns about a religious congruence fallacy. This fallacy results from assuming that religious beliefs are consistent, that religious beliefs represent a clear and consistent set of values, that an individual's actions result from those values, and that these beliefs and values are constantly held across one's lifespan (Chaves 2010). Instead, to document the "messiness" that Pastor Dave discusses, this work accounts for the fact that messiness in (and out of) religious spaces exists. In other words, this work does not presume that attendance and membership at a White evangelical megachurch automatically signifies a clear set of beliefs and practices; rather, it seeks to disrupt that notion entirely.

Organizational

I attended weekly Sunday sermons at Lakeview for two years, where I documented the context of sermons, the interactions between congregants, the leadership style of pastors, and other day-to-day details of church life. During Sunday services, I took notes on the content of the sermons and overall themes and events that occurred. I did not record any identifiable information about congregants in attendance. I also conducted observation at church-sanctioned events, such as barbeques, prayer meetings, holiday pageants, and parishioner-specific events, like weekend women's luncheons.

In analyzing the content of sermon data, the words of the leadership team, and the organizational makeup of the church structure, I was able to document the gendered (Acker 1992; Connell 1987, 2006; Martin 2004; Pascoe 2011; Risman 2004), racialized (Mueller 2017; Ray 2019), and sexualized (Jackson 2006; Kitzinger, Wilkinson, and Perkins 1992; Pascoe 2011) components of the organization; the ways in which resources and rules are connected to the ideologies of the organization (Ray 2019), and the ways practices, meanings, and actions maintain inequalities, or what Joan Acker (2006) calls their *inequality regimes.*

Lakeview Church also creates podcasts; the team that manages the sound board records the three Sunday sermons and edits them to produce one final audio version, available in podcast format for those who cannot attend services in person, or who would like to revisit the message of the week. I listened to these podcasts for the entirety of my time in the field and continued to listen online for a year after my fieldwork concluded.

These observations provided me with a nuanced and detailed understanding of many aspects of the life of the church. They also helped me document the changing life of the organization, in its subtle and more obvious forms. For example, during my time at Lakeview, I witnessed small shifts in how things like homosexuality and same-sex marriage were discussed. These subtle shifts in language were captured due to the longevity of my time in the field and are an important part of the story of the church. I also captured the changing life of the organization in its more obvious forms by witnessing a pastoral transition during my time in the field, when Pastor Dave replaced Pastor Isaac in fall 2016.

To protect the confidentiality of my field site and the research participants in this study, the data I present in the chapters to come has been edited to include pseudonyms and reflect changes to identifiable information and details shared with me or observed about others. In a few cases, to protect parishioners' identities, I have created composite personae (Hochschild 1979; Moon 2004).

As a White, feminine-presenting woman, I am afforded a certain level of invisibility in a predominantly White megachurch. Each week, I wore fitted jeans with boots or flats, a business-casual blouse with a high neckline, and, depending on the temperature, a cardigan or a scarf. I would blow dry and straighten my shoulder-length hair, accessorize my clothing with a necklace and earrings, and wear very light eye-makeup. I mirrored what other women my age wore to church events, but this mirroring did not really alter what would otherwise be my day-to-day appearance. I provide a lengthy discussion of my approach to the field in the methodological appendix, with specific attention to the ways I navigated my own positionality.

Ethnographic fieldwork is at its best simultaneously scientific, creative, and ambitious (Nippert-Eng 2015), and allows for an in-depth understanding of a group, institution, or culture. This research, along with my methodological approach to the questions at hand, documents the on-the-ground mechanisms, debates, and divides that work to shape this multifaceted but enduring relationship between evangelism and conservative politics in the United States.

This book documents the vulnerability, anxiety, and confusion that come with the identification and debate around the imagined secular, and how the debates around the imagined secular allow White evangelicals to re-create themselves as good and godly and to avoid being marked as ugly. In chapter 2, I provide a brief history of White evangelicals in the United States to set the stage for understanding the imagined secular. Each subsequent chapter explores a different element of the imagined secular: the feminist (chapter 3), the Black activist and racial justice (chapter 4), and the dual threats of uncontained heterosexuality (chapter 5) and homosexuality (chapter 6). These chapters show how the church balances its goals of growth with anxieties about being understood or marked as ugly, alongside the process of a bounded welcoming that allows both for the appearance of change in doctrine and for protections around the things they hold most dear. Through both my methodological design and analytical approach, I show how White evangelical Christians negotiate their personal beliefs alongside larger beliefs and goals of the church. In doing so, this work lends insight into the ways White, middle- and upper-middle-class evangelicals in the liberal bubble of the Pacific Northwest work to grow as a church in an era of declining religiosity and also come to support (and understand their support for) Donald Trump. These debates and conversations about a contemporary evangelical politic carry with them much larger meanings, and are indicative of larger cultural, political, and social anxieties that shape a nation.

CHAPTER 2

The Fear of Religious and Cultural Decline

Each generation meets God in its own manner.

—Tanya Luhrmann (2012:xv)

Fifteen adults sat in chairs arranged in a semicircle around the meeting room, notebooks, Bibles, and pens in their laps. All of the tables were pushed up against the walls and it was dark and rainy outside. Large easels with notepads covered in bright, haphazardly arranged sticky notes flanked either side of the white board. The scene did not look much different from an intense graduate seminar. The bright lights in the room cast a harsh glow upon the space, but the atmosphere was warm, as the members of Disciples' Journey laughed, joked, and shared both their joys and their concerns about their relationships with their children.

The names of five different generations were written up on the white board: The Builders, the Boomers, Gen X, Millennials, and "?" (what is now known as "Gen Z"). Kimberley, a White 41-year-old woman and the children's pastor at Lakeview, had just finished leading a discussion, "Raising Godly Children." Disciples' Journey spent each Thursday working through the Pathways curriculum, and the topic of this meeting was part of a larger unit in the curriculum on "Home Life."

Kimberley and Carrie, a 39-year-old White woman who often led the Disciples' Journey meetings, turned everyone's attention to the white board and easels. Kimberley and Carrie offered the group a choice: they could spend the second part of the evening discussing the questions group members had penned on sticky notes the week before about raising kids, or they could do an exercise on the different generations in the church. By a raise of hand, all 15 members of Disciples' Journey present that evening voted for the latter.

Carrie asked the room to split up by generation. After a shuffling of chairs, Kimberley prompted each group to discuss the following: the major events that defined their generation, their family, what they think of authority, what they think of faith/the church, and how their generation is misunderstood. The Boomers and Gen X'ers were the largest groups in the room. There was one Builder (aged 70–90), no one from Gen Z, and one Millennial: me.

After giving the groups about 15 minutes to talk, Kimberley brought everyone together and said that "A part of being a church is understanding where everyone is coming from. We are living longer, and the world has shaped all of us differently." In an excited tone, she added, "When have we ever had five generations in the church?!"

Without being asked, Raymond, a 55-year-old White man in a business suit with slicked-back hair, went up to the board and wrote out the population numbers for each generation off the top of his head. Ray, as he liked to be called, frequently took over the exercises led by Carrie and Kimberley. Just 20 minutes earlier, he had interrupted Carrie and gone to the board to write out statistics he had "heard somewhere" about how children learn. Carrie and Kimberley exchanged glances while Ray wrote, and the rest of the group picked up casual conversation before the leaders resumed the lesson when he took his seat again.

Kimberley asked the Gen X group to stop talking so that everyone could share their thoughts about the question prompts. Kimberley looked at the board, and read over some basic descriptors for each generation before she asked each group to share take-aways from their conversations. The Gen X'ers talked a bit about their childhoods and said they felt that the reputation of their generation was that of "apathy/nonparticipatory." Kimberley, a member of this generation, added that their childhoods and coming of age were also defined by AIDS. Everyone in the room nodded. Kimberley continued and also added, "We are the abortion generation. Isn't that so sad? It makes me want to cry just thinking about it."

Becky, Mexican American and age 52, was sitting directly next to me, and turned to her friend and said, somewhat under her breath, "Is that why there are only 58 million of them?" Katherine, White and age 55, laughed quietly in response. According to the numbers Ray had written on the board, Gen X indeed stood out as a smaller generation than of course the Boomers before them and the Millennials to follow. But she was also making what seemed to be a very flip joke in a room full of people presumed to vote for Donald Trump, in large part, due to their prolife stance.

It seemed as though Kimberley and Carrie did not hear this joke about abortion. They continued with the lesson and asked everyone in the room to talk about the reputation of younger generations. The room agreed that Millennials are defined by their "entitlement" and that the "?" (now known as Gen Z) is a bit all over the place. Parsing out themes from the conversation that ensued, Carrie wrote the following on the board under the big question mark representing what is now known as Gen Z: "Bible what? Connected [to the internet], Isolated, Lonely, No responsibility."

Kimberley circled both the Millennials and the "?" generation titles and stepped back from the board. She looked out at the group and said, "This scares me."

Katherine nodded her head vigorously, placed her pen down on top of her notebook, and said that the younger kids "will refer to the Bible as a story I heard somewhere." The second she finished her thought, Becky chimed in and said, "But we need to tell them they are NOT stories. They are TRUTHS." The room murmured in agreement. Earl, a 63-year-old White man, asked what events defined these lost, youngest generations, before answering his own question with "ISIS?"

No one disagreed with him.

Sally, a 48-year-old White woman, asked the room, "Do you think they think the world is spinning out of control?"

Shannon, a 43-year-old White woman, responded, "We don't know. We don't know how they are informing themselves. We are no longer gatekeepers. The internet changed that."

Joe, a 52-year-old White man, reminded the group that, while it may not feel that way, the home is where "we have the largest control factor in this section of our life. We can't have as much control at work, or at church." Bill, a 50-year-old White man, nodded and added, "It's where you're burdened or blessed with the greatest responsibility. The biggest reason kids leave the church is parents are preaching it, not living it." Laurie, a 47-year-old White woman, lamented, "But our kids are gone!"

The group wrapped up the conversation and moved their chairs back into a circle to conclude the evening with prayer. Kimberley suggested they focus their prayer on all generations, first, and then focus on a prayer for the lost kids.

. . .

This meeting of Disciples' Journey was held four months before Donald Trump became the presidential nominee, and eight months before he was elected the 45th President of the United States. For those at Lakeview, their concerns about religious decline long preceded the 2016 election. White evangelicals have spent the past 100 years building a cultural, religious, and political powerhouse in the United States. Now, it seems that younger generations might totally undo that work. Even if such a threat is not true in reality, the feelings that such uncertainty fuels matter for our understandings of White evangelism and its alignments with conservative politics.

In this chapter, I provide a brief historical overview of White evangelicals in the United States to highlight their engagement and embattlement in cultural and politics fights tied to gender, sexuality, and the White family. These fights set the stages for their successes, their marriage with conservative politics, and their understandings of their place in the world today.

A BRIEF HISTORY OF WHITE EVANGELISM IN THE UNITED STATES

On November 10, 2016, two days after Donald Trump was elected the 45th president of the United States, the *New York Times* ran an op-ed titled "The Rage of White, Christian America." Robert P. Jones, the chief executive of the Public Religion Research Institute, wrote that "The waning numbers of White Christians in the country today may not have time on their side, but as the sun is slowly setting on the cultural world of White Christian America, they've managed, at least in this election, to rage against the dying of the light" (Jones 2016).[1]

In order to understand what is happening in the present, we need to first rewind and look at the history of the evangelical movement in the United States. White evangelicals have long been invested in the religious, social, and political fabric of the United States. But putting faith into a Republican candidate to protect their values and stand up for their rage has not always been their collective tactic for cultural influence. However, the factors that have led to that alignment are crucial for understanding the conservative bloc that White evangelicals are known as today.

Establishing Cultural Engagement

White evangelical Protestants are strongly aligned with the GOP today, but this is a political alliance markedly different from evangelicals of the past. Over the last 50 years, we have seen two major religious and politic trends flip: first, while evangelicals used to be more likely to identify as Democrat, the opposite is now true. In 1960, 60% of evangelicals in the United States identified as Democrats. By 1988, only 40% of evangelicals identified as Democrats. Today, 28% of evangelicals identify as Democrats. During this 50-year period, evangelical Republican affiliation rose from 32%, to 48% in 1988, to 56% today (Kellstedt et al. 1994; Pew 2015a). Second, while evangelicals used to be less likely to engage in American political life compared to their nonevangelical peers, the opposite is now true. As of 1980, evangelicals are just as likely, if not more likely, to be politically engaged (Malka et al. 2012; Smidt and Kellstedt 1992). These political shifts are a result of the combination of economic, sociodemographic, and social and cultural issues that have solidified a White evangelical movement distinct from secular groups and other religious groups in the United States.

The growth of evangelical political engagement could be explained in part by the socioeconomic model of political participation. Evangelicals, as a whole, grew increasingly more prosperous between 1970 and 2000 as measured by levels of income (Claassen and Povtak 2010). Evangelicals have also become more educated as a group, as measured by the highest level of education completed. By the year 2000, evangelicals were as likely as or more likely than all other religious groups (except for Jews) and nonreligious affiliates to be college-educated (Beyerlein 2004).[2] Because of these dual increases, we can expect increased political participation among evangelicals, even in the absence of both moral issues and religious candidates in an election (Claassen and Povtak 2010).

While increases in both socioeconomic status and educational levels no doubt help to drive political participation in the United States, they do not explain why White evangelicals overwhelmingly support Republican candidates, the Republican Party, and conservative ideals. Some suggest that the religiosity of political leaders helps drive an increase in evangelical support, such as the openly religious candidacy of George W. Bush, or that increased support is due to organized efforts to mobilize evangelicals by organizations affiliated with the Christian Right (Campbell 2007; Claassen and Povtak 2010; Monson and Oliphant

2007).[3] While these factors also contribute to the now long-standing marriage between White evangelism and conservatism in the United States, the foundations of this relationship become clearer when we pay attention to White evangelical political fights over questions of gender, sexuality, and the White family.

In order to understand the emergence of these politically engaged evangelicals, I begin with the conclusion of the Scopes Trial in July 1925 (formally known as *The State of Tennessee v. John Thomas Scopes*), which tested the legality of teaching the theory of evolution in schools. This trial, set in a small town in Tennessee, was broadcast via radio stations across the country. The trial became a symbol for the larger fundamentalist-versus-secular debates occurring nationwide at the time. While, in the end, fundamentalist Christians lost the legal battle to keep human evolution out of public schools' curricula, their response to the loss of this legal battle is what is most important: they began to more adamantly separate and retreat from the world around them (Laats 2010).[4] During this shift and retreat, it appeared that this strand of conservative Protestantism had become a much more defensive and reclusive version of its previous iterations in the United States (Smith 1998). This marked the start of a separation between evangelicalism and fundamentalism.

In the wake of the Scopes Trial, fundamentalist Christians were painted by the media as angry, withdrawn, paranoid, and anti-intellectual. As Christian Smith argues, "The conditions were ripe for a countermovement within" (1998:9). There were many among these young fundamentalists who felt that the negativity and isolation spurred by the Scopes Trial, as well as the mounting sense of disconnect from the larger American cultural collective, were pushing the group away from their goals of effective evangelism. Young Christian men vocally critiqued their larger group and began to shift their opinions and followers to a more moderate form of evangelicalism focused on a clear and direct engagement with, rather than retreat from, the larger world.

The more conservative fundamentalists had "lost their national audience" and someone else needed to take over the direction of the church (Morone 2003). The Christians who reformulated evangelical life in the United States did so with the goal and purpose of cultural relevance and sway, excited to establish their place and space in the larger landscape of American life. As Smith argues, "these young men wanted a true Christian faith that could hold its own in academic circles and thus provide a sound philosophical defense of the Christian world and life view" (1998:10). These young evangelical men wanted to learn, grow, and engage with the world around them.

And they were not only young men at the front of this movement. It was during this time that Aimee Semple McPherson, a young widowed single parent, was traveling across the country holding tent revivals, growing her reputation as both an itinerant evangelist and a healer (Sutton 2007). McPherson became quickly known for her religious fervor and highly theatrical performances, and, by 1923, had opened her first megachurch in Los Angeles. This church was the first of what now makes up an international Foursquare religious and business-savvy conglomerate—of which Lakeview Church is a part. Lauded as the "first religious celebrity of the mass media era" (3), McPherson was the first woman to receive a radio license to broadcast her transformation of what was otherwise, at the time, thought to be a dying religious movement. As Matthew Avery Sutton so nicely summarizes, "McPherson's religious revival caught the nation off guard. With rapid urbanization, the discovery of new technologies, the perfecting of powerful forms of mass media, the rise of the modern university system, and the growth of a celebrity-centered culture, many Americans in the early twentieth century predicted the extinction of classic evangelicalism. Yet from her location in the burgeoning show business capital of the world, McPherson changed the way American religion is practiced" (4).

The other early leaders of this new evangelical movement also found their voice through its literal amplification. These leaders gained large followings through the emergence of televangelism and the "electronic church." Following McPherson's lead, the pioneers of televangelism—Oral Roberts, Billy Graham, and Jerry Falwell—brought evangelical tenets to millions beginning in the late 1940s, setting the stage for what many call an "intense [evangelical] engagement" with the world (Wellman 2008).[5]

Oral Roberts preached on the importance of saving sexual intercourse for the confines of marriage; Billy Graham spoke out against segregation and in favor of the racial integration of social institutions, showcasing these beliefs by inviting Martin Luther King Jr. to the pulpit in front of an audience of 2.3 million people in New York City in 1955. Jerry Falwell openly questioned the tactics and motives of King and spent a good deal of time instead focusing on the importance of the family unit, and on his concerns over the secular education and values taught in public schools. Evangelicals, while growing in their membership during this period in US history, were not unified in the messaging or focus of their religious, political, or cultural beliefs.

Establishing Evangelical Institutions

However, the social upheaval and change of the 1950s to 1970s provided a useful opposition for coalition-building and cohesion. Evangelicals, especially *White* evangelicals, felt large-scale pushback on their traditional social beliefs during this time. Two back-to-back landmark Supreme Court decisions further fueled the coalescence of a White evangelical movement: in 1962 and 1963, the Supreme Court established that school-sponsored prayer in public schools violated the First Amendment, and, for similar reasons, so did school-sponsored Bible-reading in public schools. These decisions marked a cultural shift that was heightened by the media attention to them, which focused on the inflammatory theme of "Kicking God out of the public school" (Waggoner 2012). The Civil Rights Movement, the Gay Rights Movement, and the Supreme Court decision in *Roe v. Wade* in 1973 marked a time of unwelcome change for the White evangelical family. As George Marsden states, "the issues of family and sexuality proved the key to unlocking evangelical potential to become overtly political" (2006:242). Gender relations, sexuality, premarital sex, race relations, and decisions around family formation suddenly seemed up for debate and question. James Wellman argues that it was during this time, and in the wake of these events, that "the public muscle of the evangelical grassroots movement awakened" (2008:18).

As the cultural landscape around them shifted, White evangelicals felt the need to establish more institutions in which they could preach and teach *their* values. Many White evangelicals invested some of their newfound prosperity into Christian schools, expanding "to areas far removed from minority populations" (Guth 1996:14). These Christian schools were all White, and provided an institutional space in which White evangelicals could ensure that norms around gender, sexuality, and the family were taught to their liking. Further, they provided a space in which they could bring God back into their child's education.

These all-White schools are but one example of the many ways in which large portions of the White evangelical conglomerate worked to counter the goals of the Civil Rights Movement. Although Black evangelicals were among those at the forefront of the Civil Rights Movement, many White evangelicals were fundamentally opposed; some did little to nothing to support Black Americans during the 1960s (Evans 2009; Oyakawa 2019) and others actively worked to counter the goals of the Civil Rights Movement. This was especially true in the South, where, following *Brown v. Board of Education* in 1954 and the Civil Rights Act of 1964, many more White evangelical southerners turned to the Republican Party, and focused on building educational institutions to match their values and sustain de facto segregation.

Robert Wuthnow argued that, after 1960, there occurred a dramatic realignment of religious and political affiliations in the United States, whereby "the most significant ideological and social division became the one between those who take a conservative approach to both religion and politics (religious conservatives) and those who take a more liberal approach to both (religious liberals)" (O'Brien and Abdelhadi 2020:475). As Curtis J. Evans writes, "While decrying the major social and cultural revolutions of the 1960s, evangelicals looked on with envy, hoping that they were in such a position to shape the political and cultural landscape of America" (2009:249). With this realignment of conservative religious politics, they were situated to do just that.

By the end of the 1960s, as explicit attempts to uphold White supremacy waned in their political feasibility, gender became an even more salient issue for White evangelicals (Du Mez 2020). The attempt to ratify the Equal Rights Amendment (ERA) in 1972 encapsulates these moral, religious, and geographic shifts in national politics and the emergence of what were clearly becoming *White* evangelical fights over the soul of the nation. Shortly after the ERA was proposed, Phyllis Schlafly founded the "STOP ERA" group (renamed the Eagle Forum in 1975). STOP ERA focused its efforts on defeating the ERA as its first goal, but the organization had a much larger goal of promoting a long-standing, conservative, antifeminist movement under the veil of a "pro-family" agenda. STOP was an acronym for "Stop Taking Our Privileges," which Schlafly articulated more specifically as concerns over homosexual rights, a constitutional basis for abortion, and the conscription of women into the military, and as a fear that men would no longer support their wives.

Although the ERA was approved by the US House of Representatives in the fall of 1971 and the US Senate the following spring, it failed to receive the 38 state ratifications necessary to be added to the US Constitution. State resistance to ratification was larger in the South and Southwest, highlighting in part what is known as "the southern strategy," wherein the GOP capitalized on both White racial angst and, as embodied in Schlafly's work with STOP ERA, concerns over shifts in the gender order (Jenkins 2006; Marti 2020; Maxwell and Shields 2019). Historian Kristin Kobes Du Mez argues that it is hard to overstate the influence of Schlafly, who helped to unify White Christians and the Religious Right around a very conservative understanding of both the family and the nation (2020:73).

Philip Jenkins argues that we need to think about the years from 1975 to 1984 as just as crucial as the 1960s in forming and setting the stage for the United States today, an era he calls the "anti-sixties" (2006:3). According to Jenkins, the post-1975 American public was increasingly unwilling to see social dangers in terms of historical forces, and instead a new society emerged that framed its problems in terms of moral absolutes, or "dangerous, evil outsiders who can be identified and combated" (3). In understanding social problems as a matter of evil, instead of as a result of historical processes and social structures, both the problems and the solutions to said problems become much more simple. During this time, the United States saw massive shifts in discourses about criminality. What had been more support for restorative justice and understandings of redemption were replaced by an obsession with villains—evil monsters, even—who could only lose their power and status as a threat to society if they were locked away. They could not learn or be changed. As Jenkins argues, locking someone up and throwing away the key allowed for "clear-cut victories" over these evil strongholds (12). Importantly, these victories were framed in metaphors and descriptors of war and crusades against evils, a language that aligned nicely with religious rhetoric and socially conservative causes.

And, not coincidentally, the villains who received the most attention were those who targeted women and children. When these tales of criminality were focused specifically on violence against women and children, more conservative social arguments, like Schlafly's, found sympathy. As women continued to enter the workforce, and thus rely more heavily on out-of-home childcare, conservatives found a receptive audience for specific claims about sexual threats: for women, sexual harassment in the workplace; for children, fears of child abuse grew (16). While women and children have long been understood as the focus of protection during times of threat, bodies upon which national concerns are projected (Nagel 2003), there was an increasing focus on questions of masculinity during this time as well.

The Gay Rights Movement, the Feminist Movement, and this collective cultural shift to a focus on evil (instead of redemptive) men who prey on women and children, resulted in a growing urge to rethink masculinity. Philip Jenkins describes this time as the transition from the mythical John Wayne to John Wayne Gacy, the serial killer and sex offender known as the "Killer Clown" who assaulted and murdered over 30 young men and boys (2006). And, in a nation experiencing a constant deluge of rhetoric about outsider threats, a simultaneous conservative push about masculinity and men losing their ability to defend the nation both locally and on the world platform rang true for many.

This multifaceted shift, in an increasing willingness to understand the world in moral absolutes, through the binaries of good versus evil, and to pursue those evils with a war and crusade-like imaginary focused on threats related to gender and sexuality, aligned quite well with the worldview and logic of the *White* evangelical church.

The Growing Allure of the White Evangelical Church

Because of the legacy of slavery and continued patterns of racial inequality and racism in the United States, Black and White evangelicals interpret the world through theology in different ways (Emerson and Smith 2001; Lee 2015). These interpretations differ regarding understandings of individualism, or what Emerson and Smith call "accountable freewill individualism" (2001) and systematic oppression (Lee 2016). White evangelicals believe that the desire to live a positive and moral life is a personal achievement and personal responsibility. This achievement is accomplished through a personal relationship with Jesus Christ, through an immediate conversion (a born-again experience).

This logic continues, that failure to live a positive and moral life (through Christ) represents an *individual* failure; as Lee suggests, for White evangelicals, "any social problems are seen as rooted in negative relationships and poor choices . . . collective sin is typically ignored" (2016:28). And this theology of the White evangelical church reflects the larger ideology of the American Dream. If an individual's life does not embody the stereotypical successes of "making it" that is the fault of the individual. And, for those who do accrue wealth and successes, pervasive ideologies such as the American Dream justify the positions of those who have "made it" through a rhetoric of hard work and, importantly, harder work than everyone else. This ideology supports the idea that those who have worked "harder" and made it are therefore deserving of the privileges that accompany their successes. These ideologies, forged by predominantly White institutions, help to justify racial hierarchies in which White success is understood as natural, and the result of hard work, and not the structural advantages imparted onto certain groups (Edgell and Tranby 2007; Hagerman 2018; Lewis 2004).

Regardless of one's life circumstances, successes, and failures, White evangelicals profess a theology focused on love for all. This combination of a focus on individual successes and failures with a language of love as both a goal and in some cases a solution for one's problems means White evangelicals can mask and ignore structural issues with a language of individualism. This is especially true when it comes to issues of race. Paraphrasing the work of Emerson and Smith (2001), Michelle Oyakawa states that "when evangelicals focus only on individual-level changes, like confronting one's own racism and building interpersonal relationships across race, they 'unwittingly' grant power to existing social structures that divide resources unequally by race" (2019:498). In proposing that a solution to racial divides can be found in "loving thy neighbor," White evangelicals are able to ignore structural problems and solutions that might in fact "cause extensive discomfort or change to their economic and cultural lives" (Emerson and Smith 2001:130; Tranby and Hartmann 2008). And many argue that this is not an "unwitting" byproduct of their doctrine, but rather a selectively applied individualistic rhetoric preserved for those with whom they agree (Evans 2009), and an ideology that, regardless of its intent, preserves White dominance (Oyakawa 2019).

Black evangelicals, in contrast, while valuing individualism rooted in responsibility, also see this individualism as part of a system that has unfairly disadvantaged them. For many Black evangelicals, connecting being American to being Christian evokes and sustains ideals of racial justice (Perry and Whitehead 2019). Historically Black evangelical churches center a theology focused on a collective salvation that emphasizes deliverance for the oppressed (Lee 2016). Interviewing queer individuals and people of color who have returned to the evangelical church, Deborah Jian Lee describes one respondent whose mother taught her that "White evangelicals look for redemption—people who have sinned against each other look for redemption—whereas people who have been sinned against look for salvation" (21). Lee argues that churches remain segregated around these different theologies, and that, over time, these theologies have further developed in isolation, which has "helped feed White evangelical support of policies and institutions that carry out Black oppression" (25; Emerson and Smith 2001).

As cultural understandings of the evils of the world shifted, played up the growing fears among White evangelicals and White conservatives about shifts in the gender order, and aligned with already-existent frameworks for understanding (or ignoring) structural inequalities, White evangelical churches found their audience. From the mid-1960s to mid-1980s, more liberal denominations in the United States saw massive decreases in their membership. In an "anti-sixties" era in which the world was painted as crumbling and decaying, individuals sought clear and firm answers. While this era saw a drift toward cults and therapy movements because of this desire for a strict and clear orientation to the changing world, the more enduring movement proved to be evangelical religion, and the White evangelical church (Jenkins 2006:84). These churches were, like those who advocated for engagement with the world following the Scopes Trial, ready to take on more activist stances in society, and capitalize on the crusade rhetoric offered by society at large in tandem with their own apocalyptic worldviews. The White evangelical church could provide its members with a much-needed understanding of politics, the world, and their own faith simultaneously. And they did. As Jenkins argues, "Secular politics thus had a potent religious dimension. According to this worldview, America was disarming morally at a time of desperate confrontation with the literal forces of evil, symbolized by the Soviets and their radical Middle Eastern allies. In their attacks on the traditional family and gender roles, their advocacy of abortion and homosexuality, liberals were subverting the most basic components of Christian morality" (85).

The White Evangelical Conservative Voting Bloc

While the Eagle Forum gained power and received mass support from conservative politicians and church groups alike, many Christian organizations of prominence, such as the Moral Majority, the Roundtable, and the Christian Voice, emerged to provide a structure and somewhat unified voice to this growing White political and social movement. But White evangelicals experienced both successes and drawbacks during this period, as they continued to fight with the federal government over the educational institutions they had created. In 1978, the IRS stripped tax-exempt status from all-White private schools formed in the South. Falwell had established Liberty Christian Academy in Lynchburg, Virginia, which, as an all-White academy, failed to meet the IRS requirements for tax-exempt status. Falwell used this moment to mobilize solidarity and political opposition against more liberal Christians and secular society at large. White evangelical parents, teachers, congregations, and organizations alike had invested greatly in these organizations, and were distraught over yet another federal obstacle to their ways of life. As James Guth argues "for such parents it appeared that secular elites had not only pushed religious and traditional moral values out of public schools, but were trying to purge them from the private institutions where they had taken refuge" (1996:14).

In 1979, Jerry Falwell founded the Moral Majority, a political action committee, in response to the IRS's interventions and to protest legal abortion in the United States. Billy Graham refused to join the Moral Majority and stated that "Evangelists cannot be closely identified with any particular party or person. We have to stand in the middle in order to preach to all people, right or left" (Horstman 2002). Billy Graham's opposition fell to the minority as the voice of the Conservative Christian Right solidified. Falwell and his organization pushed for a prolife, pro-American, pro–traditional family, and moral agenda that positioned themselves against more liberal, secular Americans.

This combination of threats to traditional social values and threats to the White Christian institutions in which those social values were embedded, taught, and celebrated spurred the evangelical rise in conservative political life (Guth 1996). Around the 1980 congressional elections, Falwell urged ministers, "What can you do from the pulpit? You can register people to vote. You can explain the issues to them. And you can endorse candidates, right there in church on Sunday morning" (Guth 1996; Vecsey 1980). The Moral Majority became a massive political lobby group for evangelical Christians during the 1980s and, along with other organizations, began targeting prominent liberal and moderate legislators for defeat in the 1980 congressional election. The public voice of Christian liberals became much more muted than it had been in the 1960s and 1970s; evangelicals began their upward class trajectory (Claassen and Povtak 2009), and the evangelical voice became and is still the voice that the majority understand as the public voice of Christianity in the United States (Domke and Coe 2008; Wellman 2008).

The convergence of White evangelical religious values, power, and a conservative political agenda manifested in the 1980 election of President Ronald Reagan. On June 25, 1980, the *Christian Science Monitor* posited the following: "Twenty years ago the 'religion question' in the US presidential election was whether a Roman Catholic could be elected. This year the question is: Who will get the 'born-again vote?'" (Harley 1980). The period of the Reagan presidency coincided with a large increase in the number of individuals who labeled themselves as "born-again" Christians (Marti 2020). His presidency was also concurrent with the growing establishment of free-market conservatism and neoliberal policies that aligned nicely with what Gerardo Marti calls business-friendly evangelicalism and a strong advocacy for capitalism, backed further by conservative understandings of men as providers "who leave the home to aggressively contend with a competitive marketplace" (127) to sustain their good Christian homes.[6]

In addition, as Marti states, "Reagan also appealed to people concerned with protecting their families and their communities from the danger of radicalism—*radicalism* often being a code word for government programs on behalf of Blacks" (133). Reagan appealed to the continued racism central to the White evangelical conservative movement. Throughout the 1980s, as their economic and social interests were increasingly mirrored by those in political power, the "invisible army" of White conservative evangelicals grew (Green 1996).

Shortly after the disbanding of the Moral Majority in 1989, a name was given to this seemingly growing political and cultural rift in the United States. In 1991, James Hunter's book *Culture Wars* gained traction, and in 1992, Patrick Buchanan used the Republican Convention to declare a "war for the nation's soul" (Williams 1997:1). Buchanan introduced "culture wars" to the American lexicon, and it is now used as a catchall phrase to describe this conflict between more conservative, traditional, religious groups and more secular, liberal groups. While those on the democratic and more liberal side of these "wars" might have easily looked at this short historical trajectory of White evangelical Christians establishment as anti-Black, antifeminist, and antigay and thus seen clear evidence for the very ugliness that those at Lakeview seem newly engaged in avoiding, for White evangelical Christians, the lexicon of the culture wars named them as *powerful*.

The White evangelical presence in politics gained force in the 1992 presidential election, no longer an invisible army in the American political arena. White evangelicals solidified their support for the Republican Party and George Bush, while mainline Protestants in large part voted for Clinton. The 1992 presidential election was marked by a growing division between religious and nonreligious voters from all religious traditions, but the increased pairing between evangelicals and GOP support led Kellstedt et al. to suggest that "it seems as though evangelicals will only continue to grow in force" (1994:309); indeed, the authors posited that "future party historians may label 1992 the year of the evangelical" (309). In the 2000 presidential election, George W. Bush received 68% of the White evangelical protestant vote, and 78% in 2004.[7] Barack Obama, in contrast, received 24% of the White evangelical vote in 2008 and 21% in 2012. Today, White evangelicals continue to remain aligned with, and support, conservative politics in the United States, and are often described as the "base" of the Republican Party (Brint and Abrutyn 2010).

This history has led Dara Strolovitch, Janelle Wong, and Andrew Proctor to rightly suggest that Trump's election in 2016 was not an anomaly in the way many political pundits, journalists, and academics alike treat it, but rather "represents an extension of enduring and intersecting configurations of racialized and gendered power, marginalization, and oppression" (2017:354). The authors argue that the stage had been set for generations—the very generations covered in this chapter—for Trump's success. The authors suggest that Trump's election was fueled by (1) the political consequences of antifeminism and the naturalization of misogyny, (2) the construction and consequences of partisan polarization around issues of gender and sexuality, and (3) the intersections of gender, politics, and Whiteness. In other words, the very issues that the White evangelical movement consolidated around over the past century have continued to fuel their support for conservative politics.

WHITE EVANGELICALS TODAY

Columnist Amy Sullivan wrote an op-ed in the Sunday *New York Times* on April 1, 2018, that charges that "Decades of fearmongering about Democrats and religious liberals have worked. Eighty percent of White evangelicals would vote against Jesus Christ himself if he ran as a Democrat." Sullivan's point, here, is that the Moral Majority won. Their work and influence have resulted in a marriage between White evangelicals and the Republican party that helps explain a whole host of their behaviors in our contemporary cultural and political climate.

Political life and political participation—and specifically participation in Republican politics—are now understood as a key component of a White evangelical identity. Evangelicals increasingly see that voting is what members of their group "do on election day" (Gerber, Green, and Shachar 2003; Smith and Walker 2013). Further, "Evangelicals have come to believe that engagement in public debate is part of what it means to be a faithful Christian" (Wellman 2008:18). Evangelicals are almost twice as likely as mainline Protestants to say that their faith informs their politics, and by similar proportions relative to mainline Protestants, they are also more likely to say they are committed to transforming American society. Finally, an overwhelming majority, more than 90% of evangelicals, believe that religious people should "fight evil," leading Wellman to suggest that "the old notion of separation from the world has given way to intense engagement with the world" (Wellman 2008:18).

Today, White evangelicals make up one-fifth of all registered voters and about one-third of all voters who identity with or lean toward the GOP (Pew 2015b). White evangelical Protestants continue to vote more Republican than mainline Protestants (Green 2007; Layman 2001; Lockerbie 2013). And in 2016, the election "showed that White evangelical Protestants are one of the most stable electoral coalitions, as well as the most important" (Burge and Lewis 2018).

In 2016, Donald Trump received 81% of the White evangelical vote, which represented the largest share of the evangelical vote in US history (Smith and Martínez 2016).[8] In 2020, Trump received about 76% of the White evangelical vote (Mayes et al. 2020). Unlike George W. Bush or Mitt Romney, Trump did not present himself as a highly religious candidate. Perhaps partially because of this, most did not predict such a strong White evangelical voter turnout for Trump, and instead assumed that their participation would wane when candidates like Cruz and Rubio dropped out of the race. Trump's misquoting of biblical verses, a tumultuous family and marital history, numerous allegations of sexual harassment and assault, and video and audio footage of him describing grabbing women by the "pussy" surely ran antithetical to the majority of evangelical Christian's views and values. To circle back to Sullivan's *New York Times* op-ed, her response to what many understand as a puzzle when it comes to White evangelical support for Trump is simple, a story of party over person: he ran as a Republican.

Perhaps, then, one of the external threats with which the White evangelical church is currently embattled is the Democratic Party itself. And for many White evangelicals that is true. The story in many parts of the United States is more complicated, however, and a better understanding might emerge if we center the "evils" that White evangelicals believe they are still fighting.

FEAR AND POLITICS

Over the last 100 years in the United States, White evangelicals have witnessed increasing economic gains, increasing political influence, and, in a country in which, by many measures, religiosity is on the decline, fairly steady attendance and membership in church. These status gains are especially evident in the Pacific Northwest.[9] For the most part, those who attend Lakeview Church have the jobs, cars, and homes situated in the neighborhoods they want. They are not being "cut in line" for access to the American Dream (Hochschild 2016a). To the extent that a tangible version of the American Dream exists, this group has it. And they hold on to the pervasive logic that they have *earned* it.

The history of White evangelism in the United States is one defined by a group that has gained significant political and cultural power. As such, this is a group that has dictated many larger beliefs about gender, sexuality, the White family, and their intersections. Their access to political power and their increasingly conservative beliefs represent a cyclical relationship in which power normalizes these beliefs and these beliefs help align them with a changing GOP. But as our social world is prone to do, it changes. We are currently in a period of massive polarization. Social movements are challenging the inequalities on which the pillars of the White evangelical movement rest. And while the emergence and naming of the culture wars labeled White evangelicals, it labeled them as fighters, and importantly, fighters with power. As current social movements intersect with larger religious decline, White evangelicals face the threat of dual losses: the loss of their children in church on Sundays, and the loss of their cultural status as powerful social actors, once understood as normal, and thus taken for granted and unseen, becoming a group that continually risks being marked if they respond to their perceived suffering with "ugliness."

This perceived suffering highlights an important point: for those at Lakeview, and indeed, many White evangelical protestants across the country, their feelings and beliefs are central when it comes to understanding their cultural and political positions in the United States. Arlie Hochschild argues for the importance of understanding feelings: "a full understanding of emotion in politics" (2016a:15; see also Hochschild 1979). In her work to understand the great voting paradox at the "heart" of the American Right, Hochschild introduces the concept of a deep story, the "feels-as-if" story that relies on symbols, and in many cases feelings over fact, and thus showcases the fears, hopes, shame, resentment, and anxiety central to how people understand the world, and indeed their politics (Hochschild 2016a).

One way to discuss and understand the importance of feelings in political and religious life is through an investigation into social position and status (Wald, Owen, and Hill 1989). The Christian Right emerged in the United States out of concerns for and protections for a specific value set and way of life and came together to work to influence cultural and political debates around these issues in the United States. Many scholars thus share a mutual understanding of the collective Christian Right as "social conservatives who share a style of life and who act out of interest to preserve or defend that style of life against declines in prestige and influence" (Wood and Hughes 1984:87; Wald, Owen, and Hill 1989:2). As such, sociologists might best conceptualize and understand the Christian Right through an intellectual approach that frames assumptions of status and its discontents as something that is *felt*, rather than something measurable from an objective social position (Wald, Owen, and Hill 1989). The White evangelicals at the center of this book have achieved economic, educational, and social successes. They have a lot and they want to keep it. Wald, Owen, and Hill state that "status discontent should be treated as an attitudinal property exhibited in varying degrees by persons *at all levels* of the social structure" (1989:5, emphasis mine).[10] We could thus understand White evangelicals as experiencing *feelings* of disenfranchisement and discontent, even when these feelings are not reflected in other measures of status gain, or in this case loss.

Indeed, more recent work indicates that White evangelicals feel threatened today due to a perceived collective loss in cultural status. In some cases, this feeling of status loss is directly related to religious influence. For example, the more secular a community, the more likely White evangelical Protestants are to vote Republican (Campbell 2006). Drawing on the literature on racial threat, David E. Campbell argues that we can similarly understand the "religious threat" that evangelicals perceive in their communities. As communities become more secular, White evangelicals become more aligned with Republican politicians, who they view as the best representative of their felt position in the social world. Recent research finds that individuals, a good portion of whom we know to be White evangelicals, voted for Donald Trump for president, due to a "symbolic threat that they feel" (Mutz 2018). Diana C. Mutz, the author of a study on the subject, suggests that this symbolic threat is "not a threat to their own economic well-being; it's a threat to their group's dominance in our country over all" (Chokshi 2018). Similarly, using data collected right after the 2016 presidential election, Janelle Wong finds that White evangelicals' more conservative political attitudes are driven by feelings of "in-group embattlement," a feeling distinct from economic anxiety, and one that suggests that White evangelicals believe that, as a group, they face as much or *more* discrimination than persecuted out-groups (Wong 2018).

I argue that this perceived discrimination—what Pastors Dave and Amy both allude to through their conversations about suffering—is a discomfort that stems from the work to question the normalcy of Whiteness, Christianity, heterosexuality, and masculinity. As historian Anthea Butler suggests, evangelicalism is not simply a religious group, but rather "a nationalistic political movement whose purpose is to support the hegemony of white Christian men over and against the flourishing of others" (2021:138). Other recent work finds that some may have voted for Trump because of a desire to protect and reinforce these identities.

George Lakoff argues that part of Trump's success may be what he symbolizes in a nation that we tend to understand through metaphors of the family. Lakoff (2016) suggests that, for many, Trump is seen through a metaphor of a strict father, a metaphor he argues resonates more with conservatives. But Christopher Brittain poses the following question: "If evangelicals are seeking protection from a strong man, what has led them to this point?" (2018:271). Research finds a relationship between a belief in gendered nationalism (operationalized as the feeling that American Society has grown "too soft and feminine") and a vote for Donald Trump (Deckman and Cassese 2021), suggesting that some individuals seek not protection, but a return to a more patriarchal society. In their work on a belief in Christian Nationalism as a driving force in support for Donald Trump, Andrew Whitehead and Sam Perry argue that Christian Nationalism as an ideology is about maintaining and reinstituting boundaries that protect Christianity in the public sphere, and, importantly, "it is Americans' *private* worlds that strong Christian nationalists are most desperate to influence" (2020:123), private worlds that reflect a belief in gender essentialism and complementarity, where men are the head of the house and women focus on raising obedient children (2020).

Others argue that Trump support among White evangelicals is due to racism and deep-seated feelings about race (Fea 2018; Jones 2020; Marti 2020). Darrius Hills argues that Trump was able to tap into "profound feelings of alienation, displacement, and the existential and religious angst of White evangelical voters" (2018:38), angst that, especially after eight years of the Obama presidency, is "housed in White flesh" (43). For many White evangelicals, this racist sentiment may operate through ideologies of Christian nationalism (Whitehead and Perry 2020).

Feelings, and feelings related to the gendered, racialized, and sexual political projects that have been a long-standing part of White evangelicals' collective history in the United States, are a key part of the story of their current religious and political actions. But their feelings are often undertheorized or ignored in conversations about politics. I do not mean to suggest that feelings that justify and seek to uphold inequalities should be greeted with empathy. Rather, feelings rooted in both reality and *perceived* reality are crucial to understanding this group of individuals.

When we bring feelings into our analysis of the relationship between White evangelism and conservative politics, we can see that we are asking the wrong questions by looking at this group of seemingly well-to-do individuals, puzzled about why they feel like they are losing out. To those outside of the community, White evangelicals are not losing out much at all. But when we pair their feelings with their historical trajectory in the United States, we see that they have always been driven by concern over cultural influence, especially when it comes to questions of gender, race, and sexuality. It is a core part of their theology and a core part of their practice.

And more recently, they feel that their attempts to influence national and local conversations about gender, race, and sexuality risk labels of "ugliness" and thus also risk the loss of power that has long gone hand in hand with straight, White Christian men's and women's identities in the United States.

White evangelicals at Lakeview are correct that if some of their theology and beliefs around issues of gender, race, and sexuality do not shift, they will lose membership, and experience a loss in cultural influence they want to maintain. This fear of loss is real, as is the fear of what these challenges to their doctrine mean for their privileges and power as a group. This language of fear haunts a core part of how we have theorized this group. The very idea and language of an "external threat" invoke a sense and understanding of fear, not necessarily explicit (Smith 1998), but we have not adequately paired this negotiation around both engagement and change with one of emotion. The concept of the *imagined secular—the bundling of things that threaten White evangelicals' felt status as unmarked, normal, and good*—captures these feelings, their messiness and variation. And this book documents the ways in which a White evangelical church engages with the imagined secular in a way that reflects its historical roots in the United States and upholds their modern configurations.

WHITE FEELINGS IN UNSETTLED TIMES

These are, in the words of Ann Swidler (1986), unsettled times. Donald Trump entered the political arena during an era in which the United States was experiencing declining religiosity, and at a time when the church and nation at large are wrestling with their racist, sexist, and homophobic past and present. This is a book at the intersections of cultural shifts and politics, and one that explores the ways in which an organization central to the making of American life is and is not adapting.

This is a story about how this organization, a White megachurch perched on a liberal coast, is navigating religious and cultural change. It is a story about the lure of power and privilege and the anxiety that a hint of loss of either of those things can invoke. This is about a church that is trying to gain membership when younger groups are leaving. It is about a church putting faith in a politician they aren't thrilled with, but who, importantly, doesn't seem like he will challenge issues related to sexism, racism, and heteronormativity, ideologies that reflect long-standing White evangelical projects in the United States. This is not a book about why White evangelicals fervently poured their support, time, and belief into Donald Trump as a political candidate. Because for the group of people in question—the members that make up Lakeview Church—they were not his most vocal supporters. As such, this story is as much about concerns over the growth of the church, indeed concerns that long preceded the last election, as it is about White evangelical support for Donald Trump.

And this is a story about the people who are part of that organization, who have, by many standards, achieved some semblance of an American Dream. It is about a group of people who do not respond to changing tides with rage, but those who seek to engage with the imagined secular, a group of people who seek to understand younger generations that they think are entitled, lost, and disconnected from the Bible and religion and who do whatever they can to get them to come back. This book follows a group of people for whom rage is replaced with more subtle forms of assertions of power in the name of welcoming and growth. For many White evangelicals, and indeed those at Lakeview, the light is not dying. But it will continue to fade if they do not enact some changes. They want to ensure that the visible army continues to grow and does not become invisible again as their children leave in droves.

Importantly, this is not a book that treats conservative politics as a masquerade or a form of false consciousness. This is not a story about people being duped to vote against their own interests. This is an investigation of an organization that has long been in power in the United States and whose members do not want to lose that. When we put the inability for the nation to change and progress on the conscious of the disenfranchised, the poor, those in rural communities, and those in the geographic south, and away from those who live in the areas of the "coastal elites," we miss some of the biggest reasons why inequality prevails.

The chapters to come highlight the components of the imagined secular with which White evangelicals at Lakeview are most prominently engaged. They show their threats and the political logics that emerge because of their feelings around these threats, beginning with the long-standing White evangelical fight over understandings of gender and feminism.

CHAPTER 3

The Imagined Secular

Confronting Feminism, Gender, and
Family Life

I arrived early to Lakeview on an unusually warm and sunny February morning. I entered the building and began my Sunday routine: I stopped by the visitor's desk and said hello to Carrie, and then made my way through the crowd to International Java, where I chatted with Pastor Jeff, who often helped organize the volunteers that served coffee to eager morning attendants. Latte in hand, I wandered the side hallways that lead toward the Teen Zone, a separate worship space for Lakeview youth. This was not a usual part of my pre-sermon walk of the grounds, but the church had recently hung a new art installation of parishioners' work, which showcased the artistic endeavors of children, teenagers, and retirees alike.

There was a lightness in the air that morning. Whether it was the first signs that we were finally emerging from our rainy northwest winter, the paintings of cherry blossoms and Puget Sound that now lined the halls, or, perhaps, some excitement about the Super Bowl later that afternoon, the gathering crowd at Lakeview felt energized and jovial.

I walked through the same door to the sanctuary space that I entered every Sunday. I said hello to Norm, who handed me the weekly church bulletin and smiled. Norm volunteered as one of the many doorway greeters at Lakeview. Norm always stood out from the rest of the individuals positioned at all of the internal and external doorways at Lakeview, because he wore a different Hawaiian shirt to church every weekend. This week, Norm wore a blue and green shirt, quite on theme with the blue and green lights flashing from the sanctuary.

The sanctuary is a dark space with no windows, which allows for an immediate focus on the brightly lit stage at the front of the room. This morning, the blue and green lights danced over a new art installation at the back of the stage, a wooden outline of Mt. Rainier and its surrounding foothills. The stage lights, which changed more frequently than the backdrop, were paying homage to the colors of the beloved regional NFL team, the Seattle Seahawks, even though they were not representing the Pacific Northwest in the Super Bowl game later that afternoon.

As the worship band assembled behind their instruments and microphones on the stage, I filed into a back corner of the sanctuary. I enjoyed sitting at the back for two reasons. This position gave me a full view of the audience, and it meant I could sit quietly among those who were less involved in the morning services. In my two years at Lakeview, I noticed a pattern to the ways in which individuals occupied space in the sanctuary. The first rows are always occupied by the pastoral team, the church staff, their families, and any distinguished guests who might be in attendance. This is a position of both reverence and practicality, as it allows for easy access to the stage, and easy identification by the rest of those in the audience. The most visibly energetic congregants sit in the rows immediately behind, and often spend the entirety of the 20 minutes of introductory singing standing with their arms raised in praise. The voluntary prayer team also sits (or stands) toward the front. At the conclusion of each sermon, this team descends to the base of the stage, where they are available to any wanting individual for prayer requests and laying on of hands.[1] From there, things quiet down. Larger families, especially those who bring their young children into the services with them, often sit further back for ease of exit. Because there is a children's ministry upstairs during Sunday sermons, as well as private rooms with one-way glass on the second floor for breast-feeding mothers, the noise of children seems slightly less accepted in the sanctuary. Newcomers also sit toward the back, perhaps a little less sure of being in the crowd of arm-raisers. The teenagers sit together toward the side and back, as they attend the performance of the worship band before leaving for their specialized sermon in the Teen Zone. Every Sunday I situated myself among the newcomers, the in- and out-crowd of teenagers, the new faces, and the skeptics, where I felt free to take notes and remain seated without appearing out of place.

On this Sunday morning, I sat a few rows behind a couple that stood alone in their row, and bobbed along to the first "praise song" of the morning. The couple wore matching Seahawks jerseys that had been customized, inscribed with the name "Jesus" and the number "1" on their backs. As important as football is for many at Lakeview, it will of course never be quite as important as their relationship with Jesus. This couple found a creative way to celebrate their love of both.

The worship band ended their morning set with a crowd favorite, and indeed a national evangelical favorite, "This is Amazing Grace," much to the pleasure of the audience. Those closest to the stage remained standing, and loudly exclaimed the final lines of the song, with their arms raised to the ceiling: *"You lay down your life, that I would be set free, oh Jesus I sing for all that you've done for me."* The sounds of the amplified vocals, guitar, piano, and drums faded and began to mix with the sounds of clapping and hollering as the last of the congregants filtered in from the foyer, coffees in hand, to catch the beginning of the sermon. The Youth Ministry Pastor, Pastor Adam, walked on to the stage and started chatting about the new stage backdrop and the thing on everyone's minds, it seemed: the Super Bowl. Pastor Adam made a quick, off-hand joke about the high consumption of processed cheese sure to occur among all later that afternoon. He then announced that the church would host a Ladies' Lunch the following weekend. Pastor Adam provided the following disclaimer: "This is for the women only." He then added, "I am sure there will be delicious food." Pastor Adam paused to think, and then wondered, aloud, "What do women eat? Dainty Foods. Yes, probably something dainty." He laughed and exited the stage as many in the congregation laughed in response.

Pastor Dave walked up the short steps to the stage and shook his head and smiled. He adjusted the wireless microphone on his face, and said, "For all the feminists in the room, I want to start by acknowledging that men and women eat the same food." A good portion of the room laughed, cheered, and clapped in response. Pastor Dave then added, "Wow, feminism is alive and well out there!" He paused to allow for more laughter from the audience before he continued. He said, "For some of you, I bet that in just hearing the F word, you just switched churches in your head! Ocean Side [a nearby church], here I come!" There was more laughter and applause, and then the "official" sermon began.

NAVIGATING THE F WORD

This joke, on the part of Pastor Dave, might reflect some larger anxieties during a cultural moment in which women's issues are at the forefront of the American collective conscious in new ways. Women's rights were at the center of the largest protests in US history (Chenoweth and Pressman 2017), with a reported 1% of the entire US population participating in the Women's March a month before this comment was made. (These protests were, of course, outnumbered in participation by the BLM protests beginning in June 2020, which now hold the record for participation.) Many women were embracing the phrase "nasty woman" that Trump had used disparagingly against Clinton in the presidential debates the fall before. The phrase appeared all over signs at the Women's March, on T-shirts, as a widely used hashtag on social media, and even as an activist-oriented wine club. To equal parts outcry and celebration, *Merriam-Webster's Dictionary* named "feminism" the word of the year in 2017.

Jokes, or humor more broadly, are a condensed form of meaning (Tavory 2014) that can provide a group of people with social goods: relief, control, and cohesion (Kuipers 2006). Jokes can break the ice and relieve tension in a crowded sanctuary of worshipers when an off-color comment about gender is made. Perhaps, in the case of the feminist, jokes can acknowledge a feeling of anxiety, or what sociologist Iddo Tavory (2014) calls a shared experience of tension. Jokes can also establish in- and out-groups: those who are in on the joke, and those who are the subject of the joke, or do not understand it.

This joke also works to establish boundaries in the church during a cultural moment in which a variety of issues related to gender, and, by logical extension, feminism, are on the minds of many. Who is a feminist, and who is not? And what does the church think about feminism? Cultural questions related to gender have always mobilized White evangelicals to enter the public arena for commentary and debate. Feminism is not a new issue for the church. While Millennials and Gen Z'ers might press the church in new and different ways about questions of gender, as any generation does, there are issues the church has *long* wrestled with, and gender is an issue that ebbs and flows depending on our moment in history. Because feminism and questions of gender are not a new issue for the church, it is a great place to start to document and make sense of the external threats evangelicals navigate today and how they understand their place among them.

To help navigate how we should make sense of these feelings—jokes, threats, a variety of emotions, the seeming presence of feminists and those scared of the F word in one church—I introduce the concept of the *imagined secular*. The imagined secular is the imaginary that exists in the minds of evangelicals, and is created within the confines of the White evangelical church. It is a world full of nonreligious individuals who push for access to abortion and advocate for trans rights, gay rights, "deviant" sex, Black Lives Matter, Social Justice Warriors, and marriages void of God. The imagined secular contains the Democrat, the "scary" feminist, the activist person of color, the homosexual, and the single Millennial who is not ready or willing to marry, and, worse, is thinking of leaving (or has left) the church. This is not a new imaginary, but a changing one, as amorphous as our ever-changing cultural milieu.

The imagined secular is the bundling of external threats and perceived social "evils" that require White evangelicals to articulate their own beliefs in a way that risks ugliness. In other words, the imagined secular contains the things that threaten to question the unmarked goodness of White evangelicals, and threaten to question their understanding of themselves as a group against which all others are judged and that all others (should) strive to become. As such, there is a tension inherent in the imagined secular: if White evangelicals want to hold on to an unmarked normalcy they've long felt in the United States, they need to acknowledge and engage with the social transformations that they perceive to implicate their own social standing. But doing so also runs the risk of drawing attention to the very privileges they seek to protect. The ways in which White evangelicals in this book engage with these perceived social evils suggest that the identification of external threats also creates quite a bit of internal chaos that our previous theories do not account for.

The concept of the imagined secular helps us to understand and articulate the ways in which White evangelicals internalize external threats. In this chapter, I show how questions of feminism evoke a whole host of other issues in the minds of evangelicals: things like trans rights and gay marriage, for example. In holding space to engage with the messy, intertwined threats of the imagined secular, Lakeview hopes that it will be able to avoid the specter of ugliness that walks hand in hand with an unwillingness to change.

Feminism is just one aspect of this imagined secular world. I find that evangelicals respond to feminism in one of three ways: by (1) creating an evangelical feminism, (2) seeking a middle ground, or (3) rejecting feminism. What the data in this chapter reveals is that the actual definition of feminism doesn't matter. Evangelicals at Lakeview do not agree on their understandings of feminism. There is no collective approach, and they are working to grapple with that. These varied responses are, perhaps, a perfect example of the messiness that Pastor Dave alluded to—the messiness that the church is currently untangling. Because feminism works as a symbol that is part of the larger imagined secular world, evangelicals need to deal with it now, but they are working to figure out how to do so. And the ways in which they approach feminism, much like the other central components of the imagined secular world outlined in this book, highlight much larger truths about their current political beliefs and actions.

LAKEVIEW'S RESPONSES TO FEMINISM

An Evangelical Feminism

There are many individuals at Lakeview Church who identify as feminist. A threat to the church is not a threat for all, and the words of these congregants help reveal that threats are approached in a whole host of ways. They contain key differences, and clear political similarities.

I met Katherine, a 55-year-old, White, recently divorced woman and member of Disciples' Journey, for an interview on a summer morning after church services. Katherine was often fairly shy in Disciples' Journey meetings but seemed much more relaxed in a one-on-one setting. I was looking forward to talking with her outside of the group. She told me that she identifies as an introvert and recommended books to me, some about introverts and others about women more generally. Katherine assumed that I, too, was an introvert, and wanted to connect based on that presumed shared identity. Almost everyone in my life would describe me as an extrovert, but, in Katherine's eyes, I sit quietly at Disciples' Journey and don't speak, and probably seem quite inwardly focused as I take notes. I found this perception of me amusing, and we talked about our personalities a bit more, drank coffee, and shared a scone before the interview began.

During our initial chat Katherine had recommended the book *Why Women* to me.[2] This is a book written by a man about ways to advance women in the workplace. This served as a nice transition into some of my first questions for her about feminism.

Katherine told me that she believes that Jesus was a radical feminist. When I asked Katherine to explain this to me, she said that "I mean, he's letting Mary sit there at his feet!" Katherine continued and impersonated Jesus, and said, "'Here, go! Go, serve, woman!' You know? 'Go away!' So, the first time he claimed to be the son of God out loud was not just to a woman, but a woman of ill repute and a Samaritan." Katherine is describing the biblical story in which Jesus reveals himself first to Mary Magdalene after the resurrection. Jesus tells Mary to spread the news. Many evangelicals use this passage as a way to argue that both men and women have been commissioned to spread the good news that Jesus is Savior: in other words, to evangelize. Katherine is relying on a biblical story to understand Jesus as a radical feminist.

I asked Katherine if she too identifies as a radical feminist, and if, because of that, she thinks she is in the minority at Lakeview. Katherine paused in her response, and first told me that she didn't know the answer to the question. She continued, though, and said, "I think, probably [she is in the minority]. I think we welcome people in." Katherine here equates my question about feminism with being welcoming, which is perhaps indicative of the knowledge that, for White evangelicals to appear welcoming to those they haven't appeared welcoming to in the past, they need to embrace new ideals.

Katherine immediately followed this thought with, "But the gay rights issue, I'd have to say I don't believe in gay marriage, unless it's classified as differently in terms of whether it's a social marriage or a covenant." Katherine would like to see a distinction between marriages sanctioned by the church (covenant) and those sanctioned by the state. This was a common theme the church wrestled with following the legalization of same-sex marriage at the federal level in June 2015, which is the subject of chapter 6. Much less common is Katherine's connection between a radical feminism and the upholding of the institution of marriage, as radical feminism is a strand of feminism notable for its positioning of patriarchy and its destruction as its central goal. There is a large disconnect between a radical feminist agenda and the protection of a nuclear family setup. I let Katherine continue before I asked her for clarification. Katherine ended her thoughts on feminism by saying that "The thing is that, the problems with gay marriage and divorce and all these things, they are a satanic attack on the family." We can conclude with a degree of certainty that two different understandings of radical feminism are at play here. That is, Katherine's definition of radical feminism differs from someone who identifies as a radical feminist outside of the evangelical church. In contrast to many of her fellow parishioners' beliefs, Katherine may indeed see her views as radical because she believes women should have equality in the workplace and in opportunities to evangelize.

Katherine looked at me with a smile. I asked her how she might further elaborate on her understanding of feminism, one that seems to include both Jesus as radical and a real concern over satanic attacks on the family. Katherine took a sip of her coffee and said, "The family group is a good thing, but if you have somebody that's not a good persuasion sexually in your family, you don't deny them your family. You don't deny them if they don't believe in Christ. Jesus wasn't gonna do that kind of thing." Katherine also seems to suggest that those who don't identify as straight must not follow or believe in Christ. Katherine again goes back to Jesus to help explain, and perhaps understand, her own beliefs. For Katherine, feminism is about equal standing for women, but feminism, as part of the imagined secular, also seems to quickly evoke deep concerns about gays and gay marriage. While Katherine identifies as a feminist, she is quick to draw the line around protections of the heterosexual family.

However, Katherine suggests that, just as Jesus must do, gay individuals should be welcomed into families. Katherine is working to be more accepting and is wrestling with what that might mean in a time in which definitions of marriage and the family seem to be changing. Feminism no longer means the commissioning or recognition of women as godly charges in the church. It also means something else.

I interviewed Maggie, a White, married mother of three in her midthirties. Maggie has a master's degree in early childhood education, but she is currently out of the paid workforce while she raises her children. Maggie is using her educational background to start a group for mothers of young children at Lakeview. I met Maggie for the first time on a July morning in 2016 while her children were attending a summer Bible camp at Lakeview. Maggie told me about her recent negotiations with her husband around childcare, and the frustration she was experiencing that morning with her children and their behavior. Maggie and I spoke for a while about her family dynamics and the ways in which she and her husband are working to balance their parenting duties, and to better communicate about their shared frustrations with the difficulties that come with the daily realities of parenthood. In the context of this conversation, Maggie told me that she identifies as a feminist. Like Katherine, Maggie jumped to politics and gay rights when I asked her more about this identification. Maggie reminisced that her childhood church would directly tell their congregations who to vote for, and said that while she thinks a lot of churches still approach politics in this way, she sees that Lakeview is not so explicit, and wishes Pastor Dave would provide more guidance for her. Maggie said that "With some of those things like gay rights, I think Pastor Dave just tried not to go there, good or bad I'm not sure. Sometimes you know it would be nice to hear a little bit like, from the Bible, but I don't know, can you tie that in, can you find something to talk about Hillary or Trump from the Bible, I'm not sure how that would sway us one way or the other." Maggie laughed and ended her thoughts here. Maggie might be caught between her feminism and political beliefs, and while she has some uncertainty about how to navigate these views, she is also unsure about what the church thinks, too.

Self-identified feminists Katherine and Maggie are quick to bring up politics, issues related to gay rights, and family life when discussing their feminisms. It is common to have feminism and a feminist identity stand in for and encapsulate a multitude of beliefs and an orientation to the world. Indeed, for many a feminist identity is a political identity. However, Katherine and Maggie equate feminism with questions about gay rights, and, in Katherine's case especially, the connection between the two feels threatening. The imagined secular world contains a variety of liberal projects that are bundled and interconnected, and for many feminists, these are not just imagined but very real and important connections. Maggie and Katherine have probably come across many non-evangelical feminists who also advocate for gay rights. But these two women are trying to find a way to weave women's equality into their belief system without also including broader rights for other groups of people they may not approve of, but also feel like they can't explicitly disprove of anymore. And as they work to disentangle and articulate these beliefs, Katherine and Maggie turn to the Bible for answers, and in doing so highlight the centrality of a biblical literalism key to the evangelical identity and orientation to the world, especially when trying to make sense of a changing world.

Previous work documents that Katherine and Maggie are not unusual; there are many evangelical women who identify as feminist but find it difficult to pair their religious beliefs with their own feminist identities (Brasher 1998). Sally Gallagher finds that very few evangelical women are engaged in "any sort of culture war with feminism" (2004b: 460). Rather, almost two-thirds of the evangelical women in her work showed a cautious appreciation for the feminist movement and the accompanying rights gains for women, such as shedding light on issues of domestic abuse. Gallagher frames these findings as a focus on the personal and individual gains of women, rather than an acknowledgment of the fight for structural inequalities in the United States.

This individualistic appreciation for the feminist movement is due in part to the class and race privilege of many evangelical women that can ignore the larger structural inequalities specific to working-class women and women of color (Gallagher 2004b). The second-wave feminist movement is critiqued for its privileging of White women's concerns over others, and then for understanding those concerns as representative of the concerns of all women. These White evangelical women are not alone in their selective appreciation and read of feminist dialogue and beliefs. Feminism has long contained exclusionary components. Feminism, as a political identity, body of thought, and approach to the world, mirrors the interests and needs of those voicing their feminist beliefs, and we should not think of evangelicals as operating differently. However, paying attention to the shifts in exclusionary components of feminism, or, in other words, paying attention to what feminism does and does not represent for White evangelicals at different moments in history, can tell us about their other political fights.

For Maggie and Katherine, feminism might symbolize gains for women, perhaps in the household, workplace, and church, but both seem less comfortable with other feminist rights and fights, especially in more recent history. And for Maggie especially, understandings of these other perceived feminist fights are also tied to our current political moment and most recent presidential election.

Pastor Dave frequently embraced and shared feminist statements in his sermons. His comment about the "F word" and its divisiveness during that Sunday morning before the 2017 Super Bowl was not entirely unusual. In the summer of 2017, Pastor Dave began a Sunday sermon with an update on his children. Pastor Dave is the father of four, and he was ruminating on a recent conversation about career options with his two oldest daughters. Pastor Dave shared with the congregation the sentiment that he had shared with his daughters earlier that week. He said, "I think it's ridiculous that women are not paid the same amount as men, and not afforded the same opportunities as men in our country. And if that's not your theology this isn't your church!" People cheered when Pastor Dave, red in the face and visibly upset at the world his daughters were born into, exclaimed this to the crowd. Pastor Dave was angry, and this anger didn't allow as much room for the presence or acknowledgment of the nonfeminists, or those scared of the F-word, in the room.

While a sociologist like myself would code this statement as feminist, we need to think about what feminism does and does not encapsulate for White evangelicals, and what that can tell us about other cultural fights and discourses. If we take Maggie's and Katherine's statements in tandem with Pastor Dave's words, we can begin to separate statements understood as fights for equality for women and gains in the workplace from what feminism may symbolize for White evangelicals, something equated with gay rights. There are many strands of feminism in the history of the United States, and that remains true today. But Pastor Dave's words may highlight what kind of feminism is appropriate at Lakeview: one focused solely on the gains of women, with a language of equality as its justification and framing. Fights for women in conservative spaces, such as the White evangelical church, are not new either, but what the F word evokes changes.

After Pastor Dave told his congregants that they were in effect in the wrong church if they didn't believe in equal pay for women, he, under his breath, and with a smile on his face, joked, "I mean come on, we're not Baptists!" Such sentiment, and distancing from seemingly more conservative religious groups, became an increasingly common phenomenon during my two years at Lakeview. In an effort to grow and appear more welcoming, especially to those in the younger cohorts, those at Lakeview want to establish and distance themselves within larger conservative religious communities. If Lakeview wants to engage with the messiness of change, they need to do so with open doors, and do so at a great distance from those perceived to be on the Far Right in a nation divided.

The following weekend, Pastor Dave kicked off the Sunday with an apology about this statement. Pastor Dave reminded the audience of his comments from the previous weekend by summarizing his anger at the thought of his daughters being treated as "second-class citizens." He explained his Baptist joke, and said, "You all didn't hear it but it got picked up on the podcast.[3] I apologize for that. I went to Baptist seminary! That was wrong and thank you for sticking with me." In his joke about Baptists, Pastor Dave showed the ugliness, in the words of Pastor Amy, that accompanies change. As Pastor Amy reminded the congregation months before, they must not show that ugliness when they feel squeezed. Pastor Dave might want desperately to grow as a church by comparing their more "open" views with those of other religious groups, but by the teachings of his very own leadership team, a joke and disparaging comparison to another religious group are not the appropriate way to go about doing so.

Seeking a Middle Ground

Many of the individuals I spoke with at Lakeview acknowledge and embrace certain feminist ideals, in the way that Pastor Dave does, for example, but actively work to distance themselves from feminist as an identity or label. I interviewed Becky, a 52-year-old Mexican American woman and an active member of Disciples' Journey, on a hot spring afternoon. Becky and I met at a Starbucks of her choice on her day off from her new job as a receptionist. Becky, who jokingly describes herself as a "half tree-hugger" devotes quite a bit of her week to her essential oils and earth-friendly home-cleaner business. Becky mainly uses both of these business opportunities to get discounts for her family and her friends. She does not rely on them for her primary income. While we waited for our drinks, Becky struck up a friendly and lively conversation with the barista. She looked at the barista's name tag and called her by her name, yet another small moment that highlights Becky's outgoing and warm personality that draws so many to her, me included. When we received our drinks Becky pulled two metal straws from her purse before I could grab a plastic one from the shelf. She gave me her "spiel" (in her words) on the environmental and health concerns related to the copious numbers of plastic straws we use and discard daily.[4] While we walked to a nearby park to enjoy the sun, Becky joked that she cannot identify as a "full tree-hugger" as she hasn't been dedicated to the environment her entire life. While Becky creates personal stipulations around her environmental and activist identity, she fully and happily identifies as a Christ-loving evangelical.[5]

We sat together on a park bench, and over the course of a two-hour interview, I asked Becky about her thoughts on feminism. Becky responded to my question with a story. Becky told me that, at her previous church, the lead pastor left quickly in the midst of a financial scandal, and the church rushed to find an interim replacement for him. Becky told me that the church hired a woman pastor, and that Becky was "not hip to that." Becky described getting to know this pastor quite well, as Becky was working as a staff assistant for the church during this time. Becky told me that this blossoming relationship with the new pastor changed her thoughts on women in positions of leadership. The pastor came from a Lutheran church, which Becky described as "all socially supportive . . . you know, it's the gay-lesbian church, so that was kind of, probably, a softening for me." Becky told me that the new pastor's views, and the ideals she brought with her from her previous denomination, changed her thoughts on women pastors.

Becky continued,

> I do still have that traditional outlook that one man, one woman, the male, the head of the household brings up the happy family, and we all attend church together. You know, to me that's the way it should be. That's the

perfect life. So those traditional values of that are really strong for me. You know, I believe in equality. On the feminist side, I want to be given an opportunity just like anybody else. I have something valuable to say, potentially, just like anybody else, regardless if I am a woman, or Black, or White, or gay, or whatever.

Becky espouses certain feminist beliefs for her rights and the rights of others and seems to understand her fight for her rights as a woman in line with other identity politics. However, Becky also seeks a disconnect between feminism and the traditional family life she considers ideal. Becky told me that she "wants the church to be open to feminism" but, "at the same time, I think of the nuclear family. It should be a triangle. We are both corners of the triangle, and God is leading us to the right solution. It's more about a partnership than taking my stand as a woman. I don't want people to take a stand because they're a woman, or take a stand because they're gay, or to take a stand because they're Black. I want people to be people and be treated right because they're people." Becky wants her rights as a woman to be recognized, but, at the same time, does not want them to be recognized *because* she is a woman. Becky wants gains for women but, unlike Katherine and Maggie, does not want the label of feminist and what it might evoke. In some ways, Becky's sentiments are not that different from Katherine's and Maggie's, as they put such strict parameters around what feminism means to them.

Further, Becky quickly equates feminism with threats to a heterosexual relationship, perhaps because she does not feel comfortable claiming specific things as a woman. Becky refers to the triangle of a relationship, what evangelicals often talk about as a relationship between a husband, wife, and God, and Becky does not want feminism to disrupt that. Some of the existing research on conservative Christian religious responses to the feminist movement finds that, for evangelicals, second-wave feminism is understood as hostile to evangelical life and values (Gallagher 2003, 2004a, 2004b). Specifically, many evangelicals believe that feminism promotes a form of selfishness that detracts from the important focus on the family, which carries with it very specific notions of gender and gender identity: (1) a belief in gender essentialism and complementarity, that is, that gender differences are a reflection of God's creation, and these differences between men and women reflect incomplete opposites that can complete each other through marriage; (2) a belief in headship, that is, that part of God's ordained characteristics for men and women include that men are the authority within the household, family life, and society (Bartkowksi 2001; Gallagher 2004a: Irby 2014b; Kelly 2012; Moon, Tobin, and Sumerau 2019; Scholz 2005). Most evangelicals believe strongly that men and women are inherently different, and that men have the ultimate authority in the home. For many evangelicals, to adopt a feminist identity is to question beliefs in both gender complementarity and heterosexuality, foundations of the church.

Take for example a sermon Pastor Dave delivered on the topic of gender and marriage. Pastor Dave began by telling Lakeview that "I know we're near Seattle, and it's a politically correct area, and a pretty liberal area.[6] But let's stay close to the scriptures this morning and see what we can hear them saying and maybe it's time for us to take a different turn." Pastor Dave continued, "At the same time, I don't like issues that divide people. I don't presume to have all the answers up here. There are plenty of portions of the Bible that I would deem controversial. . . . However, I am going to argue this morning that there is a clear difference in roles between a man and a woman in marriage. The last thing I want to do though is reinforce any stereotypes that are broken or give fuel to any relationships in the room that are suffering right now." Pastor Dave introduced his belief in gender complementarity with many qualifiers to set the stage for the sermon to come, and he did so with reference to the looming, liberal city nearby.

Pastor Dave continued, "God created male and female as equals but they are not equivalent. They are not supposed to do the same things, although they are equals to one another." This was a common refrain in the church when discussing gender complementarity, that difference did not imply an unequal status between men and women. This is a logic that might work for some until the second major understanding of gender, headship and women's submission, is considered.

Pastor Dave tackled this concern head-on: "And let's be careful with cultural norms when we talk about submission." Pastor Dave then talked about "Communist Russia" and how Christianity was subversive in Russia during the reign of communism when Paul taught people about Christianity there 2000 years ago. Pastor Dave provided examples for how conservative the culture was in Russia during that time, "with women wearing veils," and went on to state that when Christianity was introduced in Russia, it liberated people. "So let's remember that about the heart of Christianity, that it sets people free. It liberates people." In treating Christianity as the liberating agent in a longer sermon about submission, Pastor Dave can create the argument that the submission they talk about in the church is not a "bad" kind of submission, like, say, wearing a veil or communism.

Pastor Dave asked the congregation to think about what liberation might look like in the context of Ephesians 5, which includes the long-controversial Bible verse about wives submitting to their husbands.[7] Pastor Dave said that "Some in Seattle may read this scripture at first glance and say that's oppression. And I can understand that argument. But also understand that I have three daughters. And I'm about as much of a feminist as you can be when it comes to my perspective on their life, their calling, their leadership, their potential, as I do my son." In claiming a feminist identity, and one that is "about as much of a feminist as you can be," Pastor Dave ends a conversation on concerns over oppression before it begins; if he is a feminist and believes in specific definitions of submission, others in the church can hold these beliefs too.

Pastor Dave's message as part of this Sunday sermon is an example of the church's bounded welcoming of external threats. As the lead pastor, Pastor Dave incorporates, holds space for, and devotes entire sermons to the messiness of the imagined secular. But Pastor Dave does that while both claiming a feminist identity and preserving the church's belief in gender complementarity. Pastor Dave reminded his congregation that Christianity is liberating, and that while the Lakeview community is situated near (and, really, against) the more liberal and "PC" forces of Seattle, he, as an identified feminist, can hold beliefs that support headship and submission, so his congregation can, too. Pastor Dave is setting the terms for what feminism might mean in the church: rights for women, such as equal pay, but rights *outside* of the church and *outside* of the home. Pastor Dave puts forth a feminism that does not disrupt the understandings of women's positions within an evangelical household, a position that is, in his framing, not rooted in or representative of an unequal standing next to men. The church can claim its place in larger conversations about addressing gender inequality while simultaneously allowing gender inequality to prevail.

In his sermon on gender and marriage, Pastor Dave continued to delve into the topic of submission. He again told the audience that Lakeview understands that while men and women are created differently, this difference does not imply inferiority. He said that men and women have different jobs and different ways of being fulfilled. Pastor Dave also said that in most relationships, the issue of submission is in reality infrequent. Pastor Dave talked about how when he and his wife, Melissa, disagree, one of them usually has the better argument, and the other person concedes.

But what if there is that one time out of that 100 where you both have great arguments, you both have prayed, you both have asked the Lord, you've both sought wisdom and as you come together you say, we can't decide what to do. . . . Well who decided in that moment, and this is when that verse comes into play. If we can't decide than we each step into our roles. Equal to one another but not equivalent. She steps into her role and defers to me, and I step into my role and I decide. Now, want the truth? I don't want to submit to my role. You know what I would much rather have happen? I would much rather have Melissa decide because then it's not on me! If it goes south, well, I didn't make that call!

Many in the congregation laughed at his joke. Pastor Dave ended the sermon with a brief caveat: he mentioned that headship is something that is earned, not taken, and that if a husband is not loving his wife sacrificially he does not deserve headship. He told the congregation that "this gender stuff" does not apply to all women and men. "Are all women commanded to submit to men? Heck no! Are you kidding? Look around. Men are broken. The Bible knows it. Women are broken. The Bible is smarter than that. This is only for the context of marriage. . . . The only safe place for this to manifest is in a biblical covenant where both parties are obedient to the Lord."

Before closing, Pastor Dave again reminded the audience of his identification as a feminist, and the worship band returned to the stage. In Pastor Dave's beliefs, headship does not run counter to an understanding of gender complementarity as something that can be understood to promote gender equality. Pastor Dave dismisses concerns over submission by both comparing it to "worse" forms of submission abroad and claiming its infrequency in relationships within the church. Further, although Pastor Dave concedes that, when push comes to shove, he will be the person to make the decision in his household and his wife will submit, Pastor Dave frames this decision-making authority as a burden on *him,* not as a reflection of his wife's unequal standing in their home. This reworking of submission both to argue for its egalitarianism and to uphold the power of men was a sentiment shared in couples' interviews as well.

Pastor Dave described marriage as the relationship for appropriate and safe enactments of gender complementarity. As such, couples' interviews with members of the Lakeview congregation provide the context within which to further explore the messiness and tensions around gender complementarity and feminism. Annie, a 29-year-old White woman who works in human resources, is married to Darren, a White man and social worker of the same age. I interviewed Annie and

Darren together at a coffee shop down the street from Lakeview, where we agreed to meet after a Sunday service. Annie arrived wearing somewhat baggy, flowy clothing and had curled her long hair. Darren wore thick, hip glasses, had sleeves of tattoos on both arms, and lovingly smiled at Annie, who sat next to him while he went first in answering my questions about feminism.

Darren told me that "Feminism doesn't apply to us, because, while I am the head of the household, Annie is my better and my superior. She doesn't need to rise up with feminism." For Darren, feminism represents a potential disruption to their family life and understandings of gender within the household. Darren espoused a cultural view of feminism that assumes innate differences between men and women, and also works to assign and validate specific attributes to women (Alcoff 1988; Taylor and Rupp 1993). For Darren, feminism represents a movement to help women "rise up" in the public and private spheres, but this movement is rendered nonsensical if he *believes* that his wife is his superior. Darren also espouses a "good guy" rhetoric by putting his wife first, while simultaneously establishing his own dominance and headship.

This logic continues in the couple's shared understanding of the Bible. Paraphrasing Ephesians 5:25, Darren stated that, as the Bible says, "Husbands should love their wives the way Christ loved the church." Darren, somewhat in jest, asks me and Annie rhetorically, "I am supposed to love her so much that I'm going to get crucified?" Darren and Annie both laughed before Darren continued with, "That's a long way to go that I have to catch up to treating her like that." They both laughed some more in a lighthearted manner that suggested my questions represented settled issues for them both. Feminism does not apply to their relationship or make sense for them. And, if anything, men are the ones who are in the more difficult position in an evangelical romantic relationship.

Darren sighed and said that "It's hard in a relationship when one person is serving the other and they aren't getting reciprocated, but if both people are serving each other and putting each other first, it will balance." Here, Annie interjected with the following, "The first half of that [biblical verse] is 'wives submitting to husbands.' Sometimes that can be perceived as like, 'what?! I'm not a slave, I don't have to submit!' But you have to read the other half of the scripture, which is 'husbands love your wives as much as you love the church.'" Darren interrupted Annie with "Yeah, I would happily change positions with her and submit to her over being crucified and dying for our sins." They both laughed again.

In the end, of course, Annie will submit to Darren's wishes and authority in the household, and Darren will not get crucified. However, Darren's logic of love and crucifixion works to masculinize his love and place the emotional burden of the relationship on him. He is adopting a tactic similar to Pastor Dave. Darren reframed a conversation about feminism and submission to focus on what he feels is a burden of decision-making, not the power of authority.

Annie and Darren feel that men have a more difficult position both in marriage and in submission. Darren recodes a common part of an evangelical masculinity, headship, with an emotion often coded as feminine: love (Cancian 1987). Darren's story is in line with other work that finds that evangelical men find new and surprising alternatives for asserting their masculinity (Burke and Haltom 2020; Diefendorf 2015; Heath 2003; Wilkins 2009). Annie doesn't need to "rise up" with feminism, because to do so would suggest that Darren's masculinity does not have the strength to bear the burdens of the household and marital love. This evangelical couple's discussion of feminism also resonates with a larger cultural backlash against feminism that argues that feminism emasculates men.

Annie and Darren construct feminism in relation to their understandings of the categories of woman and man. These categories contain qualities that, embedded within a larger system of symbolic meanings, define gender positions (Butler 2006; Schippers 2007). These gendered positions are defined by difference, and a difference that is central to heterosexual desire (Butler 2006). As Mimi Schippers argues, "In contemporary Western societies, heterosexual desire is defined as an erotic attachment to difference, and as such, it does the hegemonic work of fusing masculinity and femininity together as complementary opposites" (2007:90). While Schippers suggests that there is much more to the content of both masculinity and femininity than just erotic desire, the centrality of heterosexual desire to the "essence of gender difference" is key to establishing and giving symbolic meaning to the relationship between masculinity and femininity. As such, for many White evangelicals feminism may be understood as a force that threatens the core attributes of both gender *and* heterosexuality. Annie doesn't need to "rise up" with feminism, because to do so might challenge the gendered order of difference on which the foundations of heterosexuality and an evangelical family rest.

Annie takes a similar stance to Darren but relies on different stories to explain her views on feminism. Annie told me how Darren wants to be a stay-at-home dad, while she wants to be able to focus more on her career. Darren nodded along. Annie said that "Just the other day, I was reading an article about men who go to their child's something or other [activity] and are alone in the corner, not being included." As such, Annie told me that issues of gender inequality can be viewed from "both sides." Annie said, "Because I think both roles are treated unequally." She continued and said that "Women do get paid less than men, and it depends on the type of woman you are. Something I learned through getting my master's degree, if you are a really bitchy woman, you are going to get paid way more than a woman who is really nice. For men, it's the opposite. That is really backwards, I don't think that's right, but I also don't think it's right that men are excluded from taking care of their children, that we view them as less of a parent because they are male." Annie equates discrimination of women in the workplace with a perceived discrimination of men who actively parent their children in spaces that are, for a variety of structural reasons, often mostly occupied by women.

Annie finished her thoughts by telling me that "I don't think I am the right person to ask about feminism because it's both ways, it's not feminism, it's sexism in general. You know, I hear about Trump putting down women, and that's not okay, that's not right. But it's not right to put men down either." Annie does mention that Trump's recent behaviors at the time of this interview (most notably, the press around the video leak in which Trump described "grabbing women by the pussy"), or what Annie calls "putting women down," is linked as an example to her thoughts on feminism and sexism. But much as Annie and Darren understand shifts in gendered and family dynamics as disproportionately affecting and burdening men, Annie is also quick to highlight that putting both men *and* women down is bad. Annie is uncomfortable claiming rights for herself and others as women and, as with Becky's earlier sentiment, is perhaps more comfortable taking a "humanist" approach to understandings of gendered change.

I asked Darren if he agrees with Annie's thoughts on Trump, feminism, and this idea that we should be focusing more on gender discrimination against both men and women, and not on feminist gains for women explicitly. Darren's facial expression changed a bit, and he looked nervous as he said, "To kind of just explain what I'm gonna say . . . one thing we haven't mentioned is Annie was born in the former Soviet Union. She spent the first seven years of her life there and then moved here and became more Americanized over time." I smiled and nodded to encourage him to continue, and he said, "There is a Russian saying that 'God anointed men to protect women.' That is a calling and that's something that we're supposed to be doing and I think Christianity is a patriarchal system." Annie interjected here and said, "Definitely!" Darren continued, "Where the man is the head of the household and I think we are being more conservative in that area because I do see myself as the head of the household and I don't think feminism really applies to us because again I think Annie is more valuable than I am."

It is worth noting here that the same place was used by both Pastor Dave and Darren and Annie to help explain their views on gender. For Pastor Dave, Russia was implicated as the bad, suppressive "Other" in relation to a liberating depiction of Christianity. For Annie and Darren, connections to the former Soviet Union and Russian folklore are used to explain their more conservative beliefs about gendered divisions in their household. It is important to pay attention to the lived religion and deep stories of individuals, alongside attention to the institutions and messages of the institution of which they are a part (Ammerman 2016; Edgell 2012). Symbols can be used in different ways by a group of people we might otherwise treat as a bloc, but, in this case, the use of Russia as a symbol in different ways has the same end result.

Darren reiterated to me, "I don't see her as beneath me, to need to rise up with feminism. I believe she is something to be cherished and I actually go farther than considering her my equal, I consider her my better. I think some of the things that feminism is trying to get rid of are actually good things." Feminism will make it difficult for Darren to rely on an understanding of gender essentialism that retains his position as head of the household. Darren justifies this position by "cherishing" Annie, in line with Pastor Dave's suggestion that headship needs to be earned, not taken. Darren, like many at Lakeview, wants specific gains for women, but in the household, shifts in understandings of gender would shatter the evangelical marital relations that rely on difference.

While both Annie and Darren may disagree with many aspects of what the feminist movement represents to them as a couple, they feel they need to engage in open conversations with those who have different opinions and work to understand where those perspectives come from. Annie and Darren then both told me about those in their life who are different than them, and how they cherish such interactions. They both described one of Darren's best friends, who is "a lot more conservative" than them. While Darren and his friend agree on "religious stuff," Darren said that "he and his wife are separated. His wife is very much an extreme feminist and Social Justice Warrior.[8] So we have very different opinions surrounding us." Darren wants to engage with those who hold different opinions, but the very example he gave for engaging with those who are different represents a literal threat to the marriages he and Annie seek to protect. Darren gave himself away a bit with this comment; he wants to talk to feminists, but in Darren's world, "extreme" feminists are also Social Justice Warriors, a phrase understood as derogatory to signify a person who expresses and promotes socially progressive views related to feminism and civil rights. For many who use the phrase disparagingly, it is also meant to signify that the person is too politically correct or cares too much about identity politics.

Darren went on to tell me that the *good* parts of feminism—equal pay and women's ability to lead in the church—should be celebrated, but that there is a "fine line" between evangelicals being caring, loving, and accepting of people and society becoming too "thin-skinned." For Darren, "feminism and social justice have contributed to this [society becoming too thin-skinned]." Darren added, "Don't get me wrong, I am accepting of trans rights and using bathrooms, but this whole 'did you just assume my gender' is too far." Darren talked about seeing individuals in service positions who have their preferred gender pronouns on their nametags. He provides Starbucks baristas as an example, an institution that many at Lakeview seem to frequent with pleasure. These nametags are helpful for Darren, as someone who is "trying to learn" but who gets frustrated when individuals get mad when people misgender them.

For Darren, a question about feminism brings up debates central to understandings of gender and sexuality in the United States. Debates over trans rights and a focus on bathrooms are examples of "gender panics" where conversations about trans individuals' access to sex-segregated spaces are partially about trans rights, but more largely about core beliefs about what it is to be a man and a woman today (Schilt and Westbrook 2015). And bathrooms, as one of the final sites of gender segregation in the country, become the locus of many anxieties about change. While feminism evokes an array of other issues for Darren, Darren's response is in many ways quite different from others who bring up things like gay marriage and women's rights as examples of progressive and liberal causes they do *not* agree with. Here, feminism for Darren evokes a progressive cause with which he *does* agree. Darren equates feminism with trans rights and is quick to say that he is in favor of rights and access to bathrooms for trans folks. Even if Darren complains about people being thin-skinned, his response illustrates the complicated interplay between White evangelical and secular beliefs that do not neatly align into separate camps, as the rhetoric splashed across both Fox News and CNN alike might suggest.

In a follow-up question, I asked Darren if he had experienced trans individuals getting angry for "assuming their gender." Darren had not had this experience. This is the imagined secular; questions of feminism bring up opinions on trans rights and bathroom bills, as well as perceived, but not actualized or experienced, anger on the part of those trans folks as well. This imagined anger was so powerful for Darren that it shaped his stance on an issue, even though he had never experienced this type of interaction with a trans individual.

Trans rights threaten the very binary thinking that is celebrated and central to the theology of the White evangelical church. In that vein, it is perhaps not surprising that the shifts and increasing visibility of the trans community appear as a formative part of the imagined secular world for evangelicals at Lakeview. However, as Darren suggests, he is working to figure out how to be welcoming and understanding, and he is not alone in that.

Two years after Darren discussed trans rights with me in an interview, Pastor Dave brought up the topic in a sermon about gender. While discussing the importance of gender complementarity within marriage, Pastor Dave added:

> Scripture tells us that men and women are different. I think culture backs this up in many ways. Now there's always cases of a very, very small minority of gender dysphoria. And we know they exist. Where a child is born and they are in a female body and they say "I am male" from the get-go. And yes that happens. And there are studies. I have friends who work in that field and they would absolutely verify that that exists, and we are not negating that at all but for the most part, the majority of culture would agree that boy babies are different than girl babies. They just are.

Pastor Dave's use of the phrase "gender dysphoria" refers to a diagnosis that exists in the DSM-5, and one that has received mass backlash for implying that a trans identity is linked with a mental disorder.[9] This phrasing might be more palatable in the White evangelical church, where, in this instance, Pastor Dave can "acknowledge" variation to the gender binary while simultaneously reinforcing it through a pathologizing language of disorder. Pastor Dave also makes clear that gender dysphoria is a disorder among children, and that young children, from the "get-go," are able to communicate their identity as either girl or boy. Pastor Dave treats gender as a settled, binary issue at an early age, and not something that is perhaps a very different, nonbinary, or ever-evolving experience for others along their life course.

While Darren, Annie, and Becky work to distance themselves from feminism as an identity and political project, their responses to questions of feminism, along with some of the content of Pastor Dave's sermons, highlight just how far to the political and ideological center the Christian Right has been pushed in conversations about gender. The word "feminism" evoked responses on gay rights, trans rights, women in leadership, women's positions in the family and church, and the gender wage gap. The imagined secular world, as a catchall for what evangelicals see as liberal ideals, brings up a broad range of responses to feminism within this evangelical community. A specific focus on gender as an aspect of an individual identity that deserves specific rights opens up much bigger questions about sexuality and gender-based rights they aren't fully ready to disentangle.

These connections between symbols of feminism and concerns about a changing world played out in Disciples' Journey. The night after the 2016 Presidential election, Disciples' Journey held a special "prayer and brainstorming session" during what they felt was a season of transition, in regard to both the presidential election and the church, which was undergoing a shift in some of its leadership, in the transition from Pastor Isaac to Pastor Dave. This prayer night was at best unclear in its goals. The church, in praying for a "changing" nation, was leaving space for the messiness it encourages. Indeed, in small group that night I watched some rejoice over the election results, while others appeared worried and distressed in their facial expressions and tone.

After we all arrived at Lakeview and set up chairs in one of the many conference rooms in the building, the group spent 30 minutes praying for the nation. Joe, a 52-year-old White man, led the group in an impromptu prayer. Joe suggested to the group that they pray for those in the church, and that they pray for those not yet in the church. Sally, a 48-year-old White woman, added that they also "pray for those that we can go out and attack!" The election night seemed to mobilize excitement about evangelizing, or, in Sally's words, "attacking" those not in the church, or those who are not espousing a White evangelical worldview.

There were many tears of joy, and some side conversations about being able to sleep again at night now that the election was over. One side conversation stood out. A few individuals employed in the military sector expressed a renewed sense of job security due to Trump's prowar stance. This started a lengthy debate on the connection to job security and spousal support. This group debate, only part of which is described in the excerpt below, occurred within the context of a prayer night for a changing nation. Both Jess and Kelly, two White women in their thirties, questioned Earl, a 63-year-old White man, and his comments on women and their support of their husband's careers.

> *Earl:* It takes a strong wife to make a career. As a [military officer], you need a party wife. I didn't have that, so maybe I would have been higher up, but I am happy. But same goes for the pastor's wife. She was nice but not outgoing, not open to other women. She never shook my wife's hand, and I saw that as a breakdown for women here.
>
> *Jess:* I am not sure that is a realistic expectation to put on a pastor's wife. Historically yes but that is not reasonable or fair now.
>
> *Kelly:* Yes, they are not hosting potlucks or anything now.
>
> *Earl:* Maybe it is inappropriate, but when someone is expecting that and it's not being fulfilled it's hard to be drawn in [to the church].

This conversation in Disciples' Journey is less about what specific questions of feminism invoke. Instead these observations indicate that within the church, there is often debate about women and men, and how gendered positions are changing in the social world. And this debate occurred between two younger women, part of the Millennial generation, and Earl, a baby boomer. Lakeview members are debating changes in their church against changes in the nation and doing so with concerns about their membership in mind, what Earl referred to as being "drawn in" to the church in this exchange.

In one church, generational differences exist in regard to beliefs about gender, which really get to the heart of fundamental orientations in the way evangelicals approach the world. For those engaging in conversations about feminism, we also see a clear bundling of feminism with a variety of other liberal projects. And the feeling that to deal with something like feminism also means coming to terms with or thinking through questions of sexuality, gay rights, trans rights, identity politics, and the like might lead many to reject the whole notion of feminism entirely.

Rejecting Feminism

There are of course members of the Lakeview community who do not identify as feminist or relate to specific feminist goals. Feminism is an external threat that they seek distance from. For these individuals, feminism invokes the imagined secular world in a way that brings an overwhelming constellation of debates, changes, and threats to the fore, leading them to more actively reject feminist ideals.

Monica, a 65-year-old Mexican American woman with long silver hair, black clothing, and a bright lime-colored scarf, sat across from me with an excited and warm smile as we discussed women in the church. Monica went to a different coffee shop than the one she recommended for our interview, and after some frantic back-and-forth emails on my part, we found each other. The abundance of coffee establishments in the northwest is both a blessing and a curse when trying to schedule meetings with others. I offered to buy Monica a sandwich as our morning interview was now approaching the lunch hour, and I felt badly for the confusion and added time commitment to her day. Monica seemed totally unfazed by the mix-up and told me that this is something she does regularly in her life and laughed it off.

Monica offered to split her sandwich with me, shared on one plate. While I declined, this was a quick act of intimacy indicative of her immediate openness and vulnerability, which was reflected in her interview responses. About halfway through our interview I asked Monica her thoughts on feminism. I reminded her of the jokes made on Super Bowl Sunday about women, food, and feminism as a transition to this topic in the interview. She frowned and quickly told me that being a feminist and Christian are in direct conflict. Monica said, "Men and women have certain roles. Feminism is Gloria Stein-man [sic] and abortion." Feminism is antithetical to a division of labor and family life that is central to evangelical identity, which Becky, Katherine, and Maggie all ran up against in their discussions of feminism as well. Importantly the word "feminism" immediately brings up Gloria Steinem and reproductive rights, the latter the issue many pundits named as key in the evangelical voter turnout for President Trump, and indeed something that is often treated as synonymous with feminism.

When I asked Monica to expand upon her understanding of women and men's roles, she said, "Well, men and women are equal. I do believe that. But we aren't *made* [emphasis hers] equal. Women were made from Adam's rib." Much as when Katherine went to the Bible to understand and justify women's equality via Jesus and Mary Magdalene, Monica also relies on a literal interpretation of the Bible to understand her beliefs on gendered difference. Monica also connects her literal understanding of the Bible with her belief in gender equality. This internal contradiction was a recurring theme in interviews with congregants: an apparent tension between long-held and enduring beliefs in gender complementarity and beliefs in gender equality. And for many in the church, gender complementarity is gender equality, but this view doesn't hold the same weight outside of the church walls anymore. However, unlike Monica, most individuals I spoke with at Lakeview are trying to find some type of middle ground that incorporates elements and identifications of feminism with their understandings of gender. But these tensions seemed to exist for everyone I spoke with, and while they are both consistent and multifaceted, they are all occurring within one church.

THE IMAGINED SECULAR FEMINIST

A week after the 2016 presidential election, I attended Disciples' Journey on a Thursday evening. The notion of the northwest liberal bubble popped, as the exit polls made it quite clear that many in the northwest, evangelicals included, had voted for Donald Trump. Though conservative political support had risen in the South, as Arlie Hochschild has documented, Trump backers in places like the Pacific Northwest had been largely and wrongfully ignored by many.

Disciples' Journey met in a Starbucks that evening. Lakeview had rented out a good deal of its space to a local organization for events that night, so we met outside of our usual conference room setting. Our table was crowded with Bibles, worksheets, binders, new Pathways materials for the group to discuss, and beverages. While group members drank tea and nibbled on biscotti, they casually discussed marriage and how to navigate a long-term relationship as a good Christian. Frank, a 67-year-old White military veteran, scoffed at the premise of this conversation and said the following: "You think marriage is easy? No way!" Frank's decorated military career required travel and long periods of time away from home before his retirement. Now, he makes sure that his wife "calls the shots" about their schedule, and he works to prioritize her wishes for their daily schedule and activities. Frank told the group that he tries to do everything he can to cater to her day, after she spent decades doing the same for him. In the middle of this conversation, Frank paused and said that he noticed a new ring on my finger. The group resumed its conversation when I responded "no" to Frank's question about a recent engagement.

Frank followed me into the parking lot after the meeting ended that night. Frank put on his hat that read, "Love your freedom? Thank a

Vet!" as we walked outside. He brought my ring up again, and I asked him if he felt somehow deceived or confused that I was wearing a ring on my "ring finger" without an engagement. Frank shook his head and said no, and then explained to me that part of his military training was to notice details, and to do so immediately. I frequently recorded moments in my field notes when Frank made comments about noticing things about me. For example, at the start of many Disciples' Journey meetings, Frank would comment on the model of car I had driven that evening. For the first year of fieldwork, I was using ZipCar, a car-sharing service, and thus often parked a different vehicle in the parking lot at Lakeview each week. I never saw Frank in the parking lot when I arrived, but Frank always seemed to be well aware of his surroundings. Because of this, his comment about my ring did not feel new or unusual to me.

Frank continued to talk about his military days as we walked across the large parking lot. Frank told me that he feels the US military does not act as strongly as it should today. To illustrate his point, Frank told me that women need protecting, but we do not protect them enough as a country. Frank said, "Imagine if someone brutally raped someone. I don't mean got drunk and raped her. I mean brutally raped her, and we went after him. If someone touched my wife, or hurt my wife, you better believe they would be paying for it." Frank paused here and then said, "And I don't mean a quick death. I would inflict the kind of pain I saw in Vietnam." Frank's language here harkens back to the rhetoric of the evils afoot that captured the nation in the 1970s, and whose stronghold proved so effective in mobilizing support for the answers provided by the White evangelical church (Jenkins 2006).

Frank described how these feelings of protection are especially intense among young men because of testosterone, relying on a biological framework to justify these gendered enactments. Frank invokes a form of gender essentialism that understands women as needing protection by men, but his views on sexual assault as excusable under some (still illegal) circumstances are unusual for Lakeview. Oftentimes, during Sunday sermons or in small group, sexual assault was cited as "the line" when it came to conversations about working through a relationship and upholding norms of submission. For example, in a sermon about marriage, Pastor Dave discussed the important role of forgiveness after conflict, but quickly said, "If there is ever verbal or physical or sexual assault involved, that is a different story," alluding to the caveat that headship must always be earned. For Frank a concern about women and women's rights is indeed central in this political moment, but

Frank's sentiments express a very different form of concern and dialogue than, say, the #MeToo movement.[10]

Frank kept talking, and made a quick transition to politics, no doubt on everyone's mind, given the proximity to election night. Frank told me that while he didn't love Trump, Frank was happy with the election results because Clinton could not protect the nation in the ways that he wanted. In Frank's opinion, Clinton would not increase military presence and strength to the degree Frank desired, again, an increase somehow related to Frank's feelings about the protection needed for American women. Further, Frank stated, "Again, I don't love Trump, but I *hate* Hillary. She is the most deceitful and corrupt politician out there. She surrounds herself with lesbians."

Frank and I chatted a bit more, and I asked him to expand on his claims about Hillary Clinton's associates and their sexual identities. Frank went to his truck and grabbed a book he was reading, and quickly opened up to the page that talked about how, in Frank's summary, "The [White House] staff made sure that Monica didn't get near Bill, and Bill tried to hide her from others, but it wasn't just her, there were lots of women, and Hillary knew!"

At this point, Frank held the book out toward my face and pointed to the section that he had underlined and said, "See?!" Frank closed the book and tossed it into the open passenger door of his truck.[11] Frank continued, "And it's not just that. She had a secret thing on the side too. She's had a secret lesbian relationship for 25 years." I asked Frank whom Hillary Clinton's secret lesbian relationship was with, as it was clear at this point that he had diverged from the details he had been reading on the page and was speaking from his own perspective. Frank laughed and said, "I can't divulge that to you!" Frank frequently mentioned work trips to Washington, DC, to engage in some military consulting, and here, Frank was alluding to some insider knowledge gained from those work trips.

While Frank wasn't thrilled with Trump, Trump was also promising an increased national defense, and perhaps overall sense of nationalism for Frank. For Frank, the rhetoric of Make America Great Again might invoke a sense of protection, and importantly protection over women that Hillary Clinton could not introduce. Further, this rhetoric focused on protecting women might be understood as a way Frank is reaffirming his own masculinity. Recent work finds that both men's and women's endorsement of idealized forms of masculinity—what Raewyn Connell termed "hegemonic masculinity"—helps explain support for Donald

Trump as a political candidate (Vescio and Schermerhorn 2021). For example, Robb Willer and coauthors find that men whose sense of masculinity is threatened increase their support for more aggressive foreign policy (Willer et al. 2013). And other research finds a correlation between fragile masculinity and support for Trump: that is, areas in which men exhibited online search topics associated with men's concerns about living up to certain ideals of masculinity ("hair loss," "erectile disfunction," "how to get girls," "penis size," and the like) were also areas of the country more likely to support Trump. And, importantly, fragile masculinity was unrelated to support for female candidates, leading the authors to suggest that "fragile masculinity doesn't reduce support for female candidates but rather increases support for Republican candidates of any gender" (Knowles and DiMuccio 2018). Other work finds that concerns over the United States becoming "too soft and feminine" contributed to support for Donald Trump (Deckman and Cassese 2021). Therefore, it might be the combination of both a threat to one's masculinity, especially in Frank's case, *and* something about the women candidates themselves that he and others are responding to.

For Frank and many others in the church, Hillary Clinton symbolized the imagined secular feminist they work to define themselves against. The imagined secular world includes women politicians who, in their positions of power, break a whole host of norms around gender and sexuality. Frank's concerns with the Clintons did not center on Bill Clinton's documented affair, but rather Hillary's knowledge of the affair, and rumors about her own lesbian affair as well. Evangelical Christians have a language and focus and understanding of sexual redemption for men, a sexual redemption of men that often requires the help, encouragement, and gatekeeping from women (Diefendorf 2015). For Frank, Hillary Clinton failed in her role as a woman in this way by "knowing" about the affair and not doing anything with this knowledge. In Frank's mind, Hillary Clinton's failure as a sexual gatekeeper was probably just as egregious as the rumors about her own affair.

Further, the statement that started this whole conversation was about Frank's concerns about protecting women. Clinton may have also symbolized a woman who, due to her political career and successes in life, represented the type of woman that did not signal a need for protection, an enactment of femininity antithetical to many evangelicals' understandings of gender essentialism. As Du Mez (2020) documents, disdain for Clinton among evangelicals goes back to her much earlier transgressions as a wife who initially refused to take her husband's name, and as a feminist who suggested she could have stayed home, baked cookies, and had tea instead of pursuing her law career when she received questions about it on her husband's campaign trail in 1992.

My interactions with Frank the week after the 2016 presidential election highlight something quite important: feelings, emotion, and symbolism play crucial roles in politics. Frank was not thrilled about Donald Trump as a political candidate, but Hillary Clinton's gender enactments and what they symbolized to Frank, as a White evangelical man, proved much more important in his understanding of the two candidates.

At the most basic level, feminist values, however broadly or specifically defined, stand counter to evangelical tenets of gender: headship and the belief that women and men are created differently and for different purposes by God. For those at Lakeview who identify as feminist, or for those who adopt some aspects of feminist values but reject the label, their collective focus centers on rights for women under the language of *equality*. This language works to advocate for gains in the workplace, but does so without disrupting understandings of essentialism. Feminists and nonfeminists alike at Lakeview find ways to advocate for women without explicating claiming rights *as women;* rather, they discuss and advocate for equality between men and women, a specific understanding of equality that, within the context of a heterosexual marriage, still leaves men with power over their wives.

A language of equality also allows for the erasure of individual, identity-based calls for rights while establishing the church as a welcoming place. Evangelicals at Lakeview are able to say they are not against rights for women, to appease older and younger generations alike, but they do so in a way that does not alienate those who would oppose feminism as a label and political orientation. The church engages in a *bounded welcoming* of feminism, as a component of the imagined secular. They have figured out how to talk about and parade gender equality while upholding gender inequality in the church. And they've found ways to hold space for the messiness in responses to feminism that still leave men in positions of power in and outside the household. White evangelicals have worked to adopt this language of equality over the past few decades, but now feminism symbolizes other issues they must confront as well.

Because feminism is part of the imagined secular, rights for women also mean rights for gay and for trans individuals and changes in the family. Feminism is bundled with a whole host of other liberal projects, such as fights for gay marriage, gay rights, divorce, and trans rights, and disruptions to the household and family dynamic that many evangelicals hold dear. To advocate for *women's* rights, explicitly, might lead to a logical step in which White evangelicals should be advocating for gay rights and trans rights too. At Lakeview, many express a discomfort with identity politics, and the phrase itself has become a charged signifier for what right-wing ideology in the United States vehemently opposes. While all politics are grounded in identity, acknowledging one's own identities in relation to their political beliefs and pursuits can be difficult when some identities in the church are normalized and others are made hypervisible. Heterosexual, married womanhood is rendered normal at Lakeview, and because of the bundling of liberal projects that occurs within the minds of those at Lakeview, feminism, as a broad symbol, makes other fights discernible: gay rights, trans rights, women lesbian politicians who cannot act as the sexual gatekeepers for their cheating husbands, and disruptions to the nuclear family, broadly. Advocating for the rights of women might seem strange for evangelical women and men, both because of the understandings of gender that have been normalized for the entirety of their lives, and because feminism also represents these other fights as well.

Congregants at Lakeview are talking about a range of issues on the minds of many during this cultural moment; indeed, the imagined secular appears to bring up similar questions for both Millennials and Baby Boomers alike. However, those at Lakeview are not ready to make any unified statements about these issues, as is evident in their varied responses to one word. There is an inherent tension at the center of engagement with the imagined secular, then: the church's desire to grow requires engagement with these fights, and the church's desire to remain somewhat unmarked—in this case—to avoid the label of sexist or homophobic also requires engagement. But such an engagement also runs the risk of fundamentally altering the foundations on which the White evangelical church is built, and the leadership and congregants of Lakeview have found the balancing act through their support of Donald Trump. When a presidential election feels like a choice between a deceitful, feminist, unwomanly wife and rumored lesbian, Hillary Clinton (the terrifying avatar of the imagined secular), and Donald Trump, a broken man who deserves forgiveness and grace, the choice through a White evangelical logic is clear. And what a bonus when Donald Trump also makes clear, through his own personal behaviors and public policies, that he will keep things stagnant or enact reversals in the broad category of the politics of gender. Trump is definitely not suggesting, through his comments or history with women, that he is going to introduce mass changes to the collective gendered order, if there is such a thing. Trump will do the ugly work while those at Lakeview quietly back him. Those at Lakeview can continue to work to find a balance that allows them to shed any ugliness, and to work through the messiness in a way that results in an appearance of welcoming and open doors.

Evangelicals at Lakeview aren't collectively excited about Trump, and they should not be. Many evangelicals find so much of what he represents uncomfortable and, in some cases, counter to their understandings of Christianity. But many evangelicals aren't comfortable with Hillary Clinton, either. And, in tandem with their understandings of feminism, this discomfort with Clinton matters more. Clinton did and does not enact her role as a woman correctly. She is, perhaps, in the minds of many, the embodiment of the F word: an individual who gets so much attention in her presidential bid precisely because she is a woman, and her success as the first woman presidential candidate represents its own form of women's advocacy, even just in her ability to claim that title. Clinton is the combination of the threat of the Democrat and the threat of a woman who believes strongly in what Clinton and many others would call, very intentionally, *women's* rights.

In the next three chapters, I explore how Lakeview and its members make sense of recent shifts in understandings of racial and sexual politics. Both of these areas, in some way, have a shorter history of collective understanding in the church than questions of gender. While there of course exist key overlaps between evangelical understandings of gender, sexuality, and race, exploring questions related to these areas helps highlight how recent perceived changes, such as the organization of Black Lives Matter and the legalization of same-sex marriage, provoke more anxiety and confusion in the church that they need to address.

CHAPTER 4

White Evangelicals

Emotion Work and Racial Inequality

"Hands Up, Don't Shoot." This plea became the rallying cry for a nation-wide social movement after a White police officer shot and killed Michael Brown, an 18-year-old Black high schooler, in Ferguson, Missouri, on August 9, 2014. Brown was accompanied by his friend Dorian Johnson that late summer day. Johnson recounted to the media afterward that Brown had his hands in the air in surrender when he was shot. Mass protests followed Brown's killing and spread quickly across the nation. This groundswell of mobilization came to be known as the #BlackLives-Matter movement, which had emerged following the murder of Trayvon Martin the year prior. These killings ignited long-simmering national debates on racial inequality and police accountability.

The emergence of the #BlackLivesMatter movement brought renewed awareness to, and a new language for, racial disparities in the United States that many White folks had the privilege of avoiding. The movement also triggered massive resistance to its message of racial justice: Did Black lives matter? What about blue lives (i.e., police officers' lives)? All lives? Was the upheaval in Ferguson protest or riot? Were the deaths of Trayvon Martin and Michael Brown, and the countless Black people before and after them, justified police action or murder? In the midst of these debates, Ferguson—as a word, a place, a space—became symbolic of much larger battles across the nation: fights for racial justice far from resolved, or even acknowledged in a country built on chattel slavery whose oppressive legacy remains horrifically vivid to this day.

In spring 2016, thousands of miles from Ferguson, Missouri, Pastor Isaac spoke at length about an upcoming visit from his good friend and mentor, Pastor Darryl. Darryl was an older Black man, and a pastor who would be visiting Lakeview from his hometown of Ferguson, the place where Michael Brown was killed two years before. Pastor Isaac acknowledged the importance of the visit the Sunday before Pastor Darryl arrived. As part of his morning announcements before his sermon, he declared to the audience that this visit would be a chance for the congregation to discuss the "state of race in the country." Pastor Isaac's description of the guest sermon carried much more weight than merely the excitement of a visit from an old friend.

On the cool spring morning of Pastor Darryl's guest sermon, Pastor Isaac stood with Pastor Darryl in the sanctuary's front row. Both pastors held their hands in the air while the worship band played its usual rotation of songs. On a typical Sunday morning at Lakeview, congregants filter into the sanctuary with coffees in hand and chat quietly during the first songs, often slow to take their seats. On the morning of Pastor Darryl's visit, most of the seats were filled by the beginning of the first song. The room was much quieter than usual, which gave a sense of increased anticipation from the congregation about the sermon to come.

Pastor Darryl joked about this palpable energy in the room when he took his place at the front of the stage. While Pastor Isaac is serious and quiet, Pastor Darryl told the crowd they would notice a comparable shift in tone during *his* sermon. Pastor Darryl told the audience that when his voice got loud and fast, the audience would know he was preaching. He demonstrated this difference in cadence and tone to the seated congregation. Then he laughed and said, "I'm going to try to hold back my teeny tiny afro so that I don't Blackinize everyone in prayer today!" The audience laughed along with him. Pastor Darryl began to discuss some key factors related to fellowship as evangelicals. He captivated the audience. According to the Bible, he said, in earlier times "it didn't matter what ethnicity you were, they were all working together!" This comment generated lots of loud "Amens!" from the crowd, a call-and-response style virtually unheard of at Lakeview, but much more common in Black churches. Pastor Darryl's voice heightened as he proclaimed, "I don't know what it is about Lakeview, but you all bring out my Afrocentrism!" The crowd laughed loudly.

Pastor Darryl continued his discussion of fellowship and suggested to the crowd that, when one person suffers, everyone suffers with him. Pastor Darryl then paused, Bible in hand, and looked out at the congregation intently. In a quieter voice, he said, "This isn't PC [politically correct], but I'm going to say it," to which a White woman in the audience sitting toward the front of the stage loudly said, "SAY IT!" to the response of cheers around her. Pastor Darryl smiled and continued, "I'm going to use a Mississippi-ism. I ain't interested in Black Lives Matter, I'm interested in All Lives Matter! The Devil sold us a lie!"

In this moment the congregation rose to a standing ovation. This was the only instance in two years that I witnessed this reaction at Lakeview. The audience roared in praise and applause, only quieting once Pastor Darryl started speaking again. Pastor Darryl pointed out a bald, White man sitting in the front row, and started talking about that man's "teeny tiny afro." Pastor Darryl then asked the same parishioner how he got to be so handsome. This too generated lots of laughter in the audience, and perhaps worked to diffuse any lingering tension after talking about the Black Lives Matter movement. Pastor Darryl relied on jokes of difference to lighten up the crowd before moving on with the remainder of the sermon.

Pastor Darryl is an older Black man visiting a predominantly White space thousands of miles from his home. In the words of his friend Pastor Isaac, he is quite literally a symbol of something larger: his one visit was meant to somehow encapsulate the state of race in the country.[1] And his words were meant to provide guidance to the congregants of Lakeview Church. How should they think about, in Pastor Isaac's words, "the state of race in the country"? In the two years I spent observing Lakeview Church, race only came up three times as an *explicit* and main topic during Sunday Sermons. Because race was an infrequent topic of conversation in this space, and because of the many announcements leading up to Pastor Darryl's visit, we can imagine that his sermon and its content were given extra import and significance.

Pastor Darryl's visit and message on that winter Sunday morning are part of a larger pattern at Lakeview Church: a pattern of events and discussions that protect Whiteness from the perceived threats of the imagined secular, and a pattern that sustains a logic that helps justify support for Donald Trump as a faulted White man. In this chapter, I argue that a central feature of the imagined secular is its relationship to Whiteness, in both subtle and overt forms. I then discuss the subtle mechanisms of protections of Whiteness in greater detail: (1) through a reinforcement of White racial ignorance, (2) through the instrumental acceptance of people of color and non-Christians, and (3) through a consistent re-centering of Whiteness and Christianity in conversations and practice. In the second part of this chapter, I discuss "The Problem with Trump" and how the same group of White evangelicals who bring in a pastor to talk about Black Lives Matter also justifies their support for Donald Trump. Lakeview is working to distance itself from the more inflammatory elements that currently categorize the far political and religious right, such as White Christian Nationalism and White Supremacy. In doing so, the church is able to appease younger generations who are pushing for change, but also manages to leave the racial ideology central to the church relatively untouched throughout all of it.

UNDERSTANDING WHITE SPACE

Thinking about race as something individual, unchanging, and natural in both its creation and its social costs is a pervasive rhetoric and belief system. This line of thinking is quite powerful in its consequences, as it helps obfuscate the social, economic, and political forces tied to racial inequalities that are central to racial dynamics and difference in the United States (Desmond and Emirbayer 2009). This thinking is a defining feature of the United States and a defining feature of the White evangelical church. White evangelicals have a theological orientation and cultural toolkit that focuses on individual accountability and individual explanations for social problems: that is, the sinful behaviors of individuals remain the focus and locus for change, while concerns about structural inequality, or the behaviors of institutions, are left untouched (Emerson and Smith 2001). But *Whiteness*—the privilege and social status that come with the membership in the category that we call White—is a key, albeit "unmarked," feature of organizations (Ray 2019), such as the church, and one that is stealthily and overtly protected, often through this very understanding and focus on individual instead of structural solutions to racial inequality.

Whiteness prevails as an unmarked feature of institutions and organizations in part because it is difficult for people who benefit from its privileges to see it. Feminist theorist bell hooks (1994) suggests that this is a key feature of Whiteness, and calls it a "state of unconsciousness," an invisible element of the lives of White folks. But its continued existence relies upon its denial. And this denial is not just fueled by a lack of knowledge of people of color (Lipsitz 2011) or an accidental disregard on the part of white individuals. Rather, Jennifer Mueller (2020) argues that ignorance itself is the foundation of White thinking. Through the concept of *White racial ignorance*, Mueller suggests that ignorance, like knowledge, is a social product, and "people often have interests that make *not* learning and *not* understanding rational, even when knowledge is freely available" (Mueller 2020:145). This framing of ignorance as a cognitive accomplishment (Mueller 2020) instead of a passive accident helps frame White people as active participants in what is often a subtle process of protections of Whiteness.

White racial ignorance is embedded in and reinforced by the organizations that also benefit from protecting Whiteness. Pastor Darryl, a Black man from Ferguson, Missouri, flew to the Pacific Northwest on the invitation of a White pastor. Pastor Darryl told the predominantly White congregation of evangelical Christians that the Black Lives Matter movement is a lie from the devil. Whiteness produces and reinforces a world in which White people do not know Black people (Lipsitz 2011); when a Black man, and a Black man who is revered in his position of power as a preacher, is flown in to the church for a conversation on the state of race in the country, his statement that "All Lives Matter" can carry with it a good deal of weight. His words can perhaps be understood by the White congregation as indicative of what all Black people—or what all "good," Christian Black people—think. White racial ignorance can produce a scenario in which the words of one are understood as the words of many, obfuscating the realities of racial inequity in the United States. Again, this ignorance about people of color is the twin, not the opposite, of knowledge (McGoey 2012; Mueller 2020).

White racial ignorance can also work to absolve White folks of their complicity in maintaining White supremacy at the same time that it draws attention to issues of race and racism. For example, the visibility, weight, and prestige given to Pastor Darryl's visit can be understood as what George Lipsitz (2011) calls a "spectacle": an event of "misdirection" that *attracts* quite a bit of attention while it also simultaneously *detracts* attention from structural issues of race. Pastor Darryl's visit did attract quite a bit of attention, especially as it was described as a chance for the church to talk about the "state of race in the country." However, the content of Pastor Darryl's message also represents a misdirection: his words can reinforce the idea that issues of racial inequality are settled (Lipsitz 2011). Indeed, his words pair nicely with White evangelical theological understandings and belief in individuality, and individual successes over structural concerns about inequality. His words may give the members of Lakeview the idea that there is no work to be done by White evangelicals regarding race relations in the United States because, as Pastor Darryl says, that work is the work of the devil.

The threats of the imagined secular (in this case, the Black Lives Matter movement) are sometimes approached through what appears to be an enthusiastic welcoming. Wendy Moore (2008) argues that the White evangelical church exemplifies her definition of "white institutional spaces" that are created when people of color have been excluded from an institution for a long-enough period of time that all of the influential roles are taken by White individuals, who structure policy and culture in such a way as to benefit and comfort themselves. However, to defend against accusations of racism, some people of color must be permitted into White spaces. Glenn Bracey and Wendy Moore (2017) find that race tests are used to determine when and how to integrate people of color into White evangelical churches without threatening the norms and culture of the space. The ways in which people of color are "permitted" into the church are often through overexaggerated welcomes rather than through threats. For those people of color who pass the tests of the White leadership of the church, they are then often asked to fill highly public roles that are racially stereotypical, regardless of their inclinations and talents, or to speak to congregations specifically on the subject of diversity. In some situations, these exaggerated welcomes are used to create an authentic urban experience for the predominately White audience, what Jessica Barron calls "managed diversity" (2016). Pastor Darryl passed the "race test" of the church (Bracey and Moore 2017) and provided safe snippets of the Black evangelical church for Lakeview through his jokes about preaching, Mississippi-isms, and a call and response–style sermon. But although he was the beneficiary of an "overexaggerated welcome" his visit served to further fuel and uphold White racial ignorance.

Mechanisms that protect and defend Whiteness, on the part of both individuals and institutions, also help diffuse the threats of the imagined secular. Spectacles, events of misdirection, and race tests, as concepts, all powerfully highlight the ways in which institutional protections around Whiteness are often forged through an appeal to come across as nonracist. Those in the Lakeview congregation are able to say that they heard from a Black pastor in Ferguson, Missouri, that the Black Lives Matter movement is born from the devil. They can claim their place in part of a larger national dialogue about racism in the United States, and therefore brush off concerns or criticisms of being part of the problem. As such, they can also avoid the label of racist while also removing themselves from doing any work to challenge the system that benefits them and the institution of which they are a part. A key feature of

Whiteness is that the protections around it create the illusion that issues of race are "settled" in the United States, and that racism is something that bad people employ—and, more accurate for Lakeview, something that people who respond to change with *ugliness* employ. The very mechanisms that fuel the continued power of Whiteness also absolve White people, and White evangelicals at Lakeview, from coming across as ugly during a moment in which they want to be seen as welcoming.

As Tressie McMillan Cottom argues, "whiteness has the political power to be elastic" (2019:135). Whiteness can expand to hold overt displays of white supremacy, and to hide behind a welcoming invitation of a Black male pastor from Ferguson, Missouri. Whiteness can welcome the threats of the imagined secular and nullify them through the same mechanisms that keep it afloat. Those who benefit from its elasticity can indulge in the luxury of looking beyond their own actions to understand and justify the inequalities of the social world in which they live and tell themselves they are good (and not ugly), upholding, indeed, a very White imaginary.

WHITE RACIAL IGNORANCE

In the late spring of 2016, when Disciples' Journey was about halfway through their small-group Pathways curriculum, they began their long unit on missions work. The group had just finished the unit "Life in the Home," which covered topics from individual emotional health and maturity to raising godly children to home finances. Each Pathways unit built off of the last, and now that the group had worked through the foundations of home life, they were (at least in theory) prepared to begin the unit "Life in the World." The logic, as reflected in the materials, goes as follows: with a stable, balanced, and godly home life, one can then begin to think effectively about life outside of the home, and work to bring others into relationship with Jesus.

I arrived at the Thursday-evening meeting early, as usual, and helped Carrie arrange chairs in a semicircle in the brightly lit conference room. The sun was still shining outside, an advantage of our northern latitude in the late spring. Once the group had all arrived, Carrie welcomed everyone and read the Pathways prompt for the evening:

> Our access to adventure in the world is like no other time in history. Within a matter of hours, we can walk along the Great Wall of China, run on island beaches in the Caribbean, roam the jungles of the Amazon, wander the markets of Hong Kong, search the African tundra for lions, or climb the highest

peaks. Not only can we go, but the world now comes to us. We can explore the world and communicate with people who are thousands of miles away instantly on our technological devices. Ray Bakke, author of *A Theology as Big as the City,* notes that "Yesterday, cities were in the nations; today all the nations are in our cities." Cultures from around the globe are in our neighborhoods.

The group interrupted Carrie's introduction to the lesson plan and started debating whether or not there is such a thing as the "African Tundra." Carrie, as one of the authors of the prompt, seemed both embarrassed and annoyed, as two people in the group pulled out their smartphones to help answer the question at hand, reinforcing part of the message in the passage up for debate. This started a broader conversation about how, as Marjorie, a 57-year-old White women, put it, the "world has changed now that we have smartphones at our fingertips." Pastor Jeff chimed in on the group conversation, in agreement with the sentiment being shared by others. Pastor Jeff added that his own neighborhood had changed so much, in its "ethnic makeup and demographics." Pastor Jeff referenced a Hindi cultural center and a Sikh temple now two blocks from his home as evidence of these neighborhood changes.

Katherine, who was knitting in her lap during the conversation, jumped in and recalled aloud her first memory of seeing a Black person in church. She paused and said, "Well, I guess I saw some [Black people] when we would put on our gloves and church dresses and go downtown when I was little." The urban space of the city is understood as a space of Black people, and a space far away, a relic of Katherine's childhood, and not a reality of her adulthood. Katherine continued, "People used to not want to sound foreign, but now people come in groups, and it's a patchwork quilt instead of a melting pot!" Katherine laughed and sounded excited as she said this to the group. For Katherine, a conversation about neighborhood change elicited memories and a reminder of what her neighborhood is not (home to Black people), before her newer observations of a changing suburb whose very definition of change rests on the increased numbers of people who "sound foreign."

Carrie gathered the group's attention, seeming still flustered at the conversation that had ensued from her lesson prompt. Pastor Jeff kicked off the next part of the evening activities. He asked the room full of people to break off into small groups, and each group was then assigned a card that included the information of a member of Lakeview Church serving a mission outside of the United States. Each group was supposed to read about the missionary's work, and, as homework for the following week, pray for the missionary and reach out to them over Facebook messenger or via letter. Paula, a 51-year-old White woman, read the first card out loud to her group, which detailed the information of a young woman named Lauren, stationed in Uganda. Immediately, two women from two other groups spoke up, apparently friends of Lauren. Heather, White and age 64, told the room that Lauren is working against those in Uganda who are "struggling with spirits." Becky clarified to the group that these spirits come in the form of both "voo-doo witchcraft" and "the Muslim influence." The group nodded in understanding and continued on with their conversation about who would contact Lauren directly, and who would pray for her mission.

This small group interaction at the start of their weekly gathering underscores the racialized anxieties that demographic shifts in the suburbs produce, and the ways in which those anxieties reinforce the bounds of urban and suburban, and local and global, spaces. According to Katherine, one is a space where things are changing, and the other, the closest urban center, is a stagnant place home to Black people. This understanding of place and space maintains a specific understanding of Whiteness through a distancing from Black spaces, what Lipsitz (2011) calls a racialized space. This understanding also positions those at Lakeview in the place—the suburbs—where American life is happening. This notion that the suburbs are home to the "patchwork quilt" of American life implies a sense of unification in the presence of difference, an understanding not afforded Black people in the urban center.

Pastor Jeff's mention of the Hindi cultural center and the Sikh temple references the larger (and relatively highly successful) Asian American and Asian immigrant population in the area,[2] a non-White group that is celebrated more than the Black folks of the city. Residents who identify as Asian in the area Lakeview is located report the highest average incomes in the area, and the local industry is dominated by management positions, software development, and health care. Successful, non-White, but not-Black individuals are enveloped into the White suburbs, and Lakeview can claim an understanding of diversity due to shifts in the neighborhood in which it is located. However, these claims rest on the inclusion of a successful non-White population in the neighborhood. Blackness and urban life remain part of the imagined secular, unknown but nearby. This framing of and celebration of successful non-Black immigrants in the suburbs are indicative of what Bonilla-Silva predicted as a triracial stratification system, in which there are

"Whites" at the top, "honorary whites" (in this case the Asian American and Asian immigrant population in the area), and the "collective black" at the bottom of the hierarchy (2009:179).

Successful, non-White suburbanites are celebrated through their "honorary whiteness" (Bonilla-Silva 2010). In contrast, the "African Tundra," the "Muslim influence" and "voo-doo witchcraft," and Black folks who occupy more urban spaces (relative to the Lakeview area) like Seattle are bundled together. They are all elements of life well outside of the church, rendered simultaneously both dangerous and approachable. They are places for White exploration and missionary work. But the experiences of people of color in this space are misunderstood. There is a serious lack of knowledge of people of color and places of color among White evangelicals, and among White people more generally in the United States. In the Lakeview community, some people of color are "known" and others are not. Within this lack of knowledge of people of color, there exists an equally dangerous presumed knowledge. Their lack of knowledge is not due to the lack of an ability or the resources to learn; rather, a specific form of racialized learning, through the cognitive accomplishment of White racial ignorance (Mueller 2020) occurs within the church walls. Notably, although group members had phones in hand, ready to look up the existence of the "African Tundra," no one in the group followed through with this search during the meeting or corrected Carrie as the author of the prompt. Those who can be saved or have "made it" like them are enveloped into projects of White evangelical success, while everyone else becomes the backdrop, fueled by this racial ignorance, to highlight who evangelicals at Lakeview are not—and to serve as the focus of their missionary work and love to better understand themselves as good.

This manufactured ignorance of the lives of people of color and the boundaries that this lack of knowledge creates are also deployed via more explicit and noticeable forms of racism. I interviewed Monica, a 65-year-old Mexican American woman, on the one-year anniversary of the police shooting of Philando Castile. This timing was not intentional, but I spent the entire drive to meet Monica that morning listening to NPR coverage of the shooting and the wake of continued protests in the year following. When I asked Monica about her thoughts on the election of President Trump, Monica began by discussing border control and the importance of President Trump's stance on immigration because, as Monica told me, "It has overwhelmed us and depleted us as a nation . . . you know, just sucked us dry, pretty much." Monica continued to share her thoughts on immigration to the United States, and then started talking about the "ISIS terrorists killing Christians. I mean, torturing them. It's horrible."

At this point in the interview, Monica's eyes glazed over and she turned to look out the window toward the busy parking lot outside. She apologized and asked me again what my question was. I assured her that she was answering my question and asked if she could perhaps think of any more local or national examples related to her political support for Donald Trump. Monica perked up at this rewording of the question. She said, "Like children's starvation, children being hungry, and not having opportunity. Black violence. That kinda thing. I think people get on a bandwagon and they start killing policemen, so I think that's civil unrest . . . I find it very alarming and unpleasant. You know, because innocent people get killed. You know, 'cause they're always killing policemen. They just pick them off . . . you know, it's horrible." I wonder if Monica, too, was listening to coverage of the one-year anniversary of the shooting of Philando Castile, and if that coverage affected what came to the fore during this part of our interview. If she was tuned in to this anniversary, I imagine that Monica was listening to very different media coverage than I was that morning. Monica's overt racialized stereotyping of Black folks might be driven and reinforced by the media she consumes, sustaining her racialized ideas (Jamieson and Capella 2008). As Tranby and Hartmann argue in their work on Whiteness and the evangelical "race problem," "the problems of race are also nurtured and sustained by deep-seated racialized—if not simply racist—images and ideas" (2008:346). In the Trump era, racial inequality is being mapped onto all people of color, not just along its more common Black/White color line. I imagine that, both through the media she consumes and through Lakeview as an organization, Monica is understanding the threats of the imagined secular world through a lens of Whiteness. And her opinions may also reflect her class status; research finds that attaining success can lead to shifts in self-identification toward White as a racial identity (Saperstein and Penner 2012). And as someone who would not fully fit many people's definitions of White, Monica may be engaging in extra performative work around the racialized threats of the imagined secular as a way to fit in in the very White space.[3]

Monica's focus on the existence of Black people, through her descriptions and concerns over Black violence on the one-year anniversary of the shooting of a Black man by a police officer, draws attention away from the actions of Whites and focuses on the mere existence of Black people as the locus of social problems in the United States. Whiteness often draws its fuel from the assumption that racial difference comes "from the existence of Blacks rather than the behavior of Whites" (Lipsitz 1995:369), or what Gerardo Marti succinctly calls the "White problem with Black lives" (2020). The media attention to the shooting of Philando Castile and the vastly different coverage of it also work as a type of a spectacle in these White spaces (Lipsitz 2011) similar to Pastor Darryl's visit. Although they are quite different in their manifestations, the end result remains the same. When a predominately White church welcomes a Black male pastor from Ferguson, Missouri, to tell White people that *all* lives matter, and when the media coverage of the killing of a Black man by police reinforces stereotypes of Black men as dangerous and as the ones who "kill cops," the focus is turned on Black people for the comfort and dismissal of the actions of White people. White people are absolved of their actions around structural change. To return to Pastor Amy's sponge demonstration, Monica can tell herself that the "ugly" response to suffering is tropes of violence on the part of Black people, not the inaction of White people.

Importantly, the evangelicals at Lakeview are given stories about the church's important work in saving people of color from other religions and from devil-driven social movements. They *feel* as though they are affecting change. And this feeling of affecting change, rooted in White racial ignorance, and paired with news stories that suggest that the afflictions of Black people in the United States are their own fault, or that social movements to address racial inequality are the work of the devil, aligns neatly with a White evangelical theology that advocates for individual successes and dissuades from a focus on structural problems.

INSTRUMENTAL ACCEPTANCE

The weekend before Easter in April 2017, a time of great importance for the church, Pastor Dave began the Sunday Sermon with an audible sigh. President Trump was about to sign his "Buy American and Hire American" executive order, which, among many other statutes, included the provision under "Hire American" that states that "In order to create higher wages and employment rates for workers in the United States, and to protect their economic interests, it shall be the policy of the executive branch to rigorously enforce and administer the laws governing entry into the United States of workers from abroad, including section 212(a)(5) of the Immigration and Nationality Act (8 U.S.C. 1182(a)

(5)).["4] This executive order was part of his larger "America first" initiative that defined the start of his presidency. Debates about immigration were all over the news in early April as anticipation of this order mounted.

Pastor Dave acknowledged what was likely on the minds of many that week as they arrived at church Sunday morning. He started off the morning sermon by sharing that there are "a lot of racial divides and immigration in this country. The root of these divides comes down to whether or not you love people." There were roughly 400 people in the audience at Lakeview's first sermon, and many murmured inaudibly in response. An older White woman sitting directly in front of me nodded her head enthusiastically as Pastor Dave spoke. Pastor Dave acknowledged a large national debate and simultaneously reduced it to a problem of love. Members of Lakeview Church are frequently reminded to love one another, love thy neighbor, and love their enemies. This rhetoric of love, as well as dismissal of structural inequality, is born from the history of White evangelism in the United States, as discussed in chapter 2. It is also born from a desire to continue to be seen as "good" and separate from the "bad" racists. To employ a language of love is to nullify arguments that you are complicit in the systems that harm people. The evangelicals at Lakeview continue to hold on to a rhetoric of love during a time in which they know that they cannot be understood as racist if they hope to grow as a community in the Pacific Northwest. To mitigate this, the individuals at Lakeview engage in an instrumental acceptance of non-White and non-Christian individuals. Instrumental acceptance is the phrase I employ to describe the emotion work that individuals do on the part of an organization. An organization cannot welcome people in without individuals who can help in that work and relationship-building. If the bounded welcoming of Lakeview Church is made up of the policies and messages from the leadership around who is accepted and rewarded, instrumental acceptance is the mechanism through which individual congregants approach others with a specific combination of their theological beliefs and the emotion work bound up in them. I call this acceptance instrumental for two reasons related to the goals this action accomplishes. First, instrumental acceptance is directed toward Others in an effort to make these Others more like the Christians who invoke this outreach, the closest to their God's ideal. The process of instrumental acceptance also provides an action or moment that an individual can point to as evidence of something good; it can provide an example of inclusion and love that, if read outside of the historical trajectory, missions, or goals of the organization, can indeed look a lot like inclusion and love. However, this instrumental acceptance reflects the gendered, racialized, and sexualized structures of the organization, and the organization's goals to bring others into relationship with Jesus, and therefore grow.

When White evangelicals (and White people in general) reduce global inequalities to problems of love, the more vulnerable in those equations do not find allies in the church. Lakeview Church, and countless other evangelical institutions across the United States, would of course disagree with this statement. And this is in part due to the stories we all tell ourselves, and the stories the church tells its members, and firmly believes.

In the early spring of 2016, when the first blossoms showed themselves on the sprawling Lakeview Campus, when the raw air of winter experienced its first disruptions from the warmer fronts of spring, an official from the national Foursquare organization visited Lakeview. Pastor Isaac asked his congregation that morning who needed a reminder to follow God and not "conform to evil desires." About half of the audience raises their hands in response; some arms shot up in the air immediately while others slowly rose toward the ceiling. Pastor Isaac smiled and told the crowd that their guest, a representative for "Disaster Relief" for the national Foursquare organization, would help inspire this reminder in them.

Mark, a young-looking White man in his late thirties, walked up to the stage, already wearing a wireless microphone. He had just returned from Turkey, where he was working with refugees from Iraq and Syria. He began to tell a story about a refugee boy from Iraq. The boy's father was a professor, what Mark described to the crowd as a "great job." Mark described the boy's mom as a "great mom, holding down the house and taking care of the kids as good moms do. But, when she was pregnant with this boy, with him in her stomach, her city was being bombed, and she was breathing in lots of phosphorous fumes. The boy has birth defects as a result." Mark told the congregation that the family had to leave all of their money behind when they decided that the best decision for their family would be to flee and head for Turkey. Mark told the audience that Foursquare has a children's ministry in Turkey for kids with special needs. The Ministry Outreach team went to the house of this refugee family and heard their story. The team decided they wanted to get this boy a wheelchair. Together, they prayed for the boy and for the family's situation and laid hands (the conference of a spiritual blessing via physical touch).

According to Mark, God told the outreach team that he was not going to give them a wheelchair for the boy. God was going to give the boy a walker, because he believed he would be healed. Mark then told the audience that he thought to himself, "she [the mother] is having strife. Do I tell her this? How do I tell her this?" Mark reported that he and his team ultimately decided to tell the family what God told them, but he said he left that house thinking, "Lord, you better show up! Here's a Muslim family connected to the church, and we don't want their first experience to be that we tell them our God can heal but he doesn't."

A week later, Mark got a call from the mother, "who is ecstatic." He took a deep breath and continued, imitating the mother, who told him, "Asim is walking!" Mark said, "The message spread to people in the area. *That* is what we are doing. We are not just about giving out food, but having people come to Christ. There are lots of great groups that give out food, but we don't want people to go to Hell with a full belly. We want them to meet Jesus."

Mark ended his story that morning by encouraging the audience to "act in ways you think you might not be able to do on your own but that you can do with the help of the Lord's strength." He then told the congregation that there was a missionary activity taking place in the foyer that day to support the church's mission work, which he described as "making beads like women in Africa do to support their families."[5] When I entered the foyer after the morning service, I walked over to the table Mark had referenced. There were a ton of different colors of string on the table and a large bucket of plastic beads to make bracelets. Next to the table, there were quiches, scones, and a goodbye banner to celebrate the departure of a music pastor. Many went for the postservice snacks, while a small number of individuals and families trickled by the activity table. A few kids made bracelets while their parents put money in the donation bin.

While Mark's message, as a proxy for the message of the International Church of the Foursquare Gospel, is presumably meant to showcase the power of the God in which this church believes, it also highlights a central purpose of mission work: it is not just relief work (as Mark's job title suggested) but a relief work centered on bringing individuals to Christ. Let's return to this statement: "There are lots of great groups that give out food, but we don't want people to go to Hell with a full belly. We want them to meet Jesus." This is the essence of instrumental acceptance. It relies both on an individual orientation to the world through a language of love and on a focus on the success of the church in bringing people into relationship with Jesus, nullifying the threats of the imagined secular through individual stories about who is good and bad, worthy of saving and worthy of salvation.

White evangelicals at Lakeview are encouraged to celebrate either connecting a Muslim family with the church in hopes of conversion to Christianity and the cured paralysis of a boy or the work of feeding those who are hungry. And for many White evangelicals, of course, they celebrate both. But instrumental acceptance, as a mechanism for the maintenance of Whiteness, makes it difficult for White evangelicals to see that the work they are doing in the world might be more to benefit their own needs and the goals of the institution than the needs of others. Lakeview Church is balancing a desire to help and a desire to appear welcoming, and both highlight an ultimate goal of the church: to increase the numbers of people who identify as Christian and help them in their mission.

RECENTERING WHITENESS AND CHRISTIANITY

I interviewed Jesse, a White man, and Lyndsey, a White woman, both 21 years old, Jesse a recent graduate and Lyndsey a current student from a local Christian college where they met. Jesse had responded to the interview call that Lakeview started running in their weekly church bulletin for me in the summer of 2016. I was surprised when such a young couple walked into the coffee shop, as I was used to interviewing a slightly older church demographic at that point. Jesse wore a Seahawks jersey, a common element of Sunday attire for both men and woman and even the pastors at Lakeview, especially on game day, and Lyndsey wore the outfit so common of younger women (myself included) at Sunday services: tight dark jeans, a long flowy cardigan, and a blouse. They both appeared relaxed, animated, and happy to talk.

I asked Jesse and Lyndsey about their feelings regarding the election of Donald Trump. Jesse and Lyndsey both shared stories of students of color on their Christian college campus, and specifically immigrant students who, in the wake of the election, feared deportation. Jesse stated that people voted for Trump because of "moral issues" that made him "more Christian" in his answers than Clinton.

Jesse and Lyndsey acknowledged that they believe this understanding of Trump as more Christian and moral than Clinton is specific to White people. As Jesse said, "I think there were things he was saying that I would say, like, conservative Christians did not agree with, but I think they kinda weighed what's most important and what's not to them, or in a sense maybe what's more important . . . their faith, and generalizing that they're mostly White. They're not really worried about being deported. Um, so that's not our first concern." Lyndsey agreed, and said she understood why people on her campus, where she is still a student, were worried, but simultaneously dismissed her classmates worries by saying, "Their friends aren't gonna get deported, probably" with a shrug, before drinking another sip of her coffee. Jesse then interjected and said, "Yeah, and ultimately I care more about babies who might be killed than I do, like, people who might get deported, or things like that." Both Jesse and Lyndsey establish their voting behaviors and concerns as concerns specific to them as White evangelicals. They acknowledge that they should care about the concerns of their classmates, exhibiting the messages of love expressed in Sunday sermons at Lakeview, but also simultaneously make quite clear that the concerns of others are just that—the concerns of others.

While Trump might not protect Jesse and Lindsey's classmates and friends, people that they know and seemingly care about, Trump will fight to protect their individual values, which are, in this instance, related to abortion. Individual love translates into individual concern and a relative inability to understand the plight of others. When pushed, their experiences as White Christians remain the priority, but in a way that also acknowledges and instrumentally accepts the concerns of immigrants, in this case.

Some members of Lakeview Church did express concerns about an individualist approach to race relations in the United States, but their concerns do not reflect different end results. For example, Henry, a 31-year-old White male who frequently volunteers in downtown Seattle at a homeless shelter, worries about what often feels like an insular community within the church. I interviewed Henry immediately following a Sunday sermon, a sermon that was focused on not wasting one's life. Pastor Dave ended the sermon that morning by asking everyone in the congregation to high-five the person next to them while exclaiming, "I will not waste my life!" It is this message that Henry is reflecting on in his response.

Over lattes, Henry said to me, "It was a really good message but at the same time, like, give us something to do, whether that's telling us how we can interact with others in our daily life to show them our love and then they'll look at us and be like 'Why is that person different than other people I see?' and they'll ask and you'll be like 'It's because I know

Christ,' and I'm called to be more and more like Him." Here, Henry's words reflect a central goal of the church: to connect with individuals through themes of love, and then, more importantly, to hope that those feelings of love translate into that individual coming into relationship with Jesus. At the same time, though, Henry appears frustrated by the somewhat hollow-feeling nature of the Sunday sermon. Henry continued, "For people where, like, work and the community around them is very . . . I don't know if this is the right term, but ethnocentric? Like, it's pretty much the same all around them, giving them opportunities to, I don't know, like create a soup kitchen on Wednesdays at the church for people to come in and then these people have an opportunity to come and serve." Henry talked further about how, while he feels it is his personal calling to reach outside the church, he knows many would feel uncomfortable actually doing so without a clear opportunity.

Henry then described the work he is involved in to reach outside of what he sees as his ethnocentric community: "At my university, we had Lighthouse Ministry, which was making sack lunches and going out into Seattle, and finding homeless populations and actually giving them food." Henry and others at Lakeview are working hard to find solutions to the ailments of the world around them, but, in Henry's case, he does not feel like the church is going about this as effectively as it could. As a member of the Millennial generation, Henry's words represent one of the many voices of those questioning the practices of the church. But since Henry has remained in the church, his solutions are bounded by the options and logic of love and acceptance he has learned as a White evangelical in the Pacific Northwest.

Henry worries about the ethnocentric setup of the church culture. Henry's personal solution is volunteering and outreach toward a population comprising individuals quite different from him, volunteering in downtown Seattle. For Henry and others at Lakeview, "local missions" to the "heart" of the city are appealing, most often a homeless shelter associated with a Christian nonprofit that predominantly serves people of color. Issues of race are relegated to the homeless shelters in the closest city, not the interpersonal relationships within the pews at a Sunday service. Henry wants to do good in the world and wants to help others by bringing them to Jesus Christ. And while Henry is concerned by what he calls the ethnocentrism of the church, or the insular communities in which he and many others operate, Henry's solution, a solution paraded by Lakeview, reinforces ideas of urban, Black spaces, while leaving the White suburb relatively untouched (Lipsitz 2011).

Conversations about race in the church are intertwined with conversations about missions, and about saving others by bringing them into relationship with Jesus. In this worldview, the White evangelical is placed in the position of power, equipped with the tools to make the person of color's life better, whether locally or internationally. Wasting one's life, for Henry, would mean not doing missions work. His own individual successes are connected to his ability to serve, and here serve in the "heart" of the city. The connection between a sense of purpose and missions work, a connection that both exists in Henry's mind and is supported and encouraged at Lakeview, establishes a sort of racialized and classed hierarchy that here seems to represent both the cause and the solution to the ethnocentrism Henry questions. Although Henry is concerned about some of the practices and messages of Lakeview, his agency and ability to affect change are limited by the institution of which he is a part.

Henry and his Millennial colleagues are not the only ones to question the practices of the church. Questions of change, growth, and missionary activity are a confusing project for many as the church seeks to expand outward. In the Disciples' Journey meeting the week after the group was instructed to pick missionaries out in the field to pray for, eliciting commentary about voo-doo witchcraft and fights against the Muslim influence, the group reported back on their homework for the week, which had been to contact and pray for these missionaries serving abroad.

Both Sally and Earl started the group conversation by telling the room full of people that, while they both contacted their assigned missionaries from the week prior, in Sally's words, which were then echoed and seconded by Earl, they both "felt creepy about it." This started a debate about whether or not Lakeview's leadership should have told the missionaries ahead of time that people were being asked to reach out and pray for them. Pastor Jeff responded and reminded the group that these missionaries filled out prayer cards, and "what if we told them [to expect people to reach out to them] and then people didn't reach out?!" A couple group members nodded in agreement, but Sally and Earl held Pastor Jeff's eyes as he continued and said, "They are missionaries, they will rejoice in it!" Pastor Jeff dismissed Earl and Sally's concerns, and Carrie, the group leader, interjected and proudly told the group that she contacted her assignments, and that the response she got made her weep. She exclaimed to the group, "They want to translate Pathways into Thai!" Carrie told the group that she had a long back and forth with the missionaries in Thailand, and explained in great detail the Pathways curriculum and the work of the beta-testing small group sitting in front of her. She looked at them all and said, "These awesome things are instigated by you!"

Although two of the more vocal group members (and therefore conversation leaders) vocalized their discomfort with the weekly activity in a space designed to elicit and incorporate that exact type of feedback, their unease with the assignment was squashed fairly quickly with reminders from two different church leaders about the importance of the work and larger mission of the church.

Even in moments of pushback or questioning, both Whiteness and Christianity are centered through a language about importance of missions work. This mission work is something that church members need to do to grow in their own relationship with Jesus, and to help the larger church's cause simultaneously. Here, the goals of the institution are encouraged and celebrated over any individual concerns or discomfort.

In the summer of 2016, the same summer that I met with and interviewed Henry for the first time, Pastor Isaac got up during the final song by the Worship Team and asked everyone to grab a hand of a churchgoer next to them. Pastor Isaac asked everyone, now holding hands, to join him in a prayer. He asked for a prayer for Dallas, for Minneapolis, and for Russia, "where they just passed a series of laws that will make it very hard to be a Christian and do Christian work there."

In this prayer, Pastor Isaac was referring, in order, to the shooting of five Dallas police officers, the shooting of Philando Castile in Minneapolis, and the perceived legal persecution of Christians, more specifically, evangelical Christians who wish to engage in missionary work outside of the United States. Pastor Isaac took three events that seem relatively unrelated and bundled them together. This is the creation of the imagined secular in real time. Pastor Isaac acknowledged the state of race relations in the United States, as he knows he should, and as exemplified here by two very different shootings. At the same time, Pastor Isaac made clear that he is at least equally concerned for the suffering of Christians. And this suffering is defined by Christians' inability to evangelize and live in countries outside of the United States.

Pastor Isaac then started talking about how Lakeview is a church open to everyone. He teared up and paused to take a breath, momentarily overcome with emotion. With tears visible on the large screens that project an image of his face out to the congregation, Pastor Isaac said that he welcomed someone new in the lobby this morning before the services began. He started crying more audibly, and said, "I was able to say that this is a place for everyone" before he began the Sunday sermon.

With this turn of focus, Pastor Isaac put forth a clear message in this opening prayer: he juxtaposed the church as a place of welcoming against the unwelcoming (and here, really, racist and violent) "outside" world. In a prayer that began with the acknowledgment of the shooting of a Black man, he ends by reinforcing that the church is a place where everyone can feel safe. This emphasis on welcoming and safety through Christianity centers the church's own religious beliefs and the church's own needs. The church, as an organization, is finding a way to appear welcoming to all while simultaneously protecting its "unmarked Whiteness" (Ray 2019). And, as the church grows and finds ways, as a White organization, to appear welcoming to a Black pastor from Ferguson, Missouri, it can even more easily find ways to be welcoming toward (or at least understanding of) Donald Trump.

THE PROBLEM WITH TRUMP

On the same April Sunday that Pastor Dave began the morning with an acknowledgment of issues of racial divides and immigration in the United States, when he suggested to his congregation that the problem of immigration can be solved through love, he ended his sermon with the following: "We don't bring that stuff in here. [The] race thing, age thing, gender thing, that's what's modeled for us in the outside world, we don't bring that in here." Pastor Dave, as a White man afforded a certain amount of power as he stands in front of his megachurch, told the crowd that the space they are in is absent of race, gender, and age. However, through a sustained White racial ignorance, a type of instrumental acceptance that depicts the White congregation as welcoming and inclusive, and a recentering of the experiences and needs of White folks over the rest of the population, Lakeview Church is maintained as a space defined by Whiteness. Again, though, a key feature of Whiteness is that it is often and intentionally invisible to those who benefit from it. Whiteness, as a pillar of historical and contemporary race relations in the United States, is rendered invisible within the bounds of the church, what Robert P. Jones dubs a "white supremacy induced amnesia" (2020:235), a condition especially difficult to recover from when race becomes something, in the words of Pastor Dave, "modeled for us in the outside world."

By implying that race and gender and age only exist outside of the church, Pastor Dave effectively sets Whiteness and masculinity (and perhaps middle age) as default categories within the church. This type of language and approach to race is an example of "color-blind" conversations that, through a language of not seeing race, then also erase the realities of racial inequality (Bonilla-Silva 2009; Doane 2017). Further, this approach to race marks nontypical identities for Lakeview Church as those permanently *outside* of the church. Whiteness, then, becomes something that is set up as something that can be "taken for granted" (Frankenberg 1993; Tranby and Hartmann 2008). It is not that evangelicals at Lakeview "don't bring that stuff" into the church; rather, they create and receive coded messages about race and gender. In the examples put forth in this chapter, when race is discussed in the church, it is an artifact of the urban city, or evidence of suburban change. Race is discussed as part of joyous stories of celebration at successful international missions, and race is focused on during local missions to homeless shelters and soup kitchens, and central to myths of Black violence and the killing of cops.

Whiteness is something that is simultaneously invisible, taken for granted, and mobilized to justify the position and privileges of White evangelicals over those of others in the social world. This logic also allows for the justification of the actions of White people, specifically White men. Journalists, political commentators, and academics alike have obsessed over "the problem with Trump" for evangelicals, the disconnect they see between Trump's actions and statements and what most understand to be Christian values. But Trump becomes less of a "problem" when we understand that evangelicals are making sense of him in very White space.

When Whiteness and masculinity are rendered both de facto and invisible as dominant identities within the church, so too are the structural systems that support and normalize the behaviors of White men. In an institution in which Whiteness is both upheld and hidden, the behaviors of White men become divorced from anything to do with race (and the privileges connected to race) for evangelicals. As Anthea Butler suggests, "God is always available to forgive deserving individuals, especially, it seems, if the sinner is a white man" (2021:11). The problem with Trump has quite an easy solution and common focus within the church: loving a broken (White) man who needs help and support.

In addition, White evangelicals have a track record of a collective ability to rework aspects and understandings of their own faith during times of change. As discussed in chapter 1, many religious groups have found ways to reformulate their orthodoxies to best engage with the changing social landscape they face. One of the ways that social groups, including religious groups, provide members with identity and meaning is by offering a "moral orientation" for understanding their own lives and their social world (Smith 1998:90). Oftentimes, the construction of this moral orientation is done against a selected referent out group. Groups know who they are in large measure by knowing who they are not (Smith 1998). We see this with the formulation and utility of the imagined secular. However, the symbols that groups use to help understand their moral orientation to the world shift, and at Lakeview, these internal reworkings occur within a space defined by Whiteness.

Author Stephen Prothero suggests that a great way to look at this internal reworking within a Christian group is by tracing transformations in the representation of Jesus Christ. The figure of Jesus, whom Prothero argues we should understand as a "cultural Jesus," has been "something of a chameleon" (2003:8) in the United States. Evangelicals work and rework Jesus as a cultural symbol to help make sense of him, and use him as guidance, during times of change. As Prothero argues, "To hold Jesus up to the mirror of American culture is to conduct a Rorschach test of ever-changing national sensibilities. What Americans have seen in him has been an expression of their own hopes and fears— a reflection not simply of some 'wholly other' but also of themselves and their nation" (2003:9). If we understand Jesus as, at least in part, a cultural symbol whose meanings reflect both the contemporary moment and the needs, desires, and beliefs of those reworking Jesus as a symbolic figure, we can imagine that evangelicals do (and, really, everyone does) something similar with political figures as well. We impart our greatest hopes and fears onto those with more voice and power. White evangelicals are making sense of what Donald Trump symbolizes to them in a White church, a space where norms of Whiteness prevail, and where a rhetoric of individuality and love that sits so squarely within the culture of White American evangelicalism resonates with the individual members of the congregation.

Katherine, a 55-year-old White woman, described Trump to me as a "broken man."[6] Katherine looked at me and immediately followed this comment with what felt like a reminder to me that, in Katherine's eyes and in the eyes of most evangelicals, "Sarah, we are all broken!" White evangelicals believe that everyone is broken, and that such brokenness can be fixed through an acceptance of Jesus Christ as Savior. Further, not only is this acceptance of brokenness key for an individual's identity as an evangelical, it is also intimately tied to one's ability to then evangelize to others. As celebrated evangelical author Jerry Cook notes, one can only welcome others in to relationship with Jesus Christ "if you yourself admit that you are broken."[7] For Katherine and others, accepting Trump as a flawed human is not only possible but indeed central to their own faith and ability to practice that faith effectively.

Trump, as someone understood as broken, becomes a palatable figure whose actions can be understood as a manifestation of said brokenness, and, thus, someone who needs to be supported, loved, and prayed for just like all others. Because of this, Trump is also worthy of protection and defense. Katherine talks about a meme she saw on Facebook that was distributed by "The Other 98%."[8] Katherine described the post that was making fun of Trump and making fun of his family. Katherine told me how upset this made her and reminded me that "we have to see Trump as God sees him, really." The family, for Katherine, is untouchable when it comes to political humor. Katherine highlights the centrality of the family unit to evangelical life, and the importance of protecting it, a theme discussed in chapter 3.

Katherine's narrative of Trump as a "broken man" also fits with an evangelical narrative of sexual redemption, specifically sexual redemption for men. As I discuss in more detail in chapter 5, Trump's history of failed marriages, sexual affairs, a sexual affair with an adult-film star, sexual harassment of women, and openly disparaging comments about women and women's bodies fits within a larger evangelical understanding of men as needing help and guidance when it comes to a whole range of sexual and relationship behaviors. There exists a whole range of books, websites, curricula, counseling, and even conferences for evangelical men who seek sexual redemption.[9] Some of the qualities that make Donald Trump seem antithetical to evangelical values are used by evangelicals to understand him as a man seeking redemption like all others, an ideal that permeates Christian rhetoric.

Donna, a 49-year-old White woman, told me during her interview about her work as a translator at a local hospital for primarily Spanish-speaking patients. While Donna discussed at length the sense of importance she derives from her work, and her relationship and love for her clients, when I ask Donna about Donald Trump, she immediately and defiantly told me that "I voted for Trump, 'cause I didn't want Hillary to . . . I mean, eight years of Obama?! We were fortunate to get through that 'cause . . . he really, I think, intentionally tried to destroy our nation. I was so glad to get rid of him and I did not want Hillary 'cause she was just like him. So I think, I, mean Trump . . . he's a newcomer politician, shall we say?" Donna continued, and told me,

> He's never been a politician before but I believe that he's a strong man. He is highly intelligent, and I like that during the election, or during the campaign he was reaching out to evangelicals, 'cause he wanted their influence in his life and in his governing, and so I thought that was, that was very healthy and I like that also. You know, a lot of people don't like him. You know, I work with Spanish-speaking patients and a lot of them don't like him because of his immigration stance or whatever but actually, he's trying to protect our borders which . . . I think is wise.

Like Katherine, Donna approaches her understanding of Trump through individualistic language that focuses on his lack of experience as a politician, and, when larger, structural forces at play come into question (here, concerns over immigration from the clients Donna knows and loves), Donna focuses on Trump as a "strong man" being more important than the concerns of immigrants.

Both Katherine and Donna discuss Trump in individual terms that work to justify their own support for him, and work to reinforce both symbolic and real boundaries around Whiteness for Donna. Trump symbolizes Whiteness, just as Jesus has been rendered White (Prothero 2003). These understandings of Trump highlight the individual approach and understanding of the world that are also deeply connected to evangelicals' approach to conversations on race. Further, these understandings of Trump highlight the importance of both gendered difference and the institution of the family (even if Trump's family is perhaps not totally conventional), issues that continue to seem more important to evangelicals than issues of immigration, for example. Indeed, as Kristin Du Mez summarizes, "He was the latest and greatest high priest of the evangelical cult of [White] masculinity" (271:2020).

Trump is allowed justifications and qualifiers that others are not afforded. In chapter 3, Hillary Clinton is discussed as a politician who symbolizes both the threat of the Democrat and the threat of the feminist that White evangelicals position themselves against; she is understood in the same space that Donald Trump is. Responses to the imagined secular world reinforce both Whiteness and masculinity; white men can be excused and understood for a whole host of behaviors that women and people of color cannot.

Finally, Raymond, a White 55 year old, who feels ambivalent about Trump and the church's stance on our political climate, suggested to me that Trump's election might be a sign of the end times. Katherine, whom I discuss above, told me something similar. Katherine said, "I do think it [the past presidential election] is part of the end times, which I think is coming faster than I thought. I thought we would have five or ten years. It's coming a lot faster than I thought. And, what happens, has to happen before Christ comes 'cause everything man tries has to fail. And, I'm afraid that also includes Democracy, or Republicanism." For those who are more ambivalent, or not supportive of Trump and his presidential reign, they still rework Trump within a narrative that makes sense to them, and does not require the type of work or calling out of the structural issues that may have helped elect Trump into office, and indeed benefit them. The perceived concerns or failings of a politician they are not excited about can be understood in much more positive terms: the return of Jesus Christ.

Trump, as a politician, does not have to make full sense to White evangelicals. For many, his platforms and even his election are both secondary to and reflective of other concerns with which they are engaging. Trump's support among these White evangelicals is symbolic of their larger understandings about in- and out-groups, and symbolic of their concerns over threats to their religious way of life. Like all symbols, Trump and what he represents is contested and reworked in part of these larger conversations about a church in a nation in flux. And this malleability is much more easily digested and configured in the White church.

INCLUSION FOR EXCLUSION'S SAKE

In September 2016, just two months before the presidential election of that year in the United States, Pastor Isaac transitioned out of his role as the lead pastor at Lakeview Church. He had, in the weeks prior, announced piecemeal the plans for the leadership transition, which included full information about his replacement, Pastor Dave. Pastor Isaac also shared quite a bit with the church community about how he came to this decision, and told everyone that he felt called to lead a new church in a different part of the country. The Lakeview leadership team planned a celebration to honor Pastor Isaac's decade of leadership during his final Sunday at Lakeview. Members of the congregation were selected to speak about Pastor Isaac and his wife, Stephanie. And Pastor Darryl flew back from Ferguson, Missouri, to honor his friend.

Pastor Darryl kicked off the farewell celebration that morning. The audience clapped as he walked up onto the stage, where he told the crowd that he had flown back to the Northwest to "witness and be here for the transition and to honor Stephanie and Isaac." Pastor Darryl then remarked, "I know to put Stephanie first. I am a trained husband of 38 years!" The congregation laughed.

Pastor Darryl said that the tenth chapter of the Gospel of John came to his heart that morning. He encouraged the congregation to bring out their Bibles and pens and write down the verse on their weekly handout so that it would be, in his words, "pressed into their hearts." Pastor Darryl recited verse 11: "I am the good shepherd. The good shepherd lays down his life for his sheep. Pastor Isaac. He has showed me, an African American with a TWA—a teeny weeny afro—that we can transcend culture, that it's not about Black Lives Matter, it's about Christ in our hearts that matters. Never measure your success with what you see but what God knows." Pastor Darryl then shouted, "Hallelujah!" before laughing and saying "Sorry that slipped out! My Afro-centrism slipped out! I forgot I'm not White! Let me get back to my Whitest White position." He then changed his voice and repeated "Hallelujah" in a much quieter, less excited tone.

In September, Pastor Darryl's message was slightly different than it was in the previous April: he said that Pastor Isaac was the one who taught him that "we can transcend culture, it's not about Black Lives Matter." Here, Pastor Darryl's words reveal whose idea it was, the previous April, for Pastor Darryl to speak about Black Lives Matter as the work of the devil. But, in the end, the individual or individuals who crafted and curated Pastor Darryl's visit matter a bit less than his joke following up this comment during Pastor Isaac's farewell celebration— that he forgot he is not White, and that he needed to "get back to my Whitest White position." Pastor Darryl's "joke" here underscores the physical boundaries of the church, and its symbolic boundaries around race as well. Although Pastor Darryl, as a Black man, again found himself welcomed into and speaking to a predominantly White congregation, he seems well aware that his welcoming is bounded, predicated on his ability to continue to simultaneously highlight and nullify his difference.

Dr. Martin Luther King popularized earlier observations by sociologist Liston Pope, who noted that "eleven o'clock on Sunday morning is the most segregated hour of the week" (Pope 1957; Gilkes 2010). In the United States, this adage still holds true (Gilkes 2010), although it appears to be changing slowly.[10] The White church remains a White church, as measured demographically by who fills the pews; importantly, though, even when a Black pastor from Ferguson, Missouri, is welcomed into the space to talk about race, or non-White congregants attend and are actively involved in the day-to-day life of Lakeview, the church remains a space defined by Whiteness. Evangelicals at Lakeview are "talking about race" and, specifically, topics like Black Lives Matter, immigrant rights, and migrant support.[11] But they are having these conversations in ways that dismiss structural inequalities related to race and racism. In turn, these conversations uphold their positions in the social world simultaneously as separate and removed from issues of racial inequality in the United States, and as the individuals who can and should save the racialized "other" abroad.

The church has figured out a way to talk about race and uphold Whiteness without implicating itself in White supremacy. While Monica's statements provide additional empirical evidence for research on the relationship between evangelical Christian support for Donald Trump and desires to defend White Christian nationalism (Gorski 2017; Whitehead and Perry 2020), and overarching beliefs in White Christian nationalism regardless of religious identity (Whitehead and Perry 2020), Monica's verbalization of racist stereotypes is unusual at Lakeview. While her beliefs are of course an integral part of the makeup of the imagined secular, we must pay attention more clearly to the everyday action (and inaction) of protections of Whiteness that are occurring in more subtle forms today. Evangelicals at Lakeview can manage the threats of the imagined secular world by engaging in debates that work to continue to uphold Whiteness and simultaneously mask those dominant cultural markers in the process.

Pastor Darryl's visits to talk about the "state of race in the country" were a bounded welcoming of a highly racialized component of the imagined secular; Pastor Darryl's visits and words help code the White space as being aware of racial inequality without challenging any of the norms that uphold said inequalities. In a conversation about the state of race in the country, and the Black Lives Matter movement, issues of structural racism were neutralized, and Whiteness was recentered: the one day that year devoted to conversations about race in the United States became about *all* lives. When the imagined secular is created in a space defined by Whiteness, its components centered on race become a bit less "messy."

The church is working to appear inclusive in an effort to, indeed, remain exclusive. And the ways they go about this as an institution can be difficult to see. As is often the case with social norms and values, the mechanisms of normalization are often unclear at best, or masked behind efforts toward inclusion, conversation, and debate. While there are exceptions, both the leadership and members of Lakeview Church are enacting and maintaining these boundaries around White space through discreet social means. They don't want to come across or appear racist, and most of them would of course say they are not at all racist and firmly believe that (Bonilla-Silva 2009). The church is working to grow and appear welcoming in an era of declining religiosity, and while they want to appear as a community that is open to discussing Black Lives Matter, they work to justify a political leader who will show the ugliness and uphold the boundaries that they cannot. Trump is part of this protection of Whiteness, but not central to it. Rather, the White church has the ideological tools to justify his election, support, and presidency while they work on other projects central to questions of religiosity and liberalism in the twenty-first century.

CHAPTER 5

Sacred Sex

Marriage and Heterosexuality

It was a hot and humid Sunday morning in the Pacific Northwest. It was the middle of July in 2016, and congregants mingled outside before the first of the morning services began. A group of kids stood in the grove of trees next to the parking lot, chatting and laughing with one another. A young couple sat on a bench near one of the entryways to Lakeview and held hands as they talked. A girl in a floral dress, perhaps 10 years old, escorted an elderly woman with crutches across the large parking lot. Two men were surrounded by a group of young kids all dressed up for the services, with the girls in white summer dresses and all the young boys in ties. Together with the adults, they talked animatedly about upcoming summer plans. Life outside of the church walls was bustling as I made my way indoors.

When I entered Lakeview, I ran into Heather, who greeted me warmly and asked if I had gotten coffee yet. We chatted for a couple of minutes, and she told me she was excited for Disciples' Journey to pick up again in the fall; the group had taken a break for the summer and she shared that she missed that sense of community. We parted ways and I nodded hello to Pastor Jeff, who was sipping his usual morning Starbucks while he talked with someone by the welcome booth. I stood in line to get an iced coffee from International Java before I made my way into the sanctuary.

Church attendance was fairly low that Sunday morning, not an uncommon feature of mid-summer services. And although the seats were not full, the Worship Band brought lots of energy to the room, with a young man who looked almost identical to Justin Bieber, in both physical features and style, leading the band. He led a performance of brand-new songs, which made for an unusual lineup, as the Worship Band usually only introduced one new song on a given Sunday. There were a small handful of worship songs that were sure to get almost the entire congregation on their feet each week, and these crowd favorites almost always made an appearance as part of the Sunday morning rotation.

This revitalization of the Sunday morning routine could have been due, in part, to the guests visiting that day to talk about international missions work for the church. Chapter 4 covered international missions as a vital part of the individual and collective identity of the church, and an integral force in the maintenance of Whiteness within the organization. In this chapter, I explore the ways in which gender, Whiteness, and heterosexuality are all deeply intertwined and, together, mark the central and overlapping categories with which the church is wrestling today. While it can be difficult to see, due to its relationship with other overlapping threats of the imagined secular world, this chapter centers sexuality, and, specifically, perceived threats to heterosexuality, as an integral part of the church's current understanding of politics and their place in the world.

This humid Sunday morning in the summer of 2016 is a morning I have briefly and previously described in this book. It was the morning in July 2016 when Pastor Isaac asked the congregation to pray for Dallas, to pray for Minneapolis, and to pray for Russia. It was a prayer request that was immediately followed by Pastor Isaac's emotional response wherein he declared, through tears, Lakeview as the welcoming and safe place in contrast to the outside world, where things like gun violence and Christian persecution occur. It was a morning in which the creation of the imagined secular was happening in real time. And I want to now return to that morning, to the guest sermon that followed Pastor Isaac's initial welcome.

At the conclusion of his opening remarks, Pastor Isaac invited a married couple to the stage. The large screens at the back of the stage changed from a list of announcements to display photographs of the back of a woven tapestry. While the front of a finished tapestry might display a landscape scene or abstract design in rich colors, the back of a woven tapestry looks quite different: a seemingly jumbled mess of threads, knots, and loose ends that, upon first glance, would be nearly impossible to imagine as the backbone of something quite beautiful and intentional on the other side.

The guests, Michael and Brittany, a White couple who looked to be in their mid- to late thirties, asked those in the sanctuary to describe what they saw on the screens before them. One person toward the front of the room yelled out that they saw yarn, and the couple coached the audience toward the theme they were trying to communicate: the image was very messy, and not very clear. Audience members nodded along. The image on the screen then changed and displayed the front of the tapestry: a lovely, elaborate design of a mountain range with a sun setting in the background. Brittany, smiling as she spoke into the microphone, looked back at the tapestry displayed behind her, and said, "This, here, is God's view. He sees how everything is connected."[1]

With the front of the tapestry still on display, Brittany began to share her story. She told the congregation that she had been "gently called to Thailand," and then paused and corrected herself, and added, "Well, Michael has been gently called. I have been abruptly called. We want to talk to you today about our process and bring the church in on the mission." Brittany talked about how, as an evangelical woman, she never felt particularly called to missions, but she met her now-husband, Michael, and "he was like 'well that's cool, but I am [called to missions].'" Michael stepped in here, holding a microphone of his own, and said, "The mission's pastor in me though wants to say that we are all called to missions, it just looks different for everyone." Brittany cut back in, and said, "Well it's not that I'm not, I'm just drawn to people, but I am scared of crossing borders."

Brittany continued and said that "Michael had to be patient for 13 years, and I had to grow in confidence for 13 years. We trusted in God during this time that we were meant to be together and this path we've been on has been the one the Lord has had for us. We are weaving into that tapestry."

In reflecting on her slower excitement about missions work relative to her husband's, Brittany explained this type of skepticism or reluctance as affecting her relationship with God, and, by extension, her husband's relationship with God, too: "We were in God's good, but now we are ready for God's great!"[2]

Brittany then transitioned to talk about fertility, which, in the moment, felt like an abrupt topical shift. It was not. Brittany and Michael were diagnosed with infertility a few years prior, which Brittany pronounced as "almost like a death sentence" for them. She described sitting at the back of church months later, when God spoke to her and said, "you are fertile soil." Brittany didn't know how that fit in with her story at the time, but she promised the audience that, as it eventually did to her, it would make sense to them, too.

Not long after they were diagnosed with infertility, Michael and Brittany went on a vacation with close friends. While they were all out to dinner one evening, the other couple on the trip tried to convince Brittany to go on the mission to Thailand. Brittany left the table, went to the bathroom, and broke down crying in a stall, overcome with emotion as she asked and pleaded with God for a baby first.

Michael interrupted Brittany here, although that might not be the correct word, as the telling of their story felt quite rehearsed. Michael laughed and joked that "Being a good husband I didn't notice any of this, I just thought she had to go to the bathroom." The audience laughed loudly at his joke.

Brittany continued their story and said that she knew that she was asking God the impossible. She accompanied her husband on a short introductory trip to Thailand, where someone who didn't know their circumstances prayed over the couple and told them "what has been medically difficult will be easy." Brittany was of course taken aback by this message. She wasn't feeling well on the trip, and upon her return to the United States had the notion to take a pregnancy test. Brittany then shared that "Because we were obedient and went to Thailand the Lord answered." Brittany was pregnant. Brittany had an ultrasound and the doctor told her and her husband that he thought it was "weird" that they had been previously told they were infertile, because he saw no evidence of infertility, exclaiming to her that "there are no issues with your organs!" At this point in the story, Brittany took a deep breath and began to cry. She said, "In that moment, I knew the Lord healed me." The roar of applause from the audience took over, an especially impressive amount of noise given the smaller group that day. When the audible support died down, Brittany, now laughing and crying, said, "And I also thought, oh man that means I am going to Thailand!"

Brittany and Michael looked over their shoulders to read Acts 8:26–39, "Philip and the Ethiopian" as the text appeared, verse by verse, on the screens behind them.[3] This passage, while perhaps one of the less-celebrated biblical texts, was used by Michael and Brittany in this moment to illustrate the importance of listening when God calls one to unexpected places. Brittany and Michael, now *both* ready to answer God's call, told the Lakeview audience about their upcoming move to Thailand, and requested prayer from those in front of them. As the couple discussed their excitement about their upcoming move, they were experiencing other emotions, too. The couple told those gathered that "the enemy is pissed" and that they have "received lots of spiritual attacks" since they both agreed to move to Thailand to begin their missions work. While they shared that these experiences had, of course, been very difficult for them both, they did not elaborate on what those spiritual attacks were, or who or what enemy was "pissed."[4]

Before leaving the stage, Michael and Brittany asked the audience in unison, "What has the Lord been whispering to you or showing you in your dreams and visions? With obedience comes blessing. What role is God asking you to take in his master plan?" Brittany and Michael then instructed those in attendance to think back to the image of the tapestry, before they continued with, "When God calls us he also enables us." They asked everyone to form a line and come up to the edge of the stage, to cut a piece of yarn they brought in remembrance of God and the commitment to his plan. The couple ended their guest sermon with, "It is in that beautiful mess, that messy piece of the tapestry that God is revealed, that's where the goodness is."

Brittany and Michael's story is not just a story about finding the good in the messy or being rewarded by God for doing his work. Rather, to extend Brittany and Michael's metaphor, missions work and evangelical understandings of gender, heterosexuality, and the reproduction of the White family are *interwoven*. This chapter maps sexuality onto the other projects of the church, to uncover the ways in which sexuality is often a hidden but crucial part of these stories.

While Brittany and Michael's story emphasizes the importance of doing God's work, and the rewards that can come as a result of it, what is uncovered when we examine that work and those rewards? In this story, a story celebrated and centered by Lakeview Church, at first glance the work is international missions on behalf of the church. And the reward is a baby conceived together by Brittany and Michael, the missionaries. But their deep story is symbolic and reflective of larger goals of the church, and the ways in which notions of nation and sexuality are intertwined, as things that, as Joane Nagel (2003) says, give power to each other.

NATION-BUILDING, CHURCH-BUILDING, AND SEXUALITY

In the spring of 2016, in a guest sermon about missions work, Pastor Jeff described Thailand as a "really dark nation that is being transformed in front of our eyes." Pastor Jeff then spoke to the congregation about the church's missions work in Thailand, which focuses on sex trafficking and drugs. Pastor Jeff reported that, because of the church's work and focus on the issue of sex trafficking,[5] "100,000 children have found Jesus and they are going to transform the dark nation and their communist neighbor." He then pitched an upcoming missions trip there the following fall, and encouraged those in attendance to sign up for an informational meeting. Brittany and Michael are celebrating the gift of their child as a result of not only their missions work abroad, but their missions work in a country described as "dark" by the leadership in their church.

Missions work at Lakeview Church is a specific form of nation-building: one that relies on a rhetoric and centering of Whiteness and neocolonial ideas in which the White, Christian savior conquers, or converts, those in other countries who need to be saved. Take, for example, the story shared about Asim in chapter 4. Joane Nagel's (2003) work shows the ways in which nation-building is also sexualized and gendered. Nagel provides countless historical examples to illustrate the ways in which colonialism, conquest, and war—all key components of nation-building—rely on and form constructions of the racialized and sexualized "Other."[6] As discussed in chapter 2, the White evangelical church has long been involved in core aspects of nation-building in the United States, especially around the very issues Nagel argues are key to nation-building: protections of hierarchies of race, gender, sexuality, and the White family.

This construction of the Other justifies the project of nation-building and also helps the nation-builder, the colonizer, and the conqueror understand who they are. Nation-building relies on the Othering of groups in order to understand the nation being formed and re-formed. And evangelical missions work takes on a specific form of this nation-building project. Take, for example, the ways in which Russia was used and discussed as the bad, communist nation that made women wear veils, juxtaposed against the United States, where Christians can practice the religion that liberated those in Russia. This comparison sets up Christianity and the ways it is practiced in the United States as the good religious nation that does not contribute to the submission and inequality of women.

While Pastor Dave said that the example he provided dated back to the early history of Christianity, evangelicals continue to build solidarity through changing times by identifying in- and out-groups, and in creating external threats with which the church is "embattled" (Smith 1998). Smith suggests that evangelicals know who they are by knowing who they are not. Pastor Jeff literally describes Thailand as a dark nation, in turn setting up and understanding the United States as light and, perhaps, enlightened. Brittany used war-like rhetoric to describe what happened to her and Michael when they committed to their missions work: vague language about upsetting the enemy, and receiving spiritual "attacks" as a result of their work in Thailand. This type of "us versus them" rhetoric is also central to nation-building, the "them" often serving as the symbolic and actual places and people upon which evangelicals can "stage their national dramas of self-discovery and self-invention" (Nagel 2003:155).

Pastor Jeff also focuses in on the sexual practices of this Other group of people that need to be changed. As Nagel argues, a key component of a nation-building project is to define the sexual ideologies and practices of other groups and other ethnicities as different from and inferior to ones' own "normal" sexual practices. In this way, national and sexual boundaries are mutually reinforcing, and "implicit in the idea of the nation (who we are) are certain prescriptions and proscriptions for sexual crossings— what good citizens should and should not do sexually" (141). Good citizens do not engage in the behaviors of a dark nation: sex trafficking.

Rather, good citizens, and good Christian citizens, do the work of saving those abroad in dark nations. And men and women have different places in the successful implementation of these projects. Nagel argues that "contemporary nationalist ideologies define proper places for men and women and valorize the heterosexual family as the bedrock of the nation" (166). It is not a coincidence that Brittany and Michael were encouraged to tell a story of their missions work in Thailand, and that their willingness to do missions work brought them a child. As Nagel suggests, although national scripts are written primarily for men, women have a key role in these "national dramas": as mothers of the nation, and, in this case, "as vessels for reproducing the nation" (159; Jung 2020). Brittany believes that her infertility was cured by God, and, more specifically, cured by God because of her eventual willingness to follow her husband to Thailand and to save people there. Her "role" as an evangelical woman, as well as her "role" in the building and expansion of the church, was honored because of her willingness to save other people. Brittany's story also serves as an example of what Burke and McDowell (2021) call "diversity projects," which present White women's leadership in the church as indicative of their ability to help marginalized groups. Brittany can fulfill her duties as a White Christian woman by *leading* people of color to Jesus and *following* her husband in this work, upholding both White supremacy and gender inequality.

These nation-building projects, both in their historic forms outside of the church and in their contemporary iterations in the church, are embedded with specific goals: protections of Whiteness, continued enactments of gender complementarity, and sexuality understood not only through a moral lens of what is good and bad, but through a promotion, more specifically, of *heterosexuality*.

CENTERING HETEROSEXUALITY

Efforts focused on protecting and maintaining heterosexuality are often hidden from view in our conversations about religion, politics, and the day-to-day realities of social life more generally. In the church, these efforts are sometimes disguised in conversations about marriage and the family more broadly. This is in part due to heteronormativity, the process that creates heterosexuality as the presumed, natural, and God-given sexual identity. Heterosexuality is so normalized it is rendered almost invisible in its pervasiveness. The irony here is that heteronormativity also suggests that homosexuality (or other sexual identities) are also invisible due to the assumption that everyone is straight and that everyone should be straight. The "normal" becomes difficult to see, as part of the air we breathe, and the "abnormal" goes unseen because of its presumed impossibility.

Heterosexuality and sexuality more broadly are also often overlooked because we commonly understand sexuality as something individual and apolitical, rather than as an organizing principle of social life (Green 2008; Seidman 1996). When we do focus on sexuality as a key component of the social world, the majority of both historical and contemporary efforts in the area of sexuality studies have looked to the margins, studying, classifying, and labeling "deviant" sexualities, such as homosexuality, sex work, and unconventional sexual desires. This pathology of the periphery has, in turn, both reinforced and left untouched "rather than challenged the center" (Nagel 2003:49).

More recently, scholars have called for a critical focus on heterosexuality (Burke 2016; Heath 2012; Ingraham 1994; Fischer 2013; Jackson 2006; Kitzinger, Wilkinson and Perkins 1992; Pascoe 2018; Seidman 1996; Warner 1993; Ward 2020). Some have called specifically for understanding and analyzing heterosexuality, not only as a sexual identity, but as an organizing institution in social life (Ingraham 1994), and indeed, something that institutions and organizations produce. For example, CJ

Pascoe's (2011) research shows how heterosexuality is both an unofficial and a foundational part of a high school curriculum, providing the space in which boys and girls forge gendered and sexual identities. Kelsy Burke and Trenton Haltom (2020) analyze Christian pornography addiction narratives utilized by many churches and find that such narratives protect the interests and sexual desires of White, heterosexual men.

In connecting heterosexuality to social organizations, we can uncover the ways that heterosexuality is connected to the distribution of certain economic resources, cultural power, and even social control (Ingraham 1994). However, this work has often focused on the ways in which heterosexuality and heterosexual privilege regulate homosexuality (Jackson 2006; Seidman 1996). Stevi Jackson argues that we need to move beyond the concept of heteronormativity in order to see that heterosexuality also governs the lives of those included *within* its boundaries. That is, understandings of heterosexuality can govern everyone, regardless of one's sexual identity. As CJ Pascoe (2018) suggests, it is time for scholarship to focus on heterosexuality through documenting its practices, its maintenance, its protections and celebrations.

Evangelicals have long been invested in heterosexuality, and recent scholarship recognizes this (Burke 2016; Burke and Haltom 2020; DeRogatis 2015; Diefendorf 2019; Gerber 2008). While this investment has often come through a discourse of antihomosexuality (explored in chapter 6), there is an abundance of literature on heterosexuality, beginning early on in the life course. There exists an entire industry of materials focused on fairy-tale like descriptions of the importance of purity for evangelical girls and young women (DeRogatis 2015; Moslener 2015). These materials emphasize the importance of purity and preparation for marriage. And, there also exists a large literature on the ways in which evangelical couples can best experience sexual pleasure within their marriages (Burke 2016).

This Christian amalgamation of self-help materials and how-to guides, part of what Jane Ward (2020) calls the heterosexual-repair industry, has treated heterosexuality, and heterosexual marriage, as God-given and natural. If something is indeed so natural, one might question why an entire industry of literature and self-help materials exists to explain and support it. And as heteronormative assumptions that have long helped stabilize the church's theological orientation wane, younger generations are asking more questions about how to "do" heterosexuality correctly, and are also asking what the church actually believes about heterosexuality as the cultural needle on homosexuality has moved so greatly.

While Brittany and Michael's experience with fertility and missions remains a celebrated success story, their experiences may not resonate quite so deeply with younger members of the church. Younger generations are getting married later in life than those who came before them (Pew 2018). And these younger generations who are delaying marriage are also those more likely to be questioning or leaving the church. They are also those who are more likely to approve of same-sex marriage (Pew 2019b). And as people live longer, and five generations fill the seats of Lakeview on a Sunday morning, more are questioning how to reconcile their beliefs with things like divorce, cohabitation, and remarriage. These generational shifts, in combination with larger cultural shifts in understandings of homosexuality and acceptance of the LGTBQ community, present new challenges for the White evangelical church. The dual shifts of the recognition of homosexuality and the failure for younger generations to quickly hit the ultimate marker of heterosexuality within the church (marriage) mean the church needs to address questions of sexuality in new ways. As the church moves its focus and resources from conversations on homosexuality to those of heterosexuality, it is invested in two things: (1) singleness and (2) containments of sex. The church is working to get individuals into heterosexual marriage, and make sure that sex is contained within those heterosexual marriages. But questions around singleness and sex, and the church's response to them, highlight both the church's refocusing on heterosexuality and its current inability to handle this refocusing effectively.

This is in part because this is not just a matter of "refocusing"—the church cannot and will not simply pivot in its beliefs if and when heterosexuality and heterosexual marriage are inseparable from other facets of church life and doctrine. Gender essentialism, Whiteness, and heterosexuality are all pillars of the church, inseparable from the ways in which the church understands its growth, and inseparable from, and in fact central to, the ways in which church members understand themselves. For Brittany, to agree to serve—to bring light to a dark nation—is to be named Good by her god. And, as a result of this goodness, Brittany is rewarded with a baby. Light is juxtaposed against dark, good against evil (or perhaps, to use the vernacular of this church, ugly), and missionary work and fertility against uncertainty around missions and an inability to conceive.

The relationship between heterosexuality and "goodness" relies on the erasure of heterosexuality as something that might mark you through its perceived normalcy. White evangelicals have not had to think about this gatekeeping to goodness because identifying as heterosexual has never been understood as a barrier to doing God's work if everyone is presumed to be straight. Challenges to heterosexuality, then, are about challenges to something bigger, even if those challenges to the church's understandings of heterosexuality seem minor and individually focused, like singleness and questions about appropriate sexual behavior.

SINGLENESS

Singleness is discussed in a variety of evangelical literature, but the focus of this literature is often on what happens before marriage, with the clear assumption that heterosexual marriage will happen, and will happen at a relatively young age (DeRogatis 2015). Singleness is discussed and understood as a phase, and one that, when used wisely, helps prepare women for their futures as evangelical wives. This framing in the literature mirrors evangelical teachings in the church. Singleness is referred to as a "stage of life" on Lakeview's website, along with other stages of life that are listed to help indicate to people, for example, which small groups are appropriate for them to join.

While singleness is treated as a phase and not as an identity, it is simultaneously used as a way to mark, categorize and sort people into spaces for worship and discipleship, as though there is something fundamentally different about being single versus being married. And within the church, there is: through heterosexual marriage, and the gendered enactments afforded to one through marriage, one can become fully whole (DeRogatis 2015; Gerber 2011). By this logic, of course, the church would like to get people into that marriage sooner rather than later. As the phase of singleness extends for younger generations and reopens later in life for other generations, this phase is met with perceived danger. The longer singleness lasts, the greater the potential for succumbing to temptations of sexual sins outside of marriage. As such, singleness is a phase that gets a specific type of attention in the church and something that carries with it quite a bit of work and preparation for the ultimate goal: marriage.

I interviewed Carrie, a 39-year-old woman whom I got to know quite well over my two years at Lakeview, as she was a member and frequent leader of Disciples' Journey. Carrie works for Lakeview full-time. Carrie is also single. I usually made a point to arrive early to Disciples' Journey meetings, where I would help Carrie arrange chairs, set up snacks, or just chat before the meeting began. Carrie would often update me on her dating life during these interactions, so when I interviewed her formally, over coffee and scones at a local Starbucks, I began the conversation by asking Carrie if she had any dating updates to share. Carrie shook her head, indicating a no, before telling me more about her approach to dating.

Carrie has used dating sites such as Match and eHarmony, and, at the time of the interview, had transitioned to OKCupid. Carrie had paid for subscriptions to the first two sites, and in her estimation, those memberships only yielded about one date every three months. Carrie felt like these numbers were quite low, *especially* because she had to pay to join these online communities. Carrie likes OKCupid much better. She told me that she is happier with this site because it is free, and, more importantly, because the site provides percentage matches between people based off of a series of endless questions that one can answer on their own time and at their own will. For example, when you look at someone's profile, the site will say something like, "You are an 89% match with Phillip!" The site has a fairly simple but smart design: if you want to get to know a person on the site, you can see the answers they provide to these questions. However, you can only see the other person's answers to questions that you yourself have answered. This encourages people to answer more questions, which then in turn also provides people with more information about those they are thinking about interacting with on the site or asking out on a date.

In an ideal world, Carrie would be able to filter people on OKCupid who respond to two questions in the following ways: (1) men who state that they have a personal relationship with Jesus, and she clarifies, "not just with God," because, in Carrie's words, "that would include all other religions," and (2) men who value involvement in church community. As Carrie said to me, with a laugh, "That's about as basic as it gets. That's what I am looking for!"

However, like most people, once I asked Carrie more questions about what she seeks in a relationship, she got increasingly specific in her desires. While Carrie enjoys the question-and-answer setup of OKCupid, she said that it can often feel like a lot of information about any given person. To mitigate this, "Right away I go to religion and sex . . . you get a better sense of where they are at because what is interesting to me is that sometimes you'll get someone who says they are a Christian, but then you get to the question 'Do you believe in creation or evolution?' and they'll click on evolution and I am like, OKAY, WHAT?!" Carrie sees this as a huge disconnect and conflict in beliefs, one that she could not and will not entertain in a potential date.[7]

I asked Carrie more about her comment about sex. Of the many questions OKCupid makes available to its users, one asks how quickly one is willing to have sex after a first date. The multiple-choice answer includes the following potential responses: (1) on the first date, (2) after three to five dates, (3) more than that, or (4) after the wedding night. Carrie's preferred response is after the wedding night, aligning herself with evangelical teachings about the sacredness of sexual activity in marriage (Burke 2016; DeRogatis 2015; Diefendorf 2015; Luker 2007). However, in Carrie's experience, most men on the site indicate that they would want to have sex after three to five dates. This doesn't dissuade her. Instead, Carrie told me that the people whom she matches with in terms of highest percentage skip this question altogether. Carrie thinks secular men skip this question because they do not want women to know how quickly they are willing to have sex. And Carrie believes that for some secular men, a woman who wants to wait for marriage, like her, isn't going to be of interest to them. Carrie's concern, here, highlights the sexual double standard for women, where women are expected to be virginal and pure and simultaneously sexually desirable for men (Fine 1988; Tolman 2005). These dual expectations might be further exacerbated for evangelical women, as many have grown up with a "fairy-tale like" literature that not only emphasizes chastity, but connects women's purity to men's ability to enact their "biblical gender roles" as well. As Amy DeRogatis argues in her review of evangelical purity literature, "Without virgin brides, there is no need for noble princes and there are no fairy tales. In stories in which men are the actors and women are waiting to be saved, only virgins are worth fighting for" (2015:27). In addition to the concerns of the sexual double standard, Carrie can't match with secular men who skip this question, as they would not fit her expectations for religious beliefs and commitment. But Carrie has a narrative for this dilemma.

Carrie assumes that perhaps just as many men would rather wait until after the wedding night to engage in sexual activity, but that she knows such a desire is stigmatized by the secular world, so she believes these men are skipping the sex question, too. For the most part, to be understood as normatively masculine in the United States means engaging in sexual activity with women, or at least talking about sexual activity in the company of other men (Diefendorf 2015; Pascoe 2011; Renold 2007; Wilkins 2009). Carrie is correct about the stigma associated with sexual abstinence and masculinity. For men who do and would want to delay sexual activity until marriage, such a desire can require a lot of interpersonal work and management (Diefendorf 2015). It could be easier to skip this question and the potential ensuing social stigma, and it could also be easier in certain situations to just bow out of a desire for abstinence, especially if these men are not part of a church or support group who supports this pathway. While Carrie is adamant these men exist, and of course, they do, Carrie has not had any interactions, let alone any dates, with men who have checked "after the wedding night." She thinks this may be because these men have so many dating options, with so many other women like Carrie looking for them. Carrie is deploying a narrative to understand her singleness, and it is a narrative that relies on a version of the world in which abstinent men are so sought after that she cannot get to them. This narrative is perhaps especially important in an online space in which the religious and secular worlds are coming together.

Carrie did find love once, and she left it. Carrie talked at length, quite sorrowfully, about a man she dated for months, whom she fell in love with. Based off of Carrie's retelling of their relationship, it sounds like he was quite smitten with her too, and quite committed. He asked Carrie to relocate to the South with him due to a work-related move. Carrie said no and ended the relationship. When I asked Carrie if she ended things because of the request to move, she said no; she ended things because he was Catholic. Carrie explained that he was "Christian, but not Christian enough" for her. He checked off all the other boxes and "happily respected" Carrie's desire to wait to engage in sexual activity until marriage, but Carrie wants a man who both shares her faith and shares her understanding (or at least respects) her beliefs around sexual activity.

As Carrie works at Lakeview, attends church services there, and is actively involved in the church's weekly activities, the vast majority of her world revolves around that one church campus. The online world of OKCupid has the potential to put Carrie in direct contact with many who differ dramatically from her, which might heighten this boundary work she needs to put in place to find a suitable partner. The availability and pervasiveness of online dating also require different approaches to these conversations on the part of the church. When potential couples are meeting in online spaces, and not at Sunday services, the church needs to do quite a bit of work within church spaces to prepare and equip individuals for navigating these highly secular (and sexual) spaces in other arenas. The dangers of the "phase" of singleness are heightened with the increasing and expanding opportunities for online dating. And as Lakeview works to address these issues, Carrie is going about much of this on her own.

Carrie has found that, with online dating, she has reached out to men much more than they have reached out to her. Even when she matches with someone, Carrie often reaches out more than the men reach out to her. I asked her why she thinks this is, and Carrie told me that she doesn't know, but wonders if it is because men just have "massive options" and so they don't even see her match. She shrugged and said she doesn't know what their experience is with dating. I ask Carrie if she has single male friends (who, I make sure to emphasize in my question, are *just* friends) that she talks to about their dating experiences. Carrie shook her head and said, "Nope. I used to, in my twenties. But as I've gotten older, I mean, they've all gotten married. And so, I'm really respectful of those boundaries. And, any of the single guy friends that I had that got married, I'm now friends with them as a couple."

I asked Carrie more about how she navigates those new friendship dynamics. Carrie paused, and then said, "I would just include both of them. But the thing is—yeah, I'm not even around most of those guys anymore. Everyone is going in their own direction." Here, that direction is marriage, and in addition to not having a romantic relationship, Carrie is experiencing shifts (and losses) in her social and friendship circles as a result of not being married too, and, importantly, as a result of being a single *woman*.

Carrie continued, "I'm, actually really, super careful, even at Lakeview, I work with guy pastors, and I have for eleven years. And so, you know, I'm closer to the pastors than their wives, and so I'm super careful about my interactions with them. Like, I would never, and I have never, been to coffee one-on-one with any of them, you know? Like just even to discuss work stuff. Like if I go, there is always a third or fourth party that goes with. I put that zone in place." I asked her if this is a personal decision, something she decides, and she said, "Well, we don't have to, it's understood."

Although I knew the answer to the question, I asked Carrie what would be inappropriate about having coffee with one of the male pastors and, in many cases, long-time coworkers and friends. Carrie responded, "Well, you know, obviously, that [Pastor] Jeff and I are good friends. I wouldn't want anybody to see Jeff and I at Starbucks, having coffee, even though we're talking about work stuff, and maybe going over curriculum. I don't want somebody coming in from the church, or even from the outside [not a church member], that doesn't know either one of us, or maybe just knows one of us, and making an assumption. I don't want anybody to ever question if there is something inappropriate." Carrie's rules are similar to those of Vice President Mike Pence, who received quite a bit of media attention for remarks that he will not eat a meal alone with a woman, or attend events that feature alcohol without his wife by his side (Waldman 2017).

As an evangelical woman, and an individual who has been a member of the church since childhood, Carrie has been receiving specific messages about dating and marriage for her whole life. As an adult, Carrie's imagined secular world is one full of sexually active men, but she is waiting for a sexually abstinent man who is the real prize and desire in comparison. Carrie isn't meeting someone in the church to date (and marry). She has tried. She also is not rapidly swiping through choices on a dating app, or taking a casual approach to dating that many others outside of the church report doing today (Birnie-Porter and Hunt 2015). Carrie is very focused and very methodological in her approach to whom she will date and how she will date them, because even time spent with the opposite sex well outside of a romantic context needs control. But this approach to dating, relationships, and marriage has presented significant losses for Carrie: losses in love, the ending of a serious relationship, and the loss of many of her male friends. Carrie is missing out on meaningful connections (Jackson 2006) and sustained friendships because of the boundaries around appropriate enactments of heterosexuality in the church that she cannot fulfill until she is married.

Many times over the two years I spent at Lakeview, Carrie mentioned feeling like she did not have a place in the church, a place among many of her previous friends, or a place within God's kingdom as accessed through heterosexual marriage. These comments were always especially jarring coming from someone who worked at Lakeview and spent most of her days and evenings and weekends there. And Carrie is not alone in feeling this way, although, as a 39 year old, she has perhaps sustained this "phase" longer than others. Because of Carrie's struggles, which she is not alone in experiencing, Lakeview is working on their narrative and explanations for single people in the church.

STAY MARRIED!

Marriage is a long-standing part of nation-building, and as such, the politics of marriage are heightened in times of change (Heath 2013). Marriage was a common sermon topic during my time at Lakeview. And while each sermon on marriage always promised, in its overview at the start, a discussion of singleness, the topic was always presented as a bit of an afterthought at the end of the sermons even though it was acknowledged with increasing frequency during my time conducting this research. Pastors Isaac or Dave would spend 30 minutes talking about the joys and work of a covenant marriage, and often concluded with something like the following.

In the spring of 2016, Pastor Isaac began a Sunday sermon on marriage. After his usual update on upcoming church events, he kicked off the sermon with, "Ladies you will probably never know when you affirm your husband in his identity what that means to him. Empowering. And husbands if we are telling our wives how beautiful they are in that outfit—actually, maybe you look a little too beautiful and should go change!" Here, Pastor Isaac paused while the congregation laughed in response. He continued, "Our words are prideful. For those pursuing a relationship and are not yet married, be holy. Don't buy the lie. And don't settle for a mate who isn't running your pace of faith." Pastor Isaac ended with this: "Finally, a word for those who are single or divorced, be encouraged and reminded that Christ is your spouse and he is the greatest husband we will ever have." Pastor Rachel, a 39-year-old White woman and associate pastor at the church, came up to the stage for the benediction, and before she closed out the morning prayer told the congregation that "The easy thing for ladies is the makeup and adornment, all the external stuff. But the hard work is submission." In the final minutes of this sermon, there is the encouragement of the gender complementarity with which we are now familiar, through a reminder that a woman's job within marriage is to uphold men and be beautiful, but not *too* beautiful, as the sexual gatekeepers for men, followed very briefly by a short message to those who have not gotten married and are therefore not enacting these gendered practices either.

Two years later, Pastor Dave ran an entire sermon series on relationships that spanned the better part of three months. On the first day of this series, Pastor Dave suggested that, before he could talk about singleness or sex, he needed to first lay the bedrock foundation for what a biblical marriage looks like. Pastor Dave concluded this first sermon in the series with,

> Now what do you do if you are in the room and you are single. What do you do? We are going to pray. If you are a man in the room and you are single, you will want fulfillment in what you do, married or not. Find your fulfillment in what you do as unto the Lord. Find fulfillment in what God has called you to do in your life and do it. Secondly, women, single or not, you still feel fulfilled in relationships, remember, Christ is ultimately your husband. Not some guy. Christ is ultimately your husband. Are there other relationships that God has called you to? Your fulfillment lies in Christ alone. You're his bride before anything else.

In these sermons, two years apart, both pastors acknowledge singleness, and explain its presence in the church through an understanding of said single individual's relationship with Jesus Christ, but one that is highly dependent on their gender. Men are told their fulfillment is in their work, and for women, their fulfillment is in their husbands and in the church. That description doesn't do a lot for Carrie, who already feels somewhat ostracized in the church because she is not married.

In another sermon in the same series on marriage, Pastor Dave started it off by joking about the amount of time single people have on their hands because they don't have children. Here, the assumption is that having children only occurs within marriage. Pastor Dave is also talking past any divorced (and not remarried) people in the room with children under their care. The assumption of a nuclear family pervades, even in conversations about other relationship structures. Pastor Dave continued these thoughts, "The downside to being single to me is accountability. What marriage provides for us are natural accountability structures that God has given. You are a mirror in your spouse and this mirror is reflecting back on you constantly who you really are. God uses Melissa to show me who I really am." It is not surprising that Carrie feels she does not have a place in the church, even as someone who is actively involved in its daily operations and community. Singleness is often punted to the end of sermons, and, even then, the message seems to be that, until you are married, you might not even fully know who you are as a person. Carrie's understanding of herself as a single woman is inhibited by the cultural understandings of the church and the ways heterosexuality and heterosexual marriage are institutionalized within it (Jackson 2006). And her understandings of herself as someone who belongs in the church are also inhibited by the church's understandings of marriage.

While the church works to articulate its messages to single members, and does so with varying degrees of success, the church is also being questioned about sex and sexual pleasure.

ONGOING DILEMMAS OF DESIRE

Carrie, as a 39-year-old woman, has experienced the "phase" of singleness for a great deal of time, and for much longer than many in the church, even some of the Millennials I interviewed, are experiencing. However, those who got married at a younger age still talked to me at length about the guidance they sought from the church, and often didn't get, especially around sex. While heterosexual marriage is the end goal, and treated as a given within the church, many have questions about what to do before they reach marriage, and, just as importantly, what to do once they have met that marker.[8]

Maggie is 36, White, and married with kids, and told me that sex, as a topic, came up years ago with her now husband before they were married. Maggie said,

> I can't say we've talked about it, but I can say in our relationship we've actually dealt with that [sex]. It was before we were married. We had been together for three years, and we had been living together in California, and at one point I went home, I actually left our home because I was like, you've gotta get it figured out, or I'm not coming back. Basically, my best remembrance of it, and my understanding of it, is that he felt like he had a pattern, and a major issue with pornography, and it was skewing his idea of reality and what a relationship should look like. And because of that he was not comfortable with getting married, because I don't think that he was thinking that I was going to offer what he thought, from having watched that too much. So, he did seek help, he did seek counseling while I was gone, and he did break the habit, break the addiction. And we discussed it, and that he cannot do that, that that's not within our values. And 10 years later, I don't know that we've talked about it again, just sort of fixed and broken and tossed away and down.

Maggie's experience is not unusual; while evangelical men, especially, have a language of addiction and control readily available to them to discuss issues of sexuality before marriage, a discussion of pleasure is largely absent. This becomes especially salient when evangelical couples transition to married life and are supposed to enjoy their "gift from God." To pivot from understanding sexual behavior as sinful to pleasurable is difficult, and for some, it means that conversations around sex disappear entirely (Diefendorf 2015): in Maggie's words, "fixed and broken."

And although sex is not a topic in her marriage now, Maggie told me, "I did just recently have a conversation with a friend, and her son, who is 13, she thinks she found some stuff on her phone, so we talked a lot about that. So, I almost see for me, it's going to come up with my kids, so that's the next cycle, and how to deal with that with my children, instead of that in my marriage." Maggie laughed and took a sip of her coffee while I asked her if she feels her beliefs, as a Christian, helped her navigate what she thought and thinks marriage should be like and what she wanted from her husband before she got married.

Maggie, still chuckling at my question, said,

> Maybe a little bit? I feel like we went into marriage blindly. . . . You get a lot of, it's all love, it's a Cinderella sort of thing, you don't get a lot of concrete, sort of advice. Our pastor, when we met him, he did say that the first year would be the hardest year ever. I remember him saying that. And in reality, that was so not true. Like our first year was not the hardest year. That was kind of the honeymoon. It might be the hardest year if you never lived together? If you hadn't had sex? But we lived together and we had already done that, so . . . we weren't really getting into something that new.

Maggie's story is not too unusual within the church; she is just old enough to have missed some of the more explicit and national pushes for abstinence-until-marriage education in school (Santelli et al. 2017), but also understands sex and conversations about sex as conversations about addiction. In Maggie and her husband's experience, their conversations around sex centered on elements of sex that needed to be controlled, and controlled before marriage could and did happen. Within the context of marriage, the subject hasn't come up much again. But she attributes their ability to transition more easily into marriage to the fact that they had had sex prior to marriage. Their ability to navigate this transition was because they went against the common teachings of the church.

For younger couples in the church, and younger couples who are waiting until marriage or did wait until marriage to have sex, they are looking for a bit more in the way of justification for these commitments. In a couple's interview with Annie and Darren, Annie told me she thinks it is really healthy to talk about sex, and told me about the course she took at her Christian university on the subject:

> We had a class that was human sexuality, and in that class we talked a lot about, like, "what does the church say about sexuality? And what doesn't it say? And what are we being taught? What should be taught? And what should we be talking to our kids about early on?" Because the church some-

times shames sex before marriage and things like that. How can we talk about it in a way that it's preventing sex before marriage but . . . more than just, "oh, you're sinning." I'd rather talk about, "here's what it is doing to you emotionally, and what it is doing to you cognitively." . . . Because you're gonna get tied to this person and your heart's gonna be broken, you know? There's a lot more that goes into it than just "it's bad!," you know?

Like Annie, Darren wanted more from the church than advising abstinence until marriage. He added:

I think Annie touched on it, a lot of the times the church focuses on "no sex before marriage," but it's bizarre because now that I have this ring on my finger this thing that you've been telling me is evil and a sin is now like, okay like, "Cool, go get it." . . . I don't think it's being taught the right way and I don't know what the right way is. . . . Because I was taught that this is evil and this is wrong but now it's suddenly okay, and how am I supposed to feel about that? What am I supposed to do with all of those feelings of, like, this is wrong and feelings of guilt now that I'm not supposed to apparently feel guilty?

Annie and Darren's reflections and uncertainty about how to navigate complex emotional and sexual feelings in a marriage echo findings from my previous research, in which young men talked at length about the emotional difficulty and confusion in transitioning from understanding sex as something beastly (or, in Darren's words, evil) to something that is sacred (Diefendorf 2015). The perception of sexual behavior as sinful does not magically disappear overnight; it is difficult to imagine that something that has been given so much power and attention before marriage is all of a sudden OK and even celebrated.

Annie and Darren's questioning of church teachings around sexuality is not unique, and in this case, they cause Darren to question sex and sexuality as understood only through a framing of sin and addiction. Darren continued with the kind of approach he might have preferred instead:

Again, I think Annie touched on it a little bit with talking about sex, rather, from a perspective of "it's sin, god hates it," "it's wrong" and switching that into "when you have sex with somebody else you are sharing something very vulnerable with them and the more you do that the less it's really gonna mean and the less you're going to be able to develop a better relationship with your significant other."

Annie nodded her head, agreeing with her husband, and added, "Yes, that's how it's supposed to be." Darren and Annie both agree with the church's perspective on sex and gender but also want more from the church. Darren articulates his wishes for an expanded, but still godly, approach to teaching young people about sex.

> I think talking to boys about the differences between men and women when it comes to sex, and definitely talking to girls, like that should be obvious, because for women, sex is very emotional, there's a lot of an emotional component, and I think boys don't realize all the emotion that goes into the other half of it. I know counseling is expensive, but if we could get more churches providing—I mean, it doesn't need to be one-on-one—but if they provide more peer counseling for more than just addiction.

Annie turned to Darren here and said, "Don't we have counseling at Lakeview?" Darren responded, "We have a substance abuse group, and a sex addiction group, and they have a 'my partner is in sex addition' group and a 'somebody near me has a sort of addiction' group. So, they have four different groups, which I think is fantastic, but I think it would also be good just to have group counseling on . . . I guess . . . education on how to live out Christianity and sexuality."

Darren wants to move church conversations and support around sexuality beyond a focus and assumption that, if one wants to talk about sex or sexuality, it is due to an addiction. But even as Darren questions both the efficacy of and the foundation for the belief that naming or discussing sex is to name addiction, he also relies on an understanding of sex that is very much about the differences between men and women's experiences with it, the same logic upon which church addiction materials rely. In their work on pornography addiction literature, Burke and Haltom find a language of "opposite sexualities" to explain differences in men and women. In discussing pornography addiction within the church, individuals deploy a combination of religious and scientific schemas that allow for men to fully embody their sexual desires and behaviors, and pathologize and isolate women who express, in the case of their work, an interest in pornography (Burke and Haltom 2020). This logic, that women are emotional and relational, and men are physical, aggressive, and visual, makes up part of the understandings of gender complementarity and essentialism foundational to the church. Much as questions of feminism threaten gender difference, and therefore heterosexuality, a reorientation to sex and sexuality as something that is perhaps not just emotional but pleasurable for women, and as something that is not just physical but perhaps emotional for men too, risks uncoupling the gendered difference central to heterosexual desire entirely (Butler 2006; Schippers 2007). While Darren may want to move beyond a focus on addiction in conversations about sexuality, those conversations about sexuality are still going to share a similar belief in gender difference that prioritizes and understands men's desires over women's.

Nicole and Craig brought up similar questions and desires in their couple's interview. Nicole is 19 years old and White, and Craig is 21 years old and Latino; they have been dating for two years, and are both actively involved in youth ministry at Lakeview. Nicole and Craig had responded to my call for interviews placed in the weekly bulletin. I had not met them before and did not know anything about them before their arrival, which was an unusual experience for me in this study. When I asked if they were married, they told me no, but Craig, who quickly smiled and blushed, proudly told me that he picked the coffee shop we all sat in because it was the location of his first date with Nicole. Nicole smiled too and looked down while Craig beamed at her. When I asked them both if they talk about sex, Craig said,

> It's taboo—maybe just because of traditions, just traditional ways, but it might be slowly changing. I definitely have heard more things about that changing within the church culture and definitely within society. I think it's becoming more of a spoken thing, like in society, the message is "yeah, girls are sexual too" whereas in church the message is, and maybe it's just my age group, but I think I'm hearing more about girls talking about it more but it's still, like, weird. Nicole and I love to talk about relationships and marriage, but I feel like it would be a little weird if I brought up sex, or asked her questions [about sex].

At this point, what began as a couple's interview turned into a conversation between Nicole and Craig. Nicole said that "I don't really know what guys talk about. Like is it just a casual conversation 'so, how's your sex life?' I don't know if that's how you talk about it."

Craig laughed, and responded to Nicole with, "Nah, it's more hypothetical than anything. Being at a Christian college, nobody knows what they're talking about." Nicole laughed but quickly asked Craig, "But you talk about it anyway? Do you talk about sex with guys on the floor and stuff? Is that, like, a thing?" Craig said, "Uh, not like that—me and my buddies would probably joke around about it, but . . . " Nicole cut him off here, increasingly focused and intent on getting a clear answer, "What about with a married guy? Do you ever talk about it with John or Chris or anything?" Craig said, "Yeah, I'd say that's a more normal conversation to have." Nicole, asking for more clarification, probed further, "They share because they are married?" Craig said, "Not details, obviously." Craig told both of us that he hears more about sex from his non-Christian friends, but has a feeling that when he gets engaged, "I'm gonna be given advice whether I ask or not."

I asked them both why they think it might be the case that, in some scenarios, guys are talking about sex, but women within the church are not (or are talking about it less, at least). They both ask the other if they want to share first. Craig took the lead:

> I don't know. I think I would just guess, because of the church culture, it's a known thing that maybe sex or sexual addiction or pornography, those things are tied to men. . . . I think that just because that opens doors and it's kinda just more appropriate for guys to joke about it—sex. It's just more known that they have a problem with this, or it's just assumed. . . . Whereas with girls I would say, within the church culture, I almost could say it's not really ever assumed that you have that struggle or you've ever had that struggle.

In many evangelical circles, when sex is discussed in conversation, it is with a framing of addiction, sin, or need for control. And most likely, these conversations are also embedded with the assumption that struggles with sexuality are usually men's struggles. Women are expected to act as the gatekeepers and help their husbands create space for healthy sexual activity within the context of marriage. And marriage, as an institution central to understandings of sexuality for evangelicals, and as something understood as a gift from God, is supposed to mark this transition from sex as evil to sex as something good.

What these interviews with evangelical couples also bring up, though, is a desire for change. And I use the word "desire" here quite intentionally. For many younger couples in the church, and couples who are choosing to remain abstinent until marriage, questions of desire are central. Which desires are appropriate before marriage? What does desire look like within marriage? How is, in the words of Darren, something that is evil actually transformed into something that can provide pleasure? And pleasure without guilt? What are the bounds of sexuality, and sexual pleasure, outside of or separate from a lens of addiction? And, perhaps, most poignantly for many, what does pleasure mean if it is confined and tied to the institution of marriage? And if Millennials want to talk about and understand sex outside of a language of addiction, this brings up a bigger issue: the entire project of evangelical heterosexuality. That is, if all forms of sex and sexuality except for married, monogamous, heterosexual sex are bundled together in a language of sin and addiction, long-standing elements of the imagined secular, how are conversations about pleasure and joy selectively pulled out of that bundle?

The church does have a (somewhat overlooked) history of discussing and celebrating sexual pleasure within the confines of marriage (see, e.g., Burke 2016 for an exception to this), but younger couples seek these questions outside of marriage, too. And a variety of age groups are asking this question. For example, what might a healthy sexuality look like for divorcees who still have a lot of life left to live? What might it look like for those who are now cohabiting? Cultural understandings of homosexuality have shifted, but so have the commonality and appropriateness of a variety of intimate relationship formations. Disciples' Journey, as the "beta" testing group of the Pathways Curriculum the church is developing, was working to tackle these questions, too. And as a group open to those who are married, divorced, dating, widowed, or single, Disciples' Journey became an especially interesting place for watching the underpinnings of White evangelical thought on dating, marriage, and relationships.

PROTECTING SACRED SEX

During Disciples' Journey's unit on marriage, in the early winter of 2016, the group devoted a weekly small group meeting to the topic of singleness. The meeting started like any other, as Carrie asked someone to volunteer to read the daily devotional out loud to the group: "Marriage and singleness are both gifts." The group began a casual conversation about this statement, and a bit of uncertainty arose about whether they agreed with it. There were lots of "ehhhs" and "ums" in a usually vocal and opinionated group. Steve, who is White and 47 years old, talked somewhat circularly about how this can be a difficult concept for all to remember, before he invoked the "grass is always greener" phrase to make his point. Pastor Jeff, who was there to help lead the group that night, transitioned the conversation. He reminded everyone that, at the meeting the week prior, group members were given the opportunity to write down questions about the topic of marriage in advance of this week's discussion. These questions were written anonymously on sticky notes and then placed on one of the walls of the conference room. There were seven Post-its under "Singles" written largely with a green marker. The questions read as follows:

Why does church emphasize marriage/family over singleness?

As a single person, how can I participate with life in the home?

What does the Bible say about nonmarried men/women living together?

What does the Bible say about living together?

My friends are all living together before marriage—is that ok?

Is cohabitation OK for financial reasons?

Why isn't God providing me with a partner?

Questions of singleness (singleness here really meaning a relationship formation that is not marriage) are on the minds of many in Disciples' Journey. And these questions also highlight the important space that small groups can provide for navigating questions that are not, and cannot, be answered fully during Sunday sermons. Small groups offer a space that is perhaps especially important as the church expands, reframes, and reinforces their ideas.

Pastor Jeff reminded the group of these questions about cohabitation to spur conversation. But it quickly became apparent that he was priming the group for a new activity. Over the previous week, Pastor Jeff, Carrie, Kimberley, and Bill, a 50-year-old White man and software engineer (one of the volunteer authors of the Pathways curriculum), met to prepare an "object lesson" for the night to help address the question of cohabitation.

Pastor Jeff asked someone to read over the exercise prompt out loud to the group. Eileen, a middle-aged White woman, read over the Pathways material out loud while seated in the circle next to her husband. Eileen read, "Our culture's views on premarital sex and cohabitation have significantly changed over the last few decades as they have become common practice. These new norms, however, don't change what the Bible says."

While Eileen read, Carrie started gluing together objects she had collected from the church office space. Using superglue, Carrie, with assistance from James, a 32-year-old parent-to-be in the group, glued together, in pairs, a plastic cup and tissue paper, two Styrofoam cups, and two old VHS covers, one a film titled "The Myth of Safe Sex" and the other titled "Sex and Lies." Carrie, smiling and excited, then urged the group members to pass the objects around and try to pull them apart. They were also encouraged to comment and reflect on this process.

Frank began, and pulled apart the two VHS covers triumphantly, setting both on his lap. He said, "Look, they are torn apart and still wet!" Carrie picked up the VHS covers and slowly walked them around the inside of the circle, displaying them to the group. Laurie, a 47-year-old White woman, who was sitting next to her husband, added, "One cover is more damaged than the other! The less-damaged cover must have been the instigator!"

The group passed around the tissue and plastic cup pairing next, and the tissue, not surprisingly, ripped when it was removed from the cup. The cup was left covered in both tissue and glue. Will, a 34-year-old White man, held out the cup and turned it over in his hands, careful to avoid the glue. He read from the Pathways materials, and, summarizing the text, reminded the group that the packaging superglue is sold in recommends the use of acetone in order to remove it. Steve built off of Will's comment and added, "And what does acetone do to plastic?!" Before anyone could respond, Steve excitedly yelled, "BURNS IT!" James, sitting back down next to his pregnant wife, wondered aloud, with a bright-red face and sheepish grin, what the damage to the cup might be if a third object had been glued to the other two. James giggled, and no one responded.

The running theme in this "object lesson" prepared to both start a dialogue and answer questions about cohabitation is that sex is something that is damaging unless it is contained. And the subtext, here, given the questions that prompted this lesson, is that sex within cohabitation does not allow for its containment. Carrie and Jeff reminded the group that sex between two people and within the confines of marriage makes it much easier to control. If and when sex is not contained, it will rip you apart.

Against all empirical evidence, there is a very vivid imagination at play here about what nonsacred, nonmarried sex will do to an individual. And this conversation at Disciples' Journey mirrors conversations about sex and sexuality in other evangelical spaces. In my previous research on sexually abstinent men (Diefendorf 2015), I documented the ways in which men who pledge sexual abstinence until marriage understand premarital sex as "beastly" and thus must work together to identify, discuss, and contain these beastly elements of sexuality so that they are able to avoid them before marriage.

There is a key difference between these conversations about sex in Disciples' Journey and those I documented over four years with a different adult support group, though. The men who spoke so openly about sex and sexuality in my previous research were all unmarried. Further, when I followed up with this group two years after my first round of data collection, the entire group had gotten married. In this second phase of interviews, the men described the ways in which the church, which had once actively encouraged and supported these conversations, heavily discouraged them now that the men were married. The church's logic was that such group conversations among married men were inappropriate, because these men would then be talking about real experiences, and more importantly, experiences with their wives. This type of conversation, about the sex lives of married women (and talking about married women among men), did not sit well with the church and their understandings of femininity, modesty, and sexuality (Fine 1988; Tolman 2005). These conversations would also run counter to the core beliefs that husbands need to protect their wives. Talking about their sex lives opens their wives up to judgment and vulnerability. Finally, it was assumed that these conversations were no longer needed, as the men had fulfilled their goals of abstinence and reached their ultimate goal of marriage, where sex was understood as a gift, and not assumed to be something that needed control and accountability anymore.

Even though Disciples' Journey is a group of "mixed" individuals by relationship type, there is a key similarity between these conversations and those I've documented before: although this room full of individuals and couples is, through an object lesson, working through conversations about sexuality and cohabitation, they are not actually having any explicit conversations about what sexuality and sexual pleasure might look like outside of a discourse of control or outside of the context of marriage. Rather, this object lesson is meant to provide the same lessons that abstinence-only education and the focus on the beastly are meant to do: remind individuals that sex is dangerous, heartbreaking, and potentially violent outside of a married relationship. The questions posed by the group the week prior indicate that when it comes to marriage and relationships, many in the room are wondering what exactly to do outside of marriage, and what this might mean as more and more people in their lives (some of them included) cohabitate. And the response from the church is that sex in those scenarios is wrong. This lesson reinforces clear and exclusionary boundaries around marriage and sex. Sex can be accessed in certain controlled forms through heterosexuality and marriage. Everyone else needs to wait or abstain altogether.

And this object lesson, developed and tested and flippantly explored during this beta group, is not what the younger or even older members of the church are asking for. They don't want to be told further that sex is bad and wrong or that it will rip you apart. They want to know why sex is bad in a committed but unmarried relationship. And they want to know how to make it good when they enter the phase of their life when they are supposed to be enjoying it as something pleasurable. There is a pretty vast disconnect between younger couples expressing feelings of uncertainty about their future relationships and sex lives, and how to navigate those conversations outside of a model of addiction or an understanding of sex as something that is evil, and an older group of individuals in the church, the majority of them married, laughing and joking as they rip apart glued VHS tapes about the dangers of sex.

This discomfort with and inability to have conversations about sexuality and sexual pleasure outside of a discourse of addiction and control are not sequestered to small groups. When Pastor Dave launched his three-month series on relationships and marriage, he talked quite a bit at the start about how they would build up to more "PG-13" conversations about sex in the Sunday sermons. He provided a disclaimer to parents about whom it would be appropriate for and who should sit out. He said his 13 year old and 12 year old could be there, but not his 10 year old. He joked about his nerves about talking about sex, and said he was going to ask for his wife Melissa's help in the sermon about it. He said he would even discuss the "m-word" meaning masturbation. He also made clear that they would need to set the foundation for understanding biblical marriage before they got to the topic of sex.

The sermon on sex never happened. Masturbation, one m-word, was replaced by the constant topic of marriage, the true m-word in the church. Younger and some older voices alike are pushing church leadership to have these conversations, and the leadership is acknowledging that. However, in their attempts to discuss singleness, sex, and sexuality, they are falling back on the usual conversations about the danger of what happens outside of marriage, and not the joys and struggles inherent in married life. They are falling short, and falling back, on previous understandings of gender, the dangers of uncontained sex, and a narrative for singleness that might not be sustainable for many.

UGLY SEX

At the end of the object lesson that evening at Disciple's Journey, Paula, a 51-year-old White woman and one of the quieter members of the group, tried to pull apart the two Styrofoam cups, the last of the glued objects to be circulated around the room. Thinking that she would be able to pull them apart like the other objects had been, Paula preemptively declared that "different surfaces are meant to mate, not similar ones!" before she forcefully tugged at the cups. The group laughed and a few people in the circle nodded along. Paula was not able to pull the two identically surfaced cups apart. One could have then made the argument that, perhaps, "cups with the same surface" are just fine mating, but that part of the analogy was ignored by the room. Paula placed the cups on the empty seat next to her, still clinging together, and the conversation moved forward.

The discarding of cups during this object lesson can work as a metaphor for larger shifts occurring at Lakeview. The church is realizing that in order to protect this thing that has long been a given—heterosexual marriage—they need to do some serious work around understanding what it means both to get people out of singleness and into marriage and to protect the institution once couples enter it. Church leaders and members are moving conversations about homosexuality to the side in favor of (at least attempts at) more explicit conversations about heterosexuality, which usually take the form of conversations about marriage, as a central goal of the church and a defining feature of evangelical man and womanhood.

Heterosexuality is a backbone of the White evangelical theology and church. It is central to White evangelical understandings of personhood, worthiness, and nation-building. As individuals and couples question how best to "do" heterosexuality, especially outside of a heterosexual marriage, they make it visible, at the risk of being marked or labeled as ugly. The imagined secular now contains elements of things previously presumed unnegotiable: prolonged singleness, different views about sex, and a want and desire for fulfillment across the entirety of the life course. These contested components of heterosexuality contain a specter of ugliness that haunts the very questions being asked about it: the reliance on gender difference, or what Jane Ward (2020) calls the misogyny paradox, as central to desire; an inability to talk about sex and sexuality in a meaningful way outside of a language of addition and control; and deep questions about the place, and exclusion, of those in the church who do not meet said markers of heterosexuality successfully.

As the church works to navigate these questions, and is prioritizing conversations about heterosexuality, with the ultimate goal of protecting it, the church also continues to bump up against the abstract category (Stein 2001) that heterosexuality has long been defined against: homosexuality. As an enduring feature of the imagined secular, it cannot be cast aside for any prolonged period of time, and the church's contemporary approaches to homosexuality are the topic of the next chapter.

CHAPTER 6

We Aren't the Extremists

Same-Sex Marriage and Changing
Ideas of Sin

Definitions of homosexuality remain contested terrain in
most societies including the United States, and homophobia
still haunts the boundary between heterosexuality and
homosexuality.

—Joane Nagel (2003:49)

On a Sunday spring morning in 2017, Pastor Dave addressed the congregation by acknowledging that "sexuality can be a really emotional
topic." Pastor Dave told a story from his old church, located in a large
city on the other side of the country, where, one day, he saw a lesbian
couple sitting in the front row during his sermon. Pastor Dave described
that "It was pretty obvious they were in love with each other. They were
demonstrating that with their hands." Pastor Dave said he ran up to the
couple and hugged them after the sermon, and enthusiastically thanked
them both for being there. The couple requested a meeting with him at
a later date, where they disclosed that their time together in the church
was exceedingly meaningful, so meaningful in fact that the two women
attributed their shared religious practice to saving their marriage. When
Pastor Dave told the congregation at Lakeview about this comment,
the congregation laughed. And Pastor Dave laughed too, albeit a bit
nervously.

Although Pastor Dave began this sermon by saying that sexuality is
an "emotional topic," Pastor Dave did not share this story to illustrate
how emotional sexuality and marriage can be for the couple involved
in the relationship. Rather, it appears Pastor Dave meant that sexuality
can be a really emotional topic *for those at Lakeview*. While Lakeview

is spending a good deal of time and energy focusing on protections around marriage, it is heterosexual marriage they celebrate and uphold.

Pastor Dave went on to say, "I don't know what to do with that information. We disagree on what a biblical marriage is . . . you know that, right? This is an area that is confusing and one that we are still dialoguing in." The congregation grew quiet, and after a minute, he said, "Do you hear that sound? That is the sound of the fun train screeching to a halt this morning." The audience laughed loudly, which worked to break up the tension in the room.

Pastor Dave got more serious again and said that "We want to give everyone the benefit of the doubt that they are trying to find Jesus; you don't have to be in or out of a certain box to be here. But we do need to go to the Bible for answers." Pastor Dave then put forth the following to the congregation: "As we have had 'status changes' in culture—how do we live? Jesus is not embarrassed about answering this—one of the most blessed things that we can have is sexuality. But it can have potential for great damage." Pastor Dave tied his story about the lesbian couple directly to status changes evangelicals are experiencing and, in this case, changes related to larger cultural shifts in sexuality. And he also reminded the congregation that Lakeview is welcoming, that one does not need to fit into a "certain box" to sit among them.

Pastor Dave's words also highlight the confusion that surrounds these status changes, and the time that the church needs while they figure out how to best approach questions of same-sex marriage. Pastor Dave continued this sermon with,

> How do we know that Jesus cares so much about sex? Look what he says about it. It can take you to Hell. It has the potential to do that. We can debate what Hell is—lots of debates about that going on—but one is that it's when sex becomes completely removed from its original design . . . if we misuse sex, it creates a brokenness in us. Sex changes you either way. It will warp and distort you or move you to wholeness. The second thing Jesus says is that it is part of a covenant—a covenantal marriage.[1] And I say that because at some point it is going to be different than state marriage. We might be entering a new season where the church actually separates biblical covenant from legal marriage. I don't know if that is right around the corner, but we will have to see.

Pastor Dave dismissed the feelings of the lesbian couple who found support in the church, because, in his understanding, such support would be impossible to find. Their marriage is not a marriage recognized by the church. Herein lie some of the limits to the love and welcoming espoused by many in the congregation.

But if gay couples are not only permitted to get married, but are also showing up in the church, then the church needs to think seriously about their own understandings of what marriage is and represents. As such, Pastor Dave suggested that the church might need to prepare and articulate their stance on a covenant marriage. The church is having these conversations out of necessity, and not because they necessarily want to. Importantly, Pastor Dave brings these points up in relation to the "status changes" evangelicals have experienced in a changing world.

In this chapter, I show how Lakeview claims a welcoming place for the LGBTQ community, while they also successfully reinstitutionalize homophobia through conversations about "excitement" and changing ideas of sin. Lakeview's approach to homosexuality as a long-standing and defining feature of the imagined secular represents, perhaps, the ultimate example of how the church engages in a bounded welcoming in times of change, working to avoid the label of homophobic while it focuses on protecting heterosexual marriage as the main goal.

A FORCED EXCITEMENT

I interviewed Pastor Jeff about a year into my fieldwork. We sat outside on the patio of his favorite coffee shop down the street from Lakeview. I usually didn't suggest this café as a meeting spot, as Lakeview staff frequented it on a daily basis. Indeed, after we arrived, two other members of the staff took seats indoors. Although it was 50 degrees on this July morning, Pastor Jeff and I sat outside and drank iced coffees. We talked about running, an activity we both love. Pastor Jeff and I ran the same half-marathon the fall before, and saw each other and high-fived along the course. This was a moment that allowed for a bit of bonding outside of our researcher/leader relationship in the church. I made sure to bring up the topic of running before I began the interview as a way of establishing a bit more comfort on my end around the power dynamics present in the interview, as Pastor Jeff not only represented a leader within the church, but was also my initial gatekeeper to the Lakeview community.

At the beginning of his interview, Pastor Jeff had mentioned the "tough issues" that the churched needed to "tackle" to stay relevant. I followed up and asked him what those tough issues were.

> Oh, gosh. Well, we gotta talk about same-sex attraction, gender issues, the church has not navigated that conversation well. But I think Lakeview has in its DNA. . . . If I'm gonna love, accept, and forgive people, I can accept

somebody who maybe is in a lifestyle that I don't agree with, but by accepting them does not imply that I agree, and that's a hard conversation, I think, to have sometimes, but I think as Christians, we gotta get around our own hang-ups and issues and just go, like, if a lesbian couple comes into Lakeview, I need to be OK with that. In fact, be *excited* about it. Doesn't mean that I'm going to agree with their lifestyle choices, I have some very strong opinions about biblical covenant marriage that are very countercultural. But getting back to the original question, we gotta talk about same-sex attraction, we need to talk about gender issues, gender identity, and then I think we need to talk about the things that Millennials really care about.

While Pastor Jeff may not agree with a homosexual "lifestyle," he feels not only that he needs to welcome everyone into the church, but that he needs to be *excited* about it. But Pastor Jeff also believes firmly in a covenant marriage, so this feeling, in juxtaposition to the push for excitement about welcoming the LGBTQ community, makes him also feel "countercultural." Evangelicals at Lakeview are grappling with the dual efforts to rework their beliefs and messages in an effort to regain some cultural significance in our current moment, and set themselves up for continued growth in the future, while also understanding that the beliefs they feel most strongly about posit them as distinctly counter to the very cultural body they want to influence. How to go about this presents a conundrum and many in the Lakeview community are asking questions about it.

"Is homosexuality a sin? Does homosexuality send someone to hell? Does heterosexuality send someone to heaven? Here's one—is Christianity homophobic?" A few people in the audience laughed, but the crowd was, for the most part, silent and still, as Pastor Dave posed these questions to the Lakeview congregation. Pastor Dave continued, "As a Christian, you are mandated to love your neighbor. Love those who are different than you. Who see the world differently than you do. Whether that's sexual attraction, religious background, whether that's political beliefs. That's your neighbor."

Pastor Dave presented these questions to Lakeview as examples of questions he receives as a pastor. But they are also the central questions that the church is working to understand: What constitutes a sexual sin now? Can we understand the relationship between heterosexuality and homosexuality as good versus evil? Moral versus wrong? And what does love have to do with it? How do White evangelicals love the neighbors they've been understanding themselves as against for decades? As the church focuses on its understandings of heterosexuality, and works to keep people within the protected confines of a heterosexual marriage, the church has spent less time in recent history talking about its decades-long fight against homosexuality.

Shortly after Pastor Dave posed these questions about sexual identities to the Lakeview community, he said, "Let's acknowledge also that there has been a tremendous cultural earthquake or shift that has happened in my generation. For the Millennials in the room and the Gen Z'ers in the room, this is the air you breathe, this isn't a shift for you. You're the fish in the water. You know, how's the water? What's water? You're the fish right, you don't know any different, but for my generation and generations older than me, Gen X'ers and above, we have encountered a seismic shift culturally in the area of LGBTQ and the church."

While, for some in the church, the water holds the oxygen they need to breathe, it is suffocating for others. Pastor Dave continued, "On top of those questions we engage all the time, culture has placed those with nonaffirming views on notice. And you will know this, if you have a nonaffirming view of gay marriage, you are on notice that you are now an extremist culturally."

Pastor Dave used data he found from a religious think tank to back up this claim, continuing with,

> The Barna Group estimates that 52% of people that believe that same-sex relationships are morally wrong are seen as extremists, and three-quarters of Americans believe that being religiously extreme is a threat to society.[2] So, this is the cultural shift that has taken place. So, if you hold to Orthodox Christianity with regard to sexuality, then it is easy for you to be perceived as an extremist and a danger to society writ large. Now I would argue that once you take that big idea and you distill it down to personal relationships it dissipates very, very quickly. Because in personal relationships you're allowed to engage this individual as a human being and they are allowed to engage you and know you as a person. It's not a concept or an idea, it's relationship. So, let's focus this morning on this church, Lakeview, and on ourselves. Shall we do that? Let's focus on this church and on ourselves.

Pastor Dave suggests that the cultural shift he was referencing in the first part of his sermon is not so much a shift in which LGBTQ folks are receiving more rights and recognition; rather, he focuses on a shift in which the church is now "on notice" for *not* being welcoming for LGTBQ folks. Pastor Dave also describes the church as a threat and a danger to society because of its views. This is especially remarkable given the ways that homosexuality has been described and labeled historically in the United States. In flipping this narrative, Pastor Dave centers the needs and feelings of those in the church over the rights of others, and also emphasizes that the church is the victimized entity in this ongoing debate. Pastor Dave suggests that the solution to shake the label of the "extremist" is in part through a focus on individual relationships. The church is prioritizing their concerns of being labeled as "ugly" in their response to the LGBTQ community. They do not want to be marked as the extremists in a country in which even the Supreme Court has moved. But now, in holding on to what they believe, they are at risk of appearing extreme and intolerant. And this *concern* with coming across as the homophobes takes precedence over the actual work required of allyship.

In this way, evangelicals at Lakeview church approach topics of both race and sexual identity in a similar vein: congregants know they should be talking about sexuality, much as they debated feminism and acknowledged the Black Lives Matter movement. They also know and feel that they *should care* about issues related to race and sexuality. But the ways in which they approach solutions to both racism and homophobia allow inequalities to prevail; individual emotion and a focus on individual relationship-building continue to trump the structural realities of the world.

The "excitement" that Pastor Jeff says he needs to feel is the emotional sibling of the instrumental acceptance that individuals at Lakeview profess. The Lakeview community has learned to nullify the perceived threat of the Black Lives Matter movement by celebrating their love for all and their missions work, where they are cast as saviors, upholding norms of Whiteness through which congregants frame themselves as good and thus not racist. And the ways in which this emotion work weaves in with the goals and beliefs of the church reflect the favors time can provide: the church has had more time to figure out how to navigate threats of racial justice than they have had for same-sex marriage. As I suggested in the introduction to this book, there are many (often overlooked) steps between an identification of an external threat (Smith 1998) and eventual group cohesion in response to that perceived threat. A forced excitement, then, is a step before instrumental acceptance, when the church and the individuals name a threat, acknowledge it, and begin the work of figuring out just how to pair these "status changes" with their new label as "extreme" as they reckon with larger institutional changes that might be coming.

In part because the legalization of same-sex marriage represents a newer threat, there is confusion about what this excitement should look like, and how it pairs with a White evangelical theology and belief system. For example, after Pastor Isaac left in the fall of 2016, Eileen and Eric, middle-aged White individuals, talked to me after Disciples' Journey one night about how their sadness in his departure stemmed from the fact that, in Eric's words, "Pastor Isaac knew how to love people that I don't know how to." Eileen and Eric appreciated the ways in which they could learn how to be more welcoming and more loving, and more excited and open to this loving, from Pastor Isaac, the man who, with tears in his eyes, told the congregation how good it felt to welcome someone new into church on that summer morning described in chapter 5. Congregants at Lakeview seek guidance and examples for what this welcoming might look like as they are told they are living in a world in which they are the "extremists" and a danger to society for being against same-sex marriage.

Pastor Jeff implied a generational shift that may be partially responsible for this change in approach to same-sex couples. According to Pastor Jeff, loving all is "built into the DNA" of Lakeview Church, but this DNA is more recently acknowledged through the younger generations at Lakeview. Perhaps these feelings of excitement are coming from younger members of the church, the Millennials, as Pastor Jeff suggests.[3]

Annie, who would, at age 29, be classified as a Millennial, described during an interview with me a similar observation from a small group she joined at Lakeview. The group is a generic women's Bible study. Annie told me that

> It's actually really interesting with my specific Bible study because we have three different generations. We have this older generation that are, like, in their seventies where they're very conservative, right? And so they know the Bible well and they know what is right and what is wrong and it's really hard for them to have a gray area. But what I think is really cool is that we have these other generations that are able to bring them to a place of, "Yeah, but we still love them, right? [laughs], and how can we, like, show them respect and show them love?" and they agree with that but it's also very black and white for them and so, so it's been very interesting to have those conversations and sometimes we don't, because of the differing views that we have.

Annie discusses intergenerational debates around the LGBTQ community, and also suggests that, at times, it is difficult to approach conversations on same-sex attraction due to differing views within the Bible study. Annie's words highlight a level of disagreement that, for many at Lakeview, results in some confusion on where the church stands. Small groups remain an important site of debate and locus of negotiation around evangelical identity and beliefs, but individuals still seek a certain amount of foundational guidance from the church.

During a couple's interview, Nicole, White and 19, highlighted these needs for institutional guidance from the church, and told me,

> [Gay marriage] needs to be addressed and I think that we need to know where we stand with that but also paired up with that, know how to love those people, even though we may not agree with what they're doing or how they think. So, I think it's important to have those outlets to talk about those things and to, like, come to some kind of conclusion, but also paired with the fact that we still love these people and know how to interact with them in a loving way and respectful way.

Nicole knows she is supposed to approach LGBTQ individuals with love and respect. She acknowledges the importance of the small group of which she is a part as a space to debate and articulate her beliefs around this issue. However, Nicole also seeks more guidance from the church in how to go about navigating these relationships.

Carrie reflected on the topic of same-sex relationships in regard to small group conversations: "As far as the congregation as a whole, I mean, we don't even really talk about it, and I notice how Thursday nights, it's never really come up a ton. I was surprised the week when we were talking about marriage and singleness in Disciples' Journey, I don't think it really came up. It's not something that's in the forefront." Rather, questions of heterosexual marriage and the family have remained at the forefront, even though those conversations themselves are also fraught.

The topic of homosexuality *did* come up during the five-week unit on marriage and singleness that Carrie was referring to. During one of the first evenings devoted to the topic of marriage at Disciples' Journey, Carrie directed the individuals in the room to pair off for an exercise on spousal communication. Each pair was given a prompt for a decision-making conversation a couple would need to confront. The idea behind the exercise was to practice engaging in a typical, but potentially difficult, spousal communication, take notes on the conversation, and then report the conversation to the larger group for feedback. Due to an uneven gendered split in the room, Will and Steve paired off together. Will and Steve turned their chairs to face each other and read their prompt out loud. In their exercise, Steve and Will were tasked with simulating a conversation about finding a place to live. Instead of going along with the prompt, the two men started lisping and flailing their wrists, giggling and engaging in a bit of what CJ Pascoe (2011) calls the fag discourse: a way in which men bond and connect with each other, often through jokes, and manage the anxiety around this connection by shoring up their own masculinity, often by lobbing the "fag" label at other men. This interaction between Will and Steve highlights some of the work that jokes can do, in this case perhaps working to relieve the anxiety about pretending to be in a marriage with another man (Pascoe 2011; Pascoe and Diefendorf 2019; Tavory 2014).

As this back and forth continued, the two men joked that if they were supposed to be choosing a place to live, "obviously" they would need to move to Belltown, which Will described to his friend Steve and anyone who was listening to their antics as "the gay neighborhood of Seattle." Those familiar with the social geography of life in Seattle would agree that Belltown is *not* the gay neighborhood. It is a hub of affluent, young workers in the tech industry. Capitol Hill has long been understood and recognized as the center of gay life in Seattle. These two men thought they were being funny, showing their knowledge of gay life in Seattle, while also making fun of it. However, Will and Steve entirely misunderstand what that neighborhood is.

Seattle represents the place, and space, where the gays are, acting then, in some sense, as the physical space that holds much of the imagined secular. It is a city many of them visit relatively infrequently given its proximity to Lakeview, but its proximity does quite a lot of work as a reminder about what nonevangelical life is like. In this moment of joking between Will and Steve, they are unable to imagine that gay people might live in their own neighborhoods, and perhaps even attend their church. When Will and Steve joke about being a gay couple, this pretend shift in their sexual identity also means a major physical move in order to make the relationship make sense to them. Some individuals at Lakeview talk about gay life as if they know what gay life is, even as a cultural other in relation to their own lives, because, in today's world both evangelical and secular individuals are now supposed to know the LGBTQ community. Parishioners at Lakeview are trained in this cultural knowledge, but the cultural knowledge is still deeply informed by the imagined secular.

There is a type of double imaginary at play here as well. Those who occupy the secular world often imagine conservative religious folks expressing quite a bit of hostility, and sometimes blatant hatred, toward the LGBTQ community. Given both the historical and the current violence and discrimination touted by churches, this is not an unwarranted perspective. But as we see at Lakeview, that is not its dominant approach to the LGBTQ community today.

Allison, a 24-year-old White woman who joined Lakeview Church a year prior after moving from Florida, described same-sex relationships as something she doesn't need to think much about. Allison told me, "It's so easy to be like, oh no one is ever going to ask me, so I don't need to know!" Allison laughed, as part of the joke is that I am making her think about this as a researcher. Allison paused to think, and added,

> Like, if Pastor Dave was asked about this, I don't even know what I would expect him to say. Or even what I would think if he decided to allow gay marriage here, like, not giving in to it, or not doing it could risk things—but it's kind of against God, against my religion, so I am not gonna do that, and I'm gonna trust that it's gonna work out. Like if you don't wanna marry them, that's like, legally against the law. But does it matter if it's a law or not? I know that God wants us to respect authority and laws wherever we are. If I become associated with a denomination and become pastor, like, or I had to put myself in a place where someone asked me to marry them who was not, who was like in a lesbian relationship or a gay relationship, like, what would I say?

Allison draws a distinction between the federal legality of same-sex marriage and her own religious views on same-sex marriage, but this distinction presents some confusion, as Allison's religious beliefs also suggest that she act as a law-abiding citizen, but her religious values do not align with the law. This uncertainty Allison feels reflects a larger divide between evangelical and nonevangelical stances on sexual rights, as recent work finds that society at large is becoming increasingly accepting of gay marriage, while evangelicals are not (Le Miere 2018).

Becky also described the uncertainty she felt around the church's stance on the LGBTQ community. But, unlike Will and Steve, or Carrie and Allison, Becky does feel like this is something on the forefront of her mind, as she has recently met a gay man whom she has become friendly with. Becky told me a long story about joining a Buy Nothing Group on Facebook to give away some of her plants. Becky is an avid and proud gardener, and, at the end of a successful spring growing season, wanted to give away many of her plants, which she was otherwise going to "rip up" to make room for others. It was through this process of giving her plants away in this online forum that Becky met a gay man and his partner. He took some of her plants again, and, later that same year, when Becky returned to the group to seek help finding a prop for her daughter's play, Carlos and his partner, Todd, helped Becky out. Becky needed an antique wooden picnic basket for her daughter's school production of *The Wizard of Oz*. Becky said that after Carlos had loaned her the picnic basket, "We got talking and stuff and then I posted these free plants, and he came and got some. And we had a conversation, and I always make a point of, I always put stuff out there, like, when I need to. Like, 'Can I come by and pick up your thing on my way home from church?' And, I'll put things out there, that's kind of my way of, I've now told you what I'm doing. If you want to inquire, go for it." Here, Becky is illustrating to me one of her tactics in evangelizing to her local community. Becky does not immediately invite people to church. She first likes to put feelers out to individuals to gauge their interest.

In Becky's words, "He did [get interested], and so we had this conversation. We had a long conversation, and he told me his story a little bit, and he's had some tragedy, and he's with this gay partner. And, it was a really interesting story. You know, he was married and had a son, and they got killed, in an accident, and stuff like that. And, then he ended up being with, you know, a man, and blah, blah, blah." At this point in the story, Becky is less willing, and perhaps a bit uncomfortable, in relaying any details about Carlos and Todd's relationship. Further, Becky might find the beginning of Carlos's story about his horrible tragedy more relatable, as that aligns with many evangelical narratives that equate homosexuality with earlier traumas (Gerber 2011).

Becky continued, "So, now he's in this relationship, but he is from Colombia. Colombia? Cuba. I think he's from Cuba, and you know, he was wearing a cross and stuff. Anyways, so we had this conversation, and I was really conflicted. And, it was during the time of [Pastor] Isaac, but I was really conflicted. Can I invite this man to church? Like, is he going to be welcomed? Is he going to feel awkward? You know what I mean? If he comes in with his partner, you know . . . " Becky trails off here. I imagine part of Becky's concern is that Carlos alone may of course attend church without anyone knowing he is gay, but if Carlos and Todd came together, their relationship might be more clear to others.

Becky is also concerned about the reactions of her peers at church, even though most all profess love, or at least some conditional welcoming of LGBTQ individuals. "There's the people that I know, I just don't know if I can invite this gay person to church here or not. I don't want to invite somebody and then them get a bad taste, which, potentially, prevents them from further seeking. But the conversation that I had with this guy was very much, like, he missed being in a church . . . I think that's gotta be a challenge because there's so many narrow-minded Christians out there."

I got to know Becky fairly well over the two years I spent at Lakeview, and knew Becky to be an outgoing, well-connected, and outspoken church community member. This hesitancy regarding her outreach to Todd and Carlos surprised me. I asked Becky if she talked to the pastoral team at Lakeview about her uncertainty. Becky had talked to Pastor Jeff about this predicament, and described his response as follows: "Oh, he was totally, like, 'we are here to serve people who want to know Jesus no matter what.' So, he said, 'I think that it would, frankly, make some people uncomfortable. Too bad. Bring him, you know, if you want to bring him, bring him.' You know, Pastor Dave will be one of the first to go up and shake their hand, probably. It's OK. I never brought him."

I then asked Becky if she would feel comfortable inviting Carlos to church now. Becky responded to me with the following: "Yes, I still would. I just didn't, 'cause it's not somebody, like, I *know,* know. You know what I mean? It's just somebody in the neighborhood that's come over and put plants out of my yard . . . he's not my buddy. So, if our paths cross again, and circumstances come around, I should probably just invite him." Becky then said that if the "perfect situation" arises, she will invite him to Lakeview. Becky is one of the most dominant personalities of Disciples' Journey, a force both within the small group and within the larger church. Becky is quick to talk to strangers, quick to make friends, and quick to follow up with individuals she meets. This ambivalence and hesitancy on Becky's part over Carlos, as someone who is "not her buddy," likely have less to do with her insecurities around evangelizing, and much more to do with her insecurities around inviting a gay man into the church.

In her ethnography of a small town in the Northwest at the center of battles over gay rights, Arlene Stein found and argued that "By constructing homosexuals as an abstract category, members of the community were able to separate the fate of gay people as a group from gay people as individuals. The lack of sustained contact and knowledge of homosexual culture bred feelings of repulsion and subdued hostility that were ready, given the right political rhetoric, to condense into hatred" (Stein 2001:109). Will and Steve's reliance on abstract categories (and inaccurate or outdated neighborhood stereotypes) to understand homosexuality is some of what Becky may have been trying to do when she insisted she did not "know, know" Carlos, even though she does know him. The abstract category of homosexuality crumbles when White evangelicals meet LGBTQ individuals as their neighbors and potential friends. For Becky, and others, that may feel like the symbolic line between the sacred church and the imagined secular world is crossed. When the LGBTQ community was unknown, the abstract category that blurred the realities of the actual individuals made hate and apathy easier.

FROM "PRAY THE GAY AWAY" TO
A FORCED EXCITEMENT

The combination of contact with the LGBTQ community and larger cultural shifts in regard to support for the LGBTQ community calls into question the long-standing practices and cultural fights of the church, and what is really "good" and "evil" when it comes to sexual identity. Evangelical leaders and organizations have long been at the front lines of antigay legislation, measures, and activities; debates about what constitutes right and wrong, sacred or sin, when it comes to sex represent ongoing and very long fights in the United States. Indeed, a long line of ex-gay ministries emerged in the United States after the American Psychiatric Association (APA) removed the diagnosis of "homosexuality" from the *Diagnostic and Statistical Manual* (DSM) in 1973 (Waidzunas 2015). Exodus International, the largest ex-gay ministry in the United States, was founded in 1976. Another well-known antigay evangelical movement came out of Focus on the Family, a Christian organization and international conglomerate founded in 1977 by James Dobson, and known worldwide for its radio broadcasts, conservative public policy agendas, and national campaigns, or ministries. In 1998, Focus on the Family founded their Love Won Out Ministry, which had a mission statement as follows: "To provide a Christ-centered, comprehensive conference which will enlighten, empower and equip families, church and youth leaders, educators, counselors, policy-makers, and the gay community on the truth about homosexuality and its impact on culture, family, and youth." This truth about homosexuality, according to Love Won Out, was that homosexuality was, to put it simply, something that could be overcome. The organization argued that there were no conclusive studies to support a biological or genetic cause for homosexuality. Thus, homosexuality could be framed as a choice, and a sinful choice that one could change or avoid entirely.

Those who overcame the "sin" of homosexuality, with the help of Love Won Out and other similar organizations, often identified or were identified as "ex-gays." In promoting and parading "ex-gay" individuals, prominent Christian organizations also highlighted their logic: that same-sex attraction (SSA) is a sin, and a sin that can be overcome. Many ex-gays, along with the organizations that "produced" them, often spoke out against society's messages about homosexuality as something normal and healthy. Love Won Out specifically targeted the media's "misrepresentation" of homosexuality as something predetermined, and also targeted schools' "progay" agendas, harkening back to the sentiment of the culture wars started decades before.

In discussing and promoting sexuality and sexual identity as something that can change, these Christian organizations inadvertently aligned themselves with more progressive groups who talk about sexuality as fluid. Many sociologists have documented the challenges this framing presents (Erzen 2006; Gerber 2008, 2011; Moon 2004). As Tanya Erzen finds in her work on ex-gay ministries in San Francisco, in constructing same-sex attraction as a choice, evangelicals, as a result, "point to the instability and changeability of their own identities rather than serve as a testament to heterosexuality" (2006:14).

Sometimes SSA was discussed as a product of a stunted psychological process, a lag in the appropriate development of gender identity. While SSA was then understood as an unfinished process, the behavior that resulted from this stunted phase was understood as pathological and a sign of a disorder (Gerber 2011). Often those who expressed homosexual desires were pathologized in other ways as well. Literature used and cited at a Love Won Out conference, for example, equated SSA with mental health problems, alcoholism, depression, and emotional trauma (Gerber 2009). As Amy DeRogatis argues, popular science provided a "new vocabulary" for evangelicals to link sexual sin to things like physical damage and disease (Burke and Haltom 2020; DeRogatis 2015).

But these groups also needed to curate a space in which Christian individuals experiencing SSA could feel comfortable talking about homosexuality as a sin. This was especially difficult when these groups relied on a language of pathology to embolden their claims. Lynne Gerber thus argues that one of the central, although paradoxical, tasks of ex-gay ministries was to destigmatize homosexuality. Gerber suggests that part of the success of these groups was their ability to find a solution to this paradox. Gerber (2011) argues that these groups were able to maintain this duality through the "democratizing" of sins, where homosexuality was understood as interchangeable with other sins. In labeling homosexuality and SSA on par with other sins, groups like Exodus International and churches across the country placed SSA as a priority of focus as they adapted their language to best deal with it as a sin. This move highlights the malleability of evangelical approaches to these questions, but the ways in which new tactics manifest often result in the endurance of existing hierarchies.

This democratizing of sin fits within a larger evangelical logic of both sexual sin and sexual redemption. Shortly after the *Access Hollywood* tape that showed Donald Trump commenting about "grabbing women by the pussy" leaked in October 2016, Jerry Falwell Jr., president of Liberty University (one of the largest Christian universities in the United States) and son of Jerry Falwell, the founder of the Moral Majority, commented on Trump's remarks and defended him by saying that "we are all sinners" (Whitehead and Perry 2020).[4] In taking a democratic approach to sin, homosexuality can be contextualized in a way that makes conversations about it approachable and (perhaps) less stigmatizing, but this approach also allows for the potential forgiveness of a whole host of other behaviors tied specifically to heterosexuality and masculinity.

In large and small evangelical churches alike, sexual sin was addressed in men's groups focused on sexual addiction, and antigay sentiment was often executed through specific groups focused on same-sex attraction. Although Lakeview and other large and small evangelical churches discuss SSA in Sunday sermons and church materials, small groups often provide specific forms of accountability to group members to help individuals avoid such desires (Diefendorf 2015). The church has historically advocated and supported its members in talking through these desires and struggles in smaller settings. SSA groups take the sentiment of "pray the gay away" and translate this message into tangible action and goals through prayer, materials, accountability partners, and group conversation. These groups then help reinforce and fulfill larger teachings of the church: that sex within heterosexual marriage is sacred, and all other forms of sexual activity and desire must be controlled and contained, encompassing and democratizing sexual sins.[5]

But whatever control and successes these SSA groups celebrated, cultural and national shifts put into question their feasibility and appropriateness. In 2013, after much pushback, controversy, and continued financial strain, Love Won Out was disbanded by the board of directors of Exodus International (a larger, interdenominational ex-gay Christian organization), which had purchased the organization in 2009. Exodus International disbanded shortly after dismantling Love Won Out. The then president of Exodus International, Alan Chambers, apologized to the LGBTQ community for causing them "pain and hurt" as the organization closed. This moment marked a larger reckoning for evangelicals in the United States, as the disbanding of this organization reflected a sign of changing times. Just two years later, the United States legalized same-sex marriage in the *Obergefell v. Hodges* decision in June 2015, when the Supreme Court held that the Fourteenth Amendment requires states to license and recognize same-sex marriage.

That was not the end of the White evangelical church's efforts to discourage homosexuality. There was mass backlash to the Supreme Court decision in 2015, from religious and nonreligious groups alike. Many conservative religious groups banded together to deploy the argument of "religious freedom" to fight back (Eberstadt 2016; Gorski 2017; Whitehead and Perry 2020), which some suggest was indicative of a larger shift in conservative Christians' approach to politics, emphasizing a language of individual rights that had prior been a tactic of the liberal left (Lewis 2019). Others condemned those within their own religious groups. In August 2017, a group of 150 prominent evangelicals (including James Dobson) wrote and released the "Nashville Statement," which denounced Christians who support the LGBTQ community. The statement reads that "such approval constitutes an essential departure from Christian faithfulness and witness."[6]

Indeed, it is precisely because of this long history and embattlement that I began this research project in the summer of 2015 following the federal legalization of same-sex marriage. However, where I expected to document the "angry White men and women" that Stein (2001) researched, I instead found a confused group shifting their focus, marking a stark contrast to the approaches to homosexuality taken just years before. While collective turmoil has ensued at the national level, with stories about continued backlash to the decision from 2015 receiving mass media attention,[7] something different has been happening within individual churches like Lakeview.

There are no SSA groups at Lakeview today, and none existed in the time I spent doing research there. The majority of small groups are devoted to heterosexual couples and to questions related to heterosexual marriage. For example, these groups have names such as "How to Love," which is a group that explores the book by the same name, in an effort to highlight and name "frustrating relational patterns in your marriage," and a married couples group called quite literally "Stay Married!" These groups are advertised, celebrated, and offered multiple times a year. This is a marked shift in focus within a fairly typical White evangelical megachurch compared to the subject matter of groups in the recent past.

But in a moment in which evangelicals know that ex-gay conversion is wrong, and that they are supposed to love, respect, and even be "excited" about gay and lesbian individuals joining them in church, there is still much uncertainty about what that might actually look like in practice. Parishioners at Lakeview who are thinking about and debating SSA are looking to the church for more guidance and directives on their beliefs and stance in changing times. At the same time, it appears that younger generations within the church may be pushing those conversations forward, and that Lakeview, as a church, needs to catch up, as echoed in Pastor Jeff's reflection. In some cases, Lakeview is centering its own needs and reputation over the needs and experiences of historically (and currently) marginalized folks. There are also members at Lakeview who state that SSA is not something they have thought about or need to think about. While these remarks may reflect the pervasiveness and endurance of heteronormativity in the church, regardless of larger cultural shifts, these remarks may also reflect a shift in the church's focus and decreased conversations around their collective stance on homosexuality and SSA.

This felt need for a "forced excitement" on the part of evangelicals at Lakeview is happening alongside a bundling of homosexuality with other sexual sins, and the reinstitutionalization of homophobia via the very language the church is now using to appear welcoming and "open for business" to all.

THE DANGER OF "DEMOCRATIZING" SINS

All of the parishioners I spoke with at Lakeview Church discuss homosexuality as a sin, on par with any other sin. Some rely on a language of addiction, and others don't have a very fleshed-out narrative about it. But most are bundling homosexuality together with other sexual sins in the church, again what Gerber (2011) calls the "democratizing" of sins. Lakeview and its members are working to destigmatize homosexuality and make conversations about it both welcoming and approachable. However, they also still consider homosexuality to be morally wrong. The loss of homosexuality's unique status and the disappearance of the space long devoted to dealing with it (SSA groups) highlight both its declines and its shifts as a threat. And these changes also present some uncertainty about what, exactly, to do about it.

Riley, a 37-year-old White woman, discussed same-sex attraction as something akin to addiction. Riley told me that "I did some research on it because I guess I believe it's more DNA-based, it's a more natural sort of thing." Riley explained that Pastor Isaac spoke of same-sex relationships directly following the federal legalization of same-sex marriage in the United States (2015), and that Pastor Isaac "really stuck with the idea that it wasn't [natural] and that people had the ability to change and make those choices to change." Riley didn't find this message adequate or sensical to her. Unlike Pastor Isaac (at least in 2015), Riley thinks same-sex attraction is "sort of similar to drug addiction. I guess I've always swung the other way, that it is similar to a drug addiction in that you are kind of wired that way." Riley aligns more with a born-this-way rhetoric, but with a specific rhetoric in which SSA is an addiction. For example, Riley does not talk about heterosexual attraction with a language of addiction. Riley has some clear convictions about SSA, while other members of Lakeview have a different language to discuss the LGBTQ community. The threats of the imagined secular world can change in their meaning, both for individuals and for the church. As White evangelicals recast their definitions of SSA, this allows some to feel more welcoming and accepting, and means others feel confused about the boundaries around a threat, unsure of what constitutes "good" and "evil" when it comes to sexual behavior and desire.

Darren, like many of his fellow congregants at Lakeview, believes that same-sex behavior and desire are sins no different than any other. Darren also suggested that, as a fellow sinner (like everyone else), he should not judge those who engage in same-sex behavior, because, in the end, God will be the one to judge them all. Darren stated that "I think we should be witnessing to all these people from a loving standpoint instead of, 'we're here to judge you on your mistake,' 'cause we have no mistakes apparently." Darren continued by saying,

> 'Cause what makes their sin different from our sin? I think a lot of that stems from the work I do, and the population I work with who has lots of traumatic experiences with Christians, and the church . . . I think it's a complex issue to try to navigate. I have a new coworker and I was having a lot of conversations with him, and he is openly gay and in a relationship and we're talking about our different relationships and me and Annie and how well we fit together, and he was talking about him and his partner and how well they fit together and different stuff like that and I almost feel like, I'm a Christian, but I have to let you know, like, I read the Bible as love and, "Who is without sin, cast the first stone." I'm not going to judge you because I'm not the one to judge you.

Darren seeks to accept the LGBTQ community because to not accept them is to not accept himself either. And Darren may feel some extra pressure in this regard due to his job as a social worker. When same-sex desire is bundled with all other sexual sins, like pornography, masturbation, lust, or adultery, and not given its own separate status as the Thing that stands in contrast to heterosexuality, everyone is implicated, and everyone is understood as sexually broken and in need of empathy and healing. Darren knows that the joys of heterosexual marriage require boundaries, and whether he has dealt with the temptations of these sexual sins or not, there is always the possibility he might in the future. This framing of sexuality as sinful versus not sinful behavior, rather than heterosexual versus homosexual behavior, has the potential to implicate everyone; what constitutes a relationship and what constitutes a sin are both shifting simultaneously.

Well into my interview with Nicole and Craig, I asked specifically, "If a same-sex couple came to Lakeview on Sunday, would you welcome them in?" Nicole responded first with a "For sure. Yeah. For sure." Her boyfriend, Craig, agreed and said excitedly, "That would be great!" Here, both Craig and Nicole laugh. I ask them why it would be great, and Craig responds with "Because they're there. They're coming to church. They're at Lakeview. They're just people. They're not worse than me, but I think that maybe they don't know that Christians think that, or some Christians think that. I see it as any other sin." Nicole and Craig treat SSA like any other sin, and do not immediately respond with a need or desire to fix that sin.

Becky, like Darren and Craig, agrees that same-sex behavior is understood as a sin. Becky said, "I, personally, don't believe that's the way God intended it. I don't believe that it is correct, biblically. However, it's not my place to judge that, and if that person has a heart for God, and has, I mean, you know, has the ability to speak to people that can bring other people to Christ, I don't think that that should be an obstacle, not for the church. We just have to get beyond that. We have to let people be their people and not judge them." Both Becky and Darren focus on judgment as a concern that the church should move beyond. Darren specifically references the "traumatic experiences" that the LGBTQ community has faced from Christians, perhaps referencing the previous tactics towards ex-gay ministries and conversion therapy. Becky focuses on the importance of a relationship with Jesus Christ, a primary component of evangelical identity. If someone who struggles with the sin of SSA can still bring other people to Christ, Becky doesn't see much of a problem in including them. However, at the same time Becky is wrestling with quite a bit of uncertainty about bringing LGBTQ individuals into church, a step many in the church would suggest is a prerequisite for the ability to evangelize and bring others to Christ.

In one of her interviews with an evangelical woman, Stein reports that the woman sent Stein a note after her interview that read the following: "Dear Arlene. It was a pleasure to meet you today. I enjoyed visiting with you. I do feel I went on a bit too much! I don't know what got into me. I'm kind of embarrassed that I went on so. Please forgive me. I'm not always like that." I got an almost identical response from Becky after our interview. Stein frames the response she received in the context of shame. But for Becky, I think it was a shame driven by a specific type of reflection: her understanding that while she talked about welcoming people into church, when it came to specific examples in her own life, she wasn't willing or able to act on that welcoming. Becky's experience and disconnect between her own stated beliefs and actions in her life highlight the larger moment the church is in, as members wrestle with this perception of excitement and welcoming and the realities of what that might mean, especially when they feel a little unclear about how to respond in a godly way without letting their ugliness show.

In the same sermon in which Pastor Dave posed questions about homosexuality to the congregation, he shared a statistic with Lakeview. He said that he had been reading some "enlightening statistics about how gender-fluid people are, meaning that the temptations of same-sex attraction or heterosexual attraction are there for many people." Pastor Dave said that "12 percent, 14 percent, something like that experience attractions to both, and so this idea of vilification of one over the other is really unbiblical. Everyone is sexually broken and struggles." Pastor Dave is equating gender fluidity with sexual fluidity here, a conflation that would not carry weight in many other spaces. However, in his essentialist and complementarian understanding of gender, a distinction between gender and sexuality doesn't really exist. If being a man means being attracted to women, and being a woman means being attracted to men, then there is not much of a meaningful difference between sexual fluidity and gender fluidity; rather, variance in either disrupts the central feature of heterosexuality and heterosexual desire (Butler 2006; Schippers 2007).

And while Pastor Dave is talking through and aligning beliefs of the church with newer narratives of sexual fluidity outside of the church, his conclusions are different. Instead of using those statistics to conclude that sexuality is a messier amalgamation of attraction, feelings, identity, and life than most care to admit, this narrative is used to center the church and the people in it. Pastor Dave suggests instead that everyone is a little bit broken, and that everyone is struggling. This narrative can then be flipped. Instead of only using it to extend empathy, as Darren does in thinking that, because he might struggle, he shouldn't judge others that do, it can also be used to put forth a logic of overcoming sins. That is, if all sexual sins are bundled together as the same, if someone can overcome a pornography addiction, someone else can overcome SSA. Those struggles can be understood as the same, and difference is erased.

But the "struggles" are different. In the same sermon, Pastor Dave suggested that while, for gay-identifying individuals, sexuality might feel like "something that is the air you breathe" he "would argue that it's not who you are, it's a part of who you are like your favorite color is a part of who you are." But people are not discriminated against for loving the color purple. In minimizing these differences, the church can work to fold everyone in to the same battles, appear welcoming in that regard, and then ignore the work required to address homophobia as both a historical and a contemporary pillar of the White evangelical church.

In their research on LGBTQ conservative Christians and their allies, Dawne Moon and Theresa Tobin introduce the concept of *sacramental shame;* they argue that conservative Christians see SSA and "gender deviance" as temptations similar to their own, and, as such, accept that feeling ashamed of these sins will work redemptively as it does for other sins. However, as the authors point out, sexual and gender identity "do not usually respond to acts of will" (2018:456), so shame remains a perpetual requirement for individuals enacting these sins. As much as Pastor Dave and the Lakeview community may want to bundle all sexual "sins," erasing their difference will not erase the power and pain that insinuating that a part of your being requires perpetual shame can invoke. And likening sexual desire and identity to a favorite color cannot undue the harm the institution has perpetuated for generations.

The Lakeview audience was very quiet during Pastor Dave's sermon on homosexuality. In what was perhaps an effort to lighten up the room, Pastor Dave laughed and said,

> Are you freaking out about that? I mean don't freak out but that's just reality. We all struggle to submit our sexuality to the cross, that's just everybody in the room. Whether you're married or single. Whether you're looking at women or men that you're married to or not married to, whether it's lust in your heart or actual lust, whether you're engaged in pornography, whether you have same-sex desire and fulfillment, or heterosexual desire and fulfillment, outside the bonds of marriage, everyone is sexually broken, and we all must continually submit our sexuality to the cross.

Here, again, in a sermon about homosexuality, Pastor Dave made clear that homosexuality is a sin on par with the other sexual sins he lists. He continued, "Here's some verbiage that I'd love to see us change in this regard. If we believe that we're sexually broken and we're all on this journey to submit our sexuality this phrase 'love the sinner, hate the sin' goes away. Can we just get rid of that one?" The audience remained quiet. Pastor Dave used a football reference to suggest, "Let's just 4th and 20, punt, no more love the sinner hate the sin. Can we change it to this: Hate my own sin, and love others. Can we do that one instead? So, no more love the sinner hate the sin, that's kind of become cliché. How about hate my own sin, and love others? Are we cool with that one instead?

While a few people clapped, the audience did not respond as collectively or loudly as they usually would at the conclusion of a sermon. Members of the Lakeview community want guidance from the church, but this lukewarm response might indicate that there is hesitancy around how to put such guidance into action. There may also be an unwillingness from some in the community to switch gears from "love the sinner, hate the sin" to "hate my sin, love others" because of a fundamental discomfort with loving someone who "sins" in a way that many still see as morally different from other sexual sins.

If there were any members of the LGTBQ community in the audience that day, hearing a pastor suggest that one hate their own sins might mean something different than, say, someone wrestling with the guilt of watching pornography. Homophobia is a central feature of the history of the United States and its nation-building projects (Puar 2007), as implemented by institutions, social groups, and individuals. To tell a gay individual that their SSA (in the words of the church) is their own sin that should be hated by them, but not others, falls in line with a long history of imposed external and internalized self-hatred and violence on the queer community. And such a message stands in direct contrast to providing a welcoming space for all.

But Pastor Dave and many members of the Lakeview community of course believe they are welcoming. Pastor Dave ended his sermon that morning by saying that "problems of sexuality" are rather issues and questions of community and people, in a very similar vein to the approach to questions of racism that presents a solution of love. Pastor Dave emphatically said,

> It's *all about people*. People wrestling with sexual orientation and gender identity cannot be "those people" they must be "our people." In fact, my target is the 14-year-old young man or young woman in our congregation

who is dealing with same-sex attraction and how do they talk about it with me or you. Is this a safe place where they can have a conversation or do we stay in our lane like we have been for decades where they've been required to simply stuff it and hide it and then later on engage in a community that accepts them and out they go from the church, which is a tragedy.

Pastor Dave wants the church to "leave their lane," and do so by promoting a new take on sexual sin. Pastor Dave wants the Lakeview community to adopt an understanding of sexual sin that both celebrates collective failure and urges a simultaneous return to individual shame. This is a different approach to the democratizing of sin that focuses on healing one's own problem and loving others (Gerber 2011). And when put to the test, this new approach to collective failure appears to still privilege some sins over others.

(RE)INSTITUTIONALIZING HOMOPHOBIA

There are churches that have received quite a bit of attention for being "open and affirming." These churches welcome the LGBTQ population without reservation and without an agenda for change. Many of these churches exist in Seattle and the surrounding suburbs, and one has received national press for its approach to questions of Christian identity and sexual identity.[8] When Pastor Dave tells his congregation that everyone should hate their own sins (which now includes SSA and the LGBTQ community), and that the real tragedy, perhaps, is that people are leaving the church to find (queer) community that is welcoming, he shows his hand: the goal of the church is to bring people in. But, in continuing to understand SSA as a sin, Lakeview's approach is markedly different from an open and affirming space. And they don't actually want to be that space. As the church wrestles with shifts in both homosexuality and heterosexuality, they are finding new ways to reinstitutionalize homophobia.

These tactics are especially clear around the question of marriage. While individuals at Lakeview discuss SSA as a sin on par with any other sexual sin, their professed love and acceptance toward the LGBTQ community have specific conditions regarding both marriage and leadership. As Craig stated bluntly after a lot of back and forth on the subject, "I don't agree with same-sex relationships, so, in turn, I don't agree with marriage." Nicole nodded her head as Craig said this, and she added, "But as far as gay and lesbian people, I don't think that they're making up the feelings. I don't think that it's not a real struggle." Nicole reinforced an individual-level support and validation of the feelings of the LGBTQ community but, much like the church's long-standing approach to SSA, differentiates between an individual's feelings of sexual desire and her beliefs about an individual's rights to act on those desires.

In a sermon over a year after Pastor Dave shared the story about the lesbian couple that came to church, Pastor Dave took a slightly different approach to the topic of marriage. He presented this statement as a "final thought" before prayer, but I imagine it was the point of the entire sermon on marriage that morning. Pastor Dave said,

> Jesus was never married. Jesus never had kids. And somehow in the church we elevate marriage and children to like this gold standard of what a disciple looks like. Eventually we'll get there—someday you'll get married, someday ... I don't know what that is, why we do that as a church but somehow that's become a thing and Jesus didn't do either one of those things. He was never married and he never had kids. And yet Jesus was able to faithfully demonstrate the highest form of love. Think about it. The highest form of love is not married love. The highest form of love is not parent-child love. Although we often preach like it is. That becomes the gold standard. But Jesus had neither one yet he was able to demonstrate the highest form of love. How did he do that? What did he say? John 15:13. Greater love has no man than this.[9] There is no greater love than this. Getting married. No. No greater love than this. Love for kids. No. No greater love than this, than the one that lay down his life for his friends. Jesus demonstrated the highest form of love by sacrificing himself for others. You wanna be like Jesus? You wanna engage the world like Jesus would engage the world? Especially those who you differ from? Lay down your life. There's no greater love.

Pastor Dave is approaching questions of same-sex marriage similar to questions about prolonged phases of singleness in the church. When it comes down to it, the focus should be on Jesus. But here, this line also allows the church to skirt any other debates about gay marriage by minimizing the very institution the church is working to uphold and protect. In telling people that the highest form of love is not married love, or love for children, but love for Jesus, the church can maintain their line that they are welcoming to all—and all who accept and center Jesus in their lives—while still supporting the institution of marriage for the heterosexual couples in the building.

While Lakeview evangelicals draw lines around homosexuality when it comes to the institution of marriage, they also do so in regard to leadership positions within the church. While Lyndsey described the importance of loving and respecting LGBTQ individuals, she said, "I wouldn't put anyone in a same-sex relationship in a leadership position." Jesse agreed with her and added, "if that outward sin is showing and present in their life, whether it be a same-sex struggle or pornography, or pridefulness, or anything . . . stealing even. If it's an outward sin, it has to be dealt with." Jesse added that "there are stipulations . . . if they walked in and were just congregants and were just there to be part of the church, fine and be there, that'd be great. We'd be inviting. We would love to have them." Jesse reinforced the more current belief that the LGBTQ community be welcome into the church, but that they join quietly and without display of their "outward sins." Jesse continued and said, "But if they wanted to start leading a small group, and leading Bible studies through the church and stuff, like, that's another conversation to have." Jesse ended by saying that "We all sin. Sin is looked at on somewhat of an equal playing field in a sense, but I think same-sex marriage or even relations is an outward sin." Jesse discussed same-sex relationships and attraction as a sin on par with any other sin, while also differentiating between inward and "outward" sins. For Jesse, and others at Lakeview, same-sex attraction and, really, acting on those desires in the form of a relationship are an outward sin that presents itself as an affront to church doctrine. Gays and lesbians are allowed into the church, but quietly. They will not be given a podium or a voice, and they will not be understood, but they are promised a certain form of love and respect. They are, in effect, being asked to turn their outward sins inward into self-hatred. The democratizing of sin becomes less democratic when access to resources and leadership are on the table in the heterosexual institution.

Joe, a White, recently widowed man in his early fifties, told me that, "while I don't agree with it [gay marriage] by any means, I think there's a proper way and an improper way to handle it." Joe added that, if a gay person were in leadership, and got married, "I would think, they're not even acknowledging that what they're doing is not OK. And we're putting them in leadership positions." Joe then told me that, in his mind, leaders should be "trying to do their best" but that, if gay individuals were in leadership, Joe would understand that individual to think "No. This is fine. I don't believe that it's a sin." Joe continued to explain his beliefs by saying that "Even if you're just gonna come down to, like, the doctrine of Lakeview, the doctrine doesn't agree. If somebody's prostituting themselves or if somebody is . . . struggling with pornography or they're having sex with their [girlfriend], living with their girlfriend. Those things like that. I wouldn't put them in leadership 'cause they're not growing. They're not. They're not able to disciple somebody else or be in that place of leadership that they need to be if they're still trying to work on something in themselves." Joe's thoughts reinforce a democratic understanding of sexual sin (Gerber 2011), understanding a whole range of sexual behaviors as sins on par with any other sins. But the difference between homosexuality and the other sexual transgressions Joe list, is that, at Lakeview, pornography, pre-marital sex, and sex work are not described as "outward sins." They are not understood as a more blatant disregard for church teachings and are not thus relegated to the newer shadows that have emerged since the legalization of same-sex marriage. Rather, we see groups devoted to sexual addiction offered at Lakeview every season, and premarital sexuality is something discussed openly and frequently in the church.

In my previous research on evangelical men who pledged abstinence until marriage, the support group of men I researched for four years all told a cautionary tale about one of the many reasons they were supporting one another in maintaining their commitments to abstinence. The young men told me of a couple, who many in the group knew quite well, who engaged in sexual activity while they were dating. One of the group members told the church leadership about their friends' activity, and the dating couple, who were both involved in the church through youth group leadership, were removed from their positions. They were deemed unfit for their leadership roles in the church because they were not setting a good example for others. This type of logic and bundling of sexual sins allows the church to say that banning LGTBQ folks from leadership positions is not an issue of homophobia, but one of sin. LGBTQ individuals can't be in leadership positions just like people who are having sex before marriage cannot be in leadership positions. But, again, the difference here is what is described as an inward and outward sin. Stein (2001) suggests that there is a sense of forbidden desire, and danger, that comes with the sense of homosexuality as something hidden or lurking in the shadows. What is interesting is that Lakeview Church is finding ways to distance itself from homophobic labels, but, in doing so, is relegating homosexuality back to the "shadows" (Stein 2001).

The LGBTQ individuals that Lakeview members describe must not be "out" with their sins. This differentiation between outward and inward sins implies that some behaviors can and should, perhaps, be hidden. Some struggles should be between a congregant and God, and talking about same-sex attraction this way, as something outward but something that congregants at Lakeview would prefer to be pushed inward, lies in stark contrast to tactics around same-sex attraction of the past. While churches like Lakeview used to have multiple groups where individuals were welcome in to talk very openly about these "out" sins, now both these groups and the conversations that occurred within them are gone. Lakeview has conditionally opened the church to LBGTQ individuals without a focus on fixing them, but they want them to be quiet about it.

Congregants at Lakeview Church approach SSA with an understanding of love, but this is a conditional understanding of love, and a type of love that both informs and is informed by their perceived status changes in the world. Lakeview understands that they must let same-sex couples, or individuals "experiencing" SSA, into the church in order to remain culturally relevant, but that welcome is bounded: LGBTQ individuals within the church are not permitted access to marriage ceremonies within the church or positions of leadership. Although all sexual sins are bundled, if we focus here on heterosexuality, heterosexuality itself is not a barrier to leadership positions, unlike an LGBTQ identity. The distribution of resources and cultural power within the church remains in the hands of those in heterosexual partnerships (Jackson 2006). Systems of inequality can transform, rather than disappear, when their foundations are questioned (Bridges and Pascoe 2014). Lakeview Church is not removing homophobia from its institutional design, but rather finding new and different boundaries around it.

On October 30, 2016, a week before being elected the president of the United States, Donald Trump kicked off a rally in Greely, Colorado, by walking around the stage with a rainbow flag with "LGBTs for TRUMP" scrawled across it in permanent marker. Images of Trump parading a rainbow flag flooded the media, but Trump did not actually mention LGTBQ rights in the speech that followed that evening. And after his election, his efforts to restrict LGBTQ rights, most notably through his opposition to the federal legalization of same-sex marriage, his pick for vice president, and his restrictions on trans rights in what seems to be every branch of the government, indicate the extent of his literal and figurative flag-waving.

As journalist Gwynn Guilford (2016) astutely points out, when he discusses the LGBTQ community, Trump often uses the language of "they," not "you," in the way he also does when discussing African Americans. This use of language reinforces the idea that the people to whom he is actually speaking are his White, straight supporters. This type of language also creates the type of abstract, other category off of which people can understand themselves. And this language mirrors the language used by pastors and congregants at Lakeview Church.

But Trump does talk about LGBTQ people, and doing so, as Guilford rightly suggests, "helps assuage worries of more socially liberal GOP voters that supporting Trump doesn't mean you're a bigot" (2016). Notably, after the shooting at the gay nightclub in Orlando, Florida, that left 49 people killed and 53 wounded (New York Times 2016), and four months before his election, Trump discussed the LGBTQ community in the context of protecting them from terrorism, as the shooter pledged an allegiance to ISIS (Callimachi 2016). At a rally four days after the shooting in Orlando, Trump cited the shooting as evidence of disrespect for America, and said, "We have to stop people with hate in their heart from coming into our country" through provisions to control immigration in the country (Jeffers 2016).

Trump's preelection lip service and literal flag-waving for the LGBTQ community align with the conversations happening at Lakeview. Lakeview knows they need to address the LGBTQ community, and they are very much against people with "hate in their hearts." But this language, in Trump's usage and in the leadership of those at Lakeview, obfuscates a focus on actual rights for the LGBTQ community. And Trump's usage of support for the queer community in the context of anti-immigration sentiment provides an example of the bundling of the threats of the imagined secular world that can trigger reactions and support among White evangelicals. This bundling acts as a symbol that he will defend them from threats they seek protection from, regardless of whether or not this protection means a loss for the others they want to "love."

NAVIGATING "SEISMIC SHIFTS"

Heterosexuality in the White evangelical church has long been understood against its moral opposite: homosexuality. But as the "seismic shifts" in the United States have moved the needle on homosexuality, on same-sex marriage, and on (increased) understandings of sexuality as fluid, so too has heterosexuality shifted. Because of their mutual reinforcement in the church, the instability of one category leads to the instability of the other. And as the church works to rebuild its understandings and explanations related to the entire heterosexual project off of which it is defined, it has both lapsed in its explicit conversations about homosexuality and shifted its language about how to approach this part of the imagined secular that now feels more present within the church walls.

Theoretically, members of the imagined secular world are now sitting among evangelicals during Sunday sermons. What does that mean, and how do evangelicals make sense of that? For some, it is grappling with how to welcome the LGBTQ community into the church, and for others, it is a welcoming and a love that are conditional. For others, it is easier to think about the LGBTQ community as part of the city, and part of the imagined city. And, according to the church leadership, the long-standing approach and rhetoric of "hate the sin, love the sinner" is now up for debate, too. Because, to hate the sinner is now to hate people who are, for many, *known*. As Arlene Stein (2001) argues, when members of the LGBTQ community are unknown, the ability to create an abstract category that defines them makes intolerance and hate much easier. Instead, the Lakeview community needs to directly engage with this component of the imaged secular world. The gays are no longer understood as the scary recruiters for the homosexual agenda, the individuals who face sin squarely and ignore it. Rather, they are showing up in church on Sunday, and even thanking the church for help with their marriage.

While the responses on the part of both the church leadership and the congregation signify the very messiness Pastor Dave feels they are embracing, the church is engaging in a bounded welcoming of members of the LGTBQ community through its focus on heterosexuality and heterosexual marriage. But focusing on marriage is not a satisfying response for all members of the Lakeview community. As the church works to maintain its stronghold on sexual behavior and identity, understandings of sexuality, desire, and pleasure, more broadly, are being called into question as the institution of marriage expands. Members are asking questions about singleness, and about the boundaries around sexual pleasure. And as the church finds itself in flux in regard to a clear message about homosexuality, they are relying on older and dated understandings of singleness and sex that are not resonating with all of its members.

Sexual politics among evangelical elites are not as tidy within churches as other work finds when looking at national evangelical politics and movements (Moslener 2015). Upon first glance, it may appear as though the church is unified in its understandings of appropriate sexuality, but ethnographic data helps uncover a much messier picture. Even understandings of the institution of marriage have shifted. Sociologist Kristin Luker (2007) documents two different camps of people in the United States: sexual conservatives and sexual liberals. Luker argues that, in contrast to liberals, sexual conservatives treat marriage as a noun: an important life-course marker they are all working toward. But today, evangelicals at Lakeview are working to understand and treat marriage as a verb. The very plea of a small group title alone to

"Stay Married!" suggests that an institution once assumed to be both stable and stagnant is in question for members in a way it wasn't so sharply in the past.

The church is clinging to protections around the White heterosexual family. Heterosexuality, as a pillar of the theological orientation of the church, and of the institutional design and structure of the church, is interwoven with understandings of gender essentialism, Whiteness, and the family, of the ability for men and women to do God's work, and even to be fully "seen" and understood as individuals, and as *good* individuals. As such, when the stability of the God-given naturalness and ease of heterosexuality is in question as something inherently good, and when the assumption of homosexuality as inherently evil is also questioned, all of these projects risk unraveling.

The irony, though, as Nagel points out, is that heterosexuality (like Whiteness) is quite flexible (2003; see also Ward 2015). It can be the celebrated identity following a lifetime of transgressions, a justification for inequality between men and women—indeed, what Butler (2006) suggests is *the* site of gender inequality—and an excuse for the good in someone amid a whole lot of abhorrent behaviors. It can expand and shift to incorporate the protections of other identities in which it is intimately tied, namely, masculinity and Whiteness. And Lakeview Church and the myriad other similar institutions across the United States are quite flexible, too. The church is finding new ways to define its second-most precious relationship, and, in turn, is also finding new and creative language and mechanisms through which to (re)institutionalize homophobia in the process through a bounded welcoming of the LGBTQ community.

The church is navigating competing goals: it seeks to protect the institution of heterosexuality, and the institution of marriage. It also seeks to bring the single Millennial in through its doors, and get them to marry. The church is also trying to figure out how to bring the LGBTQ population in—and appear open, welcoming, and safe. But flexibility often bends in the direction and favor of those with the loudest voices, the most power, and the most resources.

As Lakeview Church works to maintain cultural relevance and grow as an institution, they are confronting the imagined secular, but doing so in a way that allows it to hold on to its core beliefs, and privileges, without reacting in a way that will mark it as "ugly." The members of the Lakeview community are not sexist because God made women to submit, and the church is advocating for a feminism that encourages workplace equality. Lakeview, as a congregation, loves Black people, and saves Brown and Black people in "dark" nations, so they are not racist. And they even had a Black pastor from Ferguson, Missouri, tell them that Black Lives Matter is the work of the devil. The Lakeview congregation is not homophobic, because everyone is a sinner, and as such, everyone must avoid indulging in such sins. They found a politician who symbolizes and bolsters the identities they seek to protect, and who will do the uglier work for them while they focus on growth as a church. Through this ongoing cultural project, Lakeview continues to focus on individuals, and individual salvation, rather than systems or structural inequalities. And the centrality of gender difference, the elasticity of Whiteness, and the flexibility of heterosexuality all help protect their theological, cultural, and political maneuvers at the same time that the church as an institution reinforces those very ideas of a normative American identity and experience.

CHAPTER 7

Enduring Inequalities in Unsettled Times

In times of change and uncertainty . . . people have trouble
believing that the divine sits still.

—Dawne Moon (2004:27)

In November 2018, two years into the Trump presidency, Ed Stetzer,
director of the Billy Graham Center at Wheaton College in Illinois,
joined Steve Inskeep, host of *Morning Edition* on NPR. Inskeep discussed White evangelicals and their support for Trump; he also talked
about Trump's comments about threats of migrant caravans crossing
into the United States, which were receiving lots of attention. Stetzer
talked about the ways in which the general public, including evangelicals, is fooled by the mass media and the politicians who provide their
content. He talked about how many evangelicals felt an "ill-ease" with
supporting Trump in the 2016 election, but that they only had two
choices, and for many, Trump's policies made more sense than Clinton's. When asked if he thought that evangelicals were hitching their
wagon to, in Inskeep's words, "a horse that is going to lose for them
over time," Stetzer replied that it was a fair question. He suggested that
perhaps evangelicals should hitch themselves to a cause: to showing and
sharing the love of Jesus Christ rather than a current politician. Stetzer
reflected, "I think, ultimately, evangelicals need to be known for what
they are for rather than what they're against" (Inskeep 2018).

White evangelicals at Lakeview Church, and at similar organizations
across the country, are working to figure out what they are for and
what they are against. Those at Lakeview are engaged in a seemingly
constant dance, working to disentangle what they support and what
they fear, and what those beliefs mean for the church they love. At the

end of a couple's interview with Darren and Annie, Darren talked with me about how the church might best market itself as a more accepting one in the future. Darren said,

> I think we are starting to see a greater divide between acceptance of everyone and hard line "we're not going to let people in." And that is kind of good. You're going to a place like Lakeview where it's like, "so glad you're here, you're welcome," or you're going to a church that's like, "no gay people are allowed here! If you don't fit our exact beliefs, we don't want you here either. Let's talk about fire raining down from heaven on the people we don't like!"

Darren and Annie both started laughing at this point. Darren and Annie, and indeed many congregants at Lakeview, understand Lakeview to be a place of acceptance. And Darren, Annie, and many of their fellow congregants importantly *want* Lakeview to feel like a place of acceptance. Others may be less excited about this welcoming and, indeed, feel as though it is a welcoming being forced upon them, but know that they are *supposed* to make the church a more inclusive space. The people that make up Lakeview Church are actively working to engage with the outside world, and to do so in a way that works to at least position the church as welcoming and accepting. They are debating who is in and who is out, and, importantly, who is out but should be in.

Sociologist Grace Yukich argues that a reliance on boundary work can create conflict for inclusive religious groups. How does a religious group that relies on the identification of the "other" and the exclusion of said other balance a need and desire to also be inclusive and welcoming? In her study on the New York Catholic Worker group, Yukich argues that when religious groups have a doctrine that opens them up to what Martin Buber calls "I-Thou" encounters, they are advantaged in their ability to find a balance between boundary work and exclusion (Buber [1923] 1958; Yukich 2010). I-Thou encounters are ones in which the whole person is acknowledged, where one treats the other not as an object, an experience, but as an entire being, a person to be respected and loved fully for who they are. Yukich (as well as Buber) argues that, in these encounters, one cannot analyze the other in the abstract. These encounters are moments of inclusion and love that cannot be forced. They are, as Yukich summarizes, both uncalculated and unintentional.

The evangelicals discussed in this book have very intentional and calculated goals of continued growth through evangelism. While Disciples' Journey or members of the larger Lakeview Congregation may be looking for encounters, to seek out said encounters with specific goals in mind renders the ability for actual, meaningful inclusion impossible.

Although Lakeview Church may have a strong desire to be welcoming and ready for growth during this time of religious decline and social and political upheaval, their efforts toward inclusion will always be hindered by the abstract categories relied on to understand others outside of their church walls.

The imagined secular is a useful concept through which to understand this interplay between exclusion and inclusion. The Lakeview community understands that they need to actively work to renegotiate the boundaries around their religious beliefs due to the presence of the imagined secular world. The evangelicals at Lakeview engage with the imagined secular as a bundled set of issues to which most of them are, at least in theory, opposed. This imagined other helps define and set the terms and symbolic boundaries for their current debates (Lamont and Fournier 1992). One aspect of this imagined other can invoke a much larger and overwhelming constellation of debates, changes, and perceived threats to White evangelical life. For some at Lakeview, this leads them to reject the components of the imagined secular world entirely. For many others within the community, the aspects of the imagined secular world produce notable variation and debate, the life and substance of what Pastor Dave calls a "messy" church during times of change. But for all, a continued focus on evangelism makes true inclusion unattainable. And true inclusion is probably not the goal.

THE SPACE BETWEEN "EXTREMISM" AND AFFIRMATION

As each chapter of this book outlines, questions of gender, sexuality, the White family, and the desire for Christianity's continued expansion are central to the debates at Lakeview. Through many highly symbolic moments and conversations, the members of Lakeview Church negotiate the boundaries around their beliefs and practices in new ways. Lakeview is talking about feminism, trans rights, same-sex sexuality, the Black Lives Matter movement, Muslims, and sexual sins, and these conversations represent the myriad ways in which some White evangelical communities have been pushed to a more ideological and political center in their debates and beliefs. The chapters in this book document the different but overlapping components of the imagined secular with which the church is currently grappling. They also document the characteristics of the imagined secular that are crucial to its understanding: its components are often bundled, as we saw in conversations about feminism, which makes it feel like an overwhelming project to tackle; it is an imaginative that is created in a specific White space and place, as illustrated in Lakeview's conversations and debates about race and missions work; and, it is an imaginative that can change and expand, as seen in shifting debates about sacred sex and homosexuality.

In part because of their relationship to the imagined secular, Darren acknowledged that many evangelicals are now understood as losing cultural sway because they are thought to be unaccepting and hateful. Darren says that "I think a big issue is, people who aren't involved in the church are like, well, I am seeing this person on TV who is identifying as Christian saying all of these hateful things, and it's hard for them to identify that as different. We also have the same kind of issue with Islam, a lot of people struggling to see the difference between this person is a Muslim, this person is a terrorist."

However, Darren also shared that "I think it is starting to shift into the two extremes which I think is going to be better . . . I think eventually . . . it will be easier to identify [the churches that preach hate] as different . . . I think more people are understanding the difference between the two, and if Christianity could push a little bit more like that, we could point and say, 'that is an extreme sect, they aren't preaching love,' which is what Jesus was teaching." Darren suggested that the church follow the teachings of Jesus, with an individual focus on love, as a way of bringing people into the church. Further, Darren wishes for certain Christian groups to continue toward the "extremes" so that he and others at Lakeview have a group to point to as ugly, to blame for and associate with the loss of status that evangelicals are experiencing, and from which they can distance themselves to avoid what they feel is an unfair label placed on them.

Darren and Annie recognize the need for the church to promote itself as more open, liberal, and willing to change if it is going to survive in the contemporary world. Of course, many at Lakeview want to distance themselves from the "extremists"; but they also want to hold on to the privileges they have. They want to distance themselves from more conservative groups in an effort to appear as the welcoming place, the place people should come and fill. Many White evangelicals want both continued growth in the United States and continued (subtle) justifications for gendered, racial, and sexual inequality. They want to shed the label of the extremist, but they do not seek a church that is welcoming to and affirming of all. They do not want to shed the theology and logic that orient their lives.

WHEN INDIVIDUAL UNCERTAINTY MEETS
THE ORGANIZATION

For people like Darren, who don't want to be understood as an extremist, but who also do not want to be a "Social Justice Warrior," the church helps navigate that position. Many within the institution may feel unsettled, but the organization is finding a way to navigate these unsettled times. The church shepherds individuals along in engaging with established components of the imagined secular, by teaching and encouraging an instrumental acceptance through a language of love and individual relationship-building that paints White evangelicals as good and paints others as like them. For newer elements of the imagined secular, like same-sex marriage, the church is encouraging a type of forced excitement that does the same type of work—the goals of the organization are mirrored in the emotional work on the part of the individuals within it. As such, in the midst and wake of these conversations and engagements with the imagined secular at Lakeview, the organization is able to initiate a bounded welcoming of components of the imagined secular: feminism, racial justice (but really, more basically, people of color), and those who are not conforming to heterosexual marriage ideals—the LGBTQ population, those who are single, and those who cohabite outside of marriage. Lakeview Church cannot portray sexist, racist, or homophobic ideals if they want to remain culturally relevant. The church is determining the best ways in which to hold on to both cultural status and change with the times.

This bounded welcoming is especially successful in an organization that is so heavily gendered, racialized, and (hetero)sexualized: the church can hold space for the messiness that responses to the imagined secular create, and do so while appearing open to these conversations while reinforcing existent beliefs about gender, race, and sexuality that continue to define them as a group. They have found a way to talk about feminism and uphold gender inequality—to even identify as feminists and do so. They have found a way to at least say they are discussing Black Lives Matter, and to continue to use missions work to justify a rhetoric of love and individuality that exempts them from conversations about racism. They are very much in the midst of the mess and chaos when it comes to changing definitions of marriage and sexuality. As the church focuses on heterosexual marriage, they are also adopting a new version of a democratizing of sin and sexual brokenness that implicates everyone and renders difference, and celebrations of difference, impossible. The church, as an organization, is upholding gender essentialism, Whiteness, and heterosexuality in its project to expand and grow.

And the church is also engaging in a bounded welcoming of Millennials, the group that was the symbol for change. I imagine this now extends to Gen Z'ers. The church is holding some of the conversations that they feel Millennials want to have, but they are by no means engaging in all of them. The church's inability to address the concerns of Millennials is especially poignant when it comes to questions of sexuality, sexual activity, and marriage. Whether the actions of the church will be enough to appease younger generations is yet to be determined.

Raewyn Connell argues that "Gender is institutionalized to the extent that the network of links to the reproduction system is formed by cyclical practices. It is stabilized to the extent that the groups constituted in the network have interests in the conditions for cyclical rather than divergent practices" (1987:141). While evangelicals at Lakeview do exhibit divergent practices in some arenas, many of their conversations circle back to the same issues that brought evangelicals together as a political and cultural force in the United States 50 years ago, exhibiting evidence for and interests in the "conditions for [the] cyclical."

The conditions for the cyclical are evident at Lakeview today. Like many White evangelical churches across the country, Lakeview confers social, emotional, and material resources on those who reflect the appropriate enactments of gender, race, and sexuality upon which the church is built. Those who reflect the goals of the organization are given voice. The women who talk about submission's benefits, the Black men who pass the "race test" of the church, and the individuals who admit they are sexually broken and not proud are those who lead. As younger generations take over leadership positions, this may of course shift. Progress is impossible without change, but this change is often quite slow. And this lethargy is embraced by those who benefit the most from the way the United States is structured today, and felt most urgently by those most affected by the White evangelical's continued conservative political support.

WHEN AN UNSETTLED CHURCH MEETS DONALD TRUMP

The White evangelical church is continuing to navigate a variety of overlapping projects. They are projects that are part of the work that builds a nation (Nagel 2003) and, for many, a Christian nation (White-head and Perry 2020) and these White evangelicals would like it to remain that way. As the church navigates perceived threats to its dominance, a political candidate entered the arena that made a bit more sense to it, in the midst of all of this perceived chaos and messiness, than others.

Donald Trump came about as a political candidate during a time in which the White evangelical church was working through a whole host of external threats. And while this group of White evangelicals by no means represents his most fervent supporters, the logic central to the upkeep of the White evangelical church aligns well with Donald Trump as a political candidate. They may not be thrilled about him, but he made sense to them as a foil to the imagined secular: he is not Hillary, the imagined feminist; he is a White man, and, as such, granted the status and understanding of the norm in the church; and even though many of his behaviors suggest questionable morals and the like, he is understood in terms of his brokenness, and in the belief that everyone is a sinner. This logic allows for both his failings and his redemption. He discussed, especially early on, the LGBTQ community through a language of love and lip service while also vowing to protect the privileging of heterosexuality central to so many institutions. The very projects with which the church has long been engaged, and is still engaged with today, set up a space in which Donald Trump can be understood and justified. He can be reworked and understood in positive terms, a sign of the end times, of the long-awaited return of a figure this community holds most central to their life: Jesus Christ. He is a symbol of their larger hopes, fights, and fears; he is not the first politician that will encapsulate their feelings and reflect their beliefs back onto them and he will not be the last.

And for those less sure, these threats and concerns over a larger decline in religiosity expand their acceptable orthodoxy, as long as the actions in question are perceived to protect said orthodoxy rather than further threaten it (Diefendorf 2019; Marti 2020:224). As Whitehead and Perry so succinctly state, "For a large swath of the American public the only thing that counts is whether they feel as though their religious and national identity is being given preference" (2020:158).

As James Guth suggests, "with some exceptions, studies of evangelicals' political views have found that they 'look like everyone else'—except on social and 'moral' issues, of course. The political alignment of evangelical votes, then, may depend on the relative salience of social and economic issues during any particular period—and on the choices offered by contending political forces" (1996:11). The evangelicals at Lakeview, in their words and actions, suggest that some of the key social issues during our particular cultural period revolve around questions of gender, sexuality, and the White family, although the relationship between these themes and evangelical support for Trump has been underinvestigated. This work helps document what those conversations look like, and how deeply intertwined evangelical understandings of gender, sexuality, the White family, and conservative politics remain today. The church is being forced to ask new questions as it expands, refocuses, and, in many cases, finds new ways to uphold enduring inequalities. It is a church that is actively working to distance itself from its historical roots described in chapter 2, but one whose current responses to our changing social world are still very much informed by its previous fights.

And while there might be a good deal of "chaos" over the term "evangelical" in the United States today, this research documents that White evangelicals are experiencing quite a bit of internal chaos as well. Evangelicals at Lakeview Church are grappling with larger cultural shifts in gender, sexuality, and the family, and this perceived external chaos is creating internal turmoil too. Scholars must continue to pay attention to this internal turmoil, these moments of debate, disjuncture, and reinforcement of specific identities and beliefs, as we work to continue to map the shifting movements of evangelical life in the United States (Green et al. 1996).

When I interviewed Pastor Jeff in the summer of 2017, I asked him point-blank why he thought so many White evangelicals voted for Donald Trump. He responded:

> Um, I think, when I look at the most recent national election, and I think about the evangelical church, I think that what I've seen is a reaction where—and this is maybe an older segment of the church, but it's probably really hard to be broad, I say it's probably, um, White, um, middle aged and older that have said, "The church that we knew doesn't exist anymore, and we want it back and we're willing to trade." What are they willing to trade? They're willing to trade maybe, some of their core beliefs for somebody to stand up for them and get it back. I don't know. Maybe that's just really broad, but that's kind of what I see going on.

In this book, I document the ways the church grapples with questions of gender, race, and sexuality against the backdrop of the imagined secular. These questions highlight the messiness that is occurring within one church around what we might otherwise assume would be unified beliefs. These questions bring up confusion and anxiety about the church's place in our social landscape. The church is trying to figure out how to be more welcoming in an era of declining religiosity. They want to speak to Millennials and Gen Z and they want to grow as an organization. But as I document throughout the book, this welcoming is bounded. In their collective efforts to dodge the label of ugly, they are working to avoid being marked and to remain an unquestioned, de facto status and existence. They are finding ways to uphold the normatively gendered White, heterosexual family without coming across as the sexists, the racists, and the homophobes, which leads us to question, in the words of Pastor Jeff, what core beliefs they really traded on in the first place.

In their efforts to remain normal, unmarked Christians, to be understood by their god and the world as "good," Lakeview Church and its members are working quite hard to avoid the label of racist, of antiracist, of homophobic, of extremist, of sexist, and of feminist; they want to continue to enjoy the unquestioned lived experiences of White Christian man- and womanhood that have long been synonymous with, and the default category for, what is understood to be American (Marti 2020). The church and its members are engaging with the imagined secular in an effort to remain "good," but this very engagement with the social "evils" that produce the imagined secular threaten to remove them from the comfort and confidence that come with the assumption that they are the standard against which all others are judged and that all others must strive to become.

PATHWAYS FORWARD

The year 2020 brought about massive social upheaval and laid bare the gross inequalities present in the United States through the devastation wrought by a mishandled global pandemic, centuries of racism and racial inequality manifested in the continued killings of Black men and women at the hands of law enforcement, and White supremacist groups attempting to take "back" the government to "Keep America Great." Through all of this, a president looked on and stirred up more hatred and violence through his tweets, speeches, and political appointments and pardons alike. And while Trump and his administration continued to reign with terror on a nation hurting, grieving, and, in many cases, literally dying, 76% of White evangelicals voted for his second term in November 2020.

When I present this research, I have been asked what a breaking point might look like, a moment, a decision, a law, that might result in White evangelicals' inability to further expand their orthodoxy in favor of a continued alignment with conservative politics. As a sociologist, I am both in practice and in principle not one for predictions. But I am not sure that the historical record of White evangelism in the United States has shown that White evangelicals have ever, collectively, found or hit those breaking points. And as long as there exist perceived moral and cultural fights over an appropriate gendered, racialized, and sexualized order, I am not sure they will.

It is unclear if younger generations will have the fortitude or desire to question and push against an organization that has retained so much power to date in the United States. Indeed, it is quite difficult to enact change within an organization whose foundations, operations, worldview, and logic—the things that both drive the everyday life of those in the church and define their divine—rest on protections of the gendered order, the White family, and the institution of heterosexuality.

But, as the nation looks ahead to our political, religious, and cultural future, those who identify as more liberal would do well to continue to treat conservative politics as quite real, not as a masquerade or form of false consciousness (Jenkins 2006:9). And we must pay attention to the ways in which conservative politics are fueled in areas presumed to be liberal or even progressive. There are no liberal bubbles free from inequalities of class, gender, race, and sexuality. Anything that suggests otherwise ignores the realities of the reproduction of inequality and furthers what is in many ways a false dichotomy between "liberal" and "conservative" regions in the first place. The MAGA hat–wearing, yelling man at the front line of a rally in Virginia, the individuals who stormed the US Capitol Building in January 2021, and the people who sit quietly in a church among the coastal elites in the Pacific Northwest and vote for someone else to do the ugly work for them bear the same reflection, though one is often given less attention.

While politics might rely on symbols, an imagined other, false promises, exaggerated threats, and a variety of surprising explanations and rationales for supporting someone, these components are quite real in the ways they are felt and experienced by individuals and groups, boldly or quietly. As such, we must keep in mind that support of a conservative political actor can come in much more muted and masked forms, sometimes as the result of a desire to hold on to a national project that, as it very well should be, is ever evolving.

Navigating Prayer, Positionality, and Institutional Review

In their article "The Feminist Ethnographer's Dilemma" Orit Avishai, Lynne Gerber, and Jennifer Randles (2013) rightly observe that the space devoted to considerations of reflexivity are often relegated to the "back burner"—in this case, the very appendix you currently read. While I worked to find a balance in centering the voices of those in this study with my own positionality and methodological decisions, I could not always do that for the sake of the reader and the narrative. For all the moments within the text I did not or could not accomplish that balance, I honor those issues here.

WATCHING EACH OTHER

Twelve adults sat around an outdoor firepit, notebooks in their laps as they took in their surroundings: it was a Thursday evening in July at a bustling pub, and the outdoor eating area was swarming with guests standing and sharing beers, wait staff zooming through these crowds as they balanced heavy trays. There were firepits where guests clustered around in chairs, outdoor tables for more private dining parties, and a few walk-up bars. Music played from speakers mounted around the outdoor complex and white lights hung from the trees, their glimmer barely yet visible in the extended light of the long summer day.

In the midst of this chaos there was quiet, as these 12 adults closed their eyes in concentration, or scribbled notes on their pads of paper before looking up at their surroundings again. The members of Disciples' Journey were visiting this restaurant as part of a local missions trip. During this evening "experiential" organized by the group leaders, their plan was to ask God for guidance about how to best pray for those in the restaurant they had not yet met. I was there to observe them doing this.

Carrie stood up and reminded the group that they were out in the world to be "open for business. We are going to serve them [the wait staff and patrons] just like they are serving us." Another group member, Marjorie, chimed in with a smile and said, "Our being out in the community shows we are regular people with regular lives and enjoyments. We aren't this strange group of people!" Pastor Jeff nodded and told the group that "Our goal for tonight is to notice and pray for people around you. Avoid judgmental words, and don't be too directional. That is not part of the exercise. Focus on the positives and be encouraging. What is the cry of their heart? It is impossible for us to know, but God knows and he might reveal if we are specific in our asking." The group rested their notebooks in their laps and looked around them. Pastor Jeff smiled and said, "How many of you are terrified?" Carrie interjected and said, "Well, missionaries that go far into the field have to deal with a lot more adversity than we will tonight." There were murmurs of agreement, but the group did look a bit uncomfortable. Eric, a 45-year-old White man, said, "People might think we are weird! Especially because there are so many of us [in this group] in relation to the people around us." Pastor Jeff nodded and said, "Right, yes. We don't want to look like we are all taking notes on people."

At this moment I felt the group's collective gaze turn to look at me, as I took notes on these interactions from the corner. The group started making jokes such as "Yes, we don't want to look like Sarah!" Two other women laughed and said, "Oh but we do want to be like Sarah!" There was lots of laughter as they continued to joke about the fact that I was doing an "experiential" on their experiential—what they came to call my "experiential on experiential." We continued to joke, and then their work began.

I often felt acutely aware of the ways in which I was being observed as a researcher while at Lakeview. Frank always knew what ZipCar I had driven to the church each week, and Carrie frequently commented on my dress, for example, asking where I got my shoes. These comments most often felt like a way to engage and connect, but what was and was not observed about me was dictated by my own identities, my own presentation of self, and the space I was in.

As a White woman, there was no "race test" for me to gain entry to Lakeview Church. Glenn Bracey and Wendy Moore (2017) study the ways in which White evangelical churches maintain racial boundaries by administering "race tests"; sometimes these tests are utility-based, wherein a person of color is permitted entry if that person is able to fit the needs of the community, as we saw with Pastor Darryl. More often, though, these tests are used to drive people away and maintain exclusion. While their work is extremely useful for understanding one of the many mechanisms through which segregation in American churches prevails, their concept is also useful to apply to a researcher's ability to gain entry to these churches—experiences Bracey centered in this work and experiences I didn't encounter as a White woman in an organizational space in which Whiteness is equated with normalcy.

In addition, I share a similar class background to many of the Lakeview congregants. And as a fairly feminine-presenting woman, it was easy for me to mirror the unsaid dress code of the other White women my age who attended Lakeview and match their aesthetic. I usually wore tight dark jeans and a blouse with a flowy cardigan over the top. I wore flats, long necklaces and earrings, and light makeup. My success in matching and blending in with the dress of the other women in this space is revealed, I think, in Carrie's frequent conversation-starters about clothing and accessories and where I found certain items.

Perhaps because this is a highly educated group, my pursuit of my PhD and focus on research were not as much of an issue as they might have been in other spaces. For example, one evening at the beginning of my fieldwork, in the late fall of 2015, Carrie and I spent a lot of time before a meeting discussing my research; she told me about how she had edited a family member's dissertation and that his research was a two-year process, so she "totally understood" when I said I was not sure how much time I would be in the field. At a meeting weeks later, Carrie included me in her head count for an experiential that required specific numbers of people in each group. Becky noticed this immediately and alerted me to it so that I could correct Carrie and remove myself from the count so that I could take notes. This was one moment of many where I felt that group members were both paying attention to my status as a researcher and, very thoughtfully, looking out for me in a way that allowed me to do this work with little issue in the group. In one couple's interview, I was asked multiple questions about my sampling size and sampling strategy before we began the interview. Another time, I found myself in a conversation that got into the weeds about differences between sociology and anthropology.

In a church in which issues of age, and generation, are especially salient, it is also important to acknowledge my age, especially because it was a result of that aspect of my identity that marked the one time I actively "participated" in my small-group observations, during the evening exercise I detail at the very beginning of chapter 2. In the early spring of 2016, Kimberley began the evening by dividing the room by generation. I remained in my seat and no one noticed, because I was the only Millennial there. Kimberley made a comment after everyone else had shuffled their chairs into groups: "Oh there aren't any Millennials in the room!" I raised both of my hands in a gesture of joking admission of surrender, "I am, I actually am!" Everyone laughed, and then Kimberley called on me to choose a question to answer; she had written up five questions on the board for each generation-divided group to work through. I answered the first question, about major life events that defined my generation. I mentioned both September 11 and the Columbine shooting—things that occurred in sixth and ninth grade for me. This felt like a fairly "neutral" way to engage as I was able to answer a question for my generation, and not for me. The irony and weight of this interaction were not lost on me as the only Millennial in the room, and I do not think it was lost on the group, either.

As an ethnographer, there were times when the moments that highlighted my role as a researcher both delighted and worried me. While I was glad at the consistent and varied ways that such remembering eased my work, especially when it came to the setup of the small group and their experientials, there were moments, too, where I worried that such noticing meant that individuals and the group might be acting and controlling their behaviors with this in mind. As Christena Nippert-Eng notes, "One becomes less noticeable by becoming more familiar, more expected, more taken for granted as time goes on. This is precisely how ethnographers overcome the worst hurdles that prevent us from learning how people normally behave" (2015:94). This low-stakes participation early on in fieldwork helped to start my pursuit of becoming more familiar.

My race, gender performance, and educational background and pursuits allowed me to fit in with this community in ways that no doubt increased my initial ability to gain access to this space, helped with my reception once I was there, and increased people's openness with me because they felt like I was "like them." The biggest exception to this, and what ended up being the most visibly salient part of my identity, as I had experienced before, was my lack of a religious identity.

DO YOU WANT TO PRAY OR WRITE NOTES?

On my very first night of fieldwork in the fall of 2015, the group closed their conversation about 10 minutes before I expected them to. Bill kept saying, "we need to cut to prayer" in the middle of an intense and engaged conversation. The group finally stopped the conversation to ensure enough time to pray, and I sat in my seat, surprised, as everyone else stood up. Carrie asked everyone to stand together at the front of the room so they could lay hands. Everyone circled around Carrie as she opened the prayer, and each individual placed either one or both arms on the shoulder or back of someone next to them, with those closest to Carrie holding their hands on her shoulders. I stood further back from him and lowered my eyes while everyone prayed. I was anxious about this unanticipated ritual and did not know how to respectfully navigate it in that moment. No one said anything about me standing outside of the circle. Once the prayer ended, I packed up my things and Bill came over to me. We chatted a bit and he asked how I liked my first evening. He then asked me about my religious background. I shared that I had grown up in the Episcopalian church, and, in a move I had learned in my previous research, then transitioned to say that, when I attended college out west, I was shocked by the sheer size of megachurches, something I had never experienced in my small church in New England, or something I had never seen in New England at all. He laughed and asked me about my research, and I explained that I was researching men who pledged abstinence until marriage. Bill said, "Yeah did you hear me having that conversation in the corner a minute ago?!" I said no and he said, "I was just talking about how we tell people sex is evil! Sex is evil! And then OK sex is good, and how do you deal with that?" I laughed quite a bit and told him that is exactly what my previous work looked at. A conversation that started about religion went back to research, and we said goodnight and parted ways.

About a month into fieldwork, at the close of a meeting in the early winter of 2016, Pastor Jeff suggested everyone pray together in small groups. Two small groups on either side of me joined up, so I was seated directly in between them. I put my pen down, closed my notebook, and put my hands on my lap. Everyone shared what they were going through that week, and one member started to cry as she shared an intense medical experience her husband had endured earlier in the week. Everyone started to pray verbally over her, and when that quieted, another person started to share, and then everyone prayed over them. Once it was clear that everyone had shared except for me, Pastor Jeff and Bill looked at me and Bill asked, "What can we pray for, for you?" I had, of course, a few minutes to see this coming. My first response was that I was happy to listen. That did not go over well. Pastor Jeff said, "Whatever, you are here to study marriage and relationships—this isn't about that, this is about community." He then reframed his first question and asked, "What would you like help achieving?" I knew it would be odd at best, and rude at worst, to further decline their requests, and upon Pastor Jeff's rephrasing of the request, I shared a detail from a part of my life they already knew about me: that I was a researcher and educator. I shared that a couple of my graduating seniors were having a rough quarter (I did not share any of the details of the situation at hand), and I could use reminders as a teacher to continue to approach the situation at hand with patience. Pastor Jeff smiled and started a prayer over asking for my continued patience. When he finished, I thanked him for his "good thoughts."

The next week, we again split into small groups for closing prayer. I was quickly jotting down a few notes as we closed, and Becky said, "Sarah, will you join us for prayer?" I said sure, smiled, closed my notebook, and apologized that I had been finishing up a note. Becky said, "Well, do you want to pray or write notes?" I scooted my chair closer to the group. Elaine, a 72-year-old White woman and the oldest member of the group, grabbed my hand in hers, and they all took turns sharing their stories for the week and receiving prayer. I listened, nodded along, and smiled when appropriate. When it was clear that everyone had spoken except for me, Becky turned to me and asked what "good thoughts" they could send out for me. In just a week, Becky had adopted the language I had used the week before. This is one of the many reasons Becky is good at evangelizing, and her use of my much more secular phrasing also worked for me, too. I navigated my space as a religious outsider; it was quite clear that the members of Disciples' Journey were quickly (and more quickly than I was) navigating how to connect with me, doing so by adopting the very language I had used instead of prayer. I wanted to take notes, and I did not want to pray—but Becky found a way to get me to engage in both.

During my first night at fieldwork, after most group members had filtered out of the room, I stayed behind to thank Pastor Jeff and Carrie for including me. We chatted for a while and Pastor Jeff said, "I don't know if you're allowed to show your hand, if you're a Christian, or are you just interested in this in terms of research?" Pastor Jeff's early question again underscores the importance, or at least strong curiosity, about my religious identities over other aspects of my life. I answered him the same way I had Bill. I told him about my childhood memories in a quaint New England Episcopalian chapel and the shock at seeing my first megachurch, to which he laughed quite hard. For Pastor Jeff, and many others in this space, showing my hand—revealing the aspect of my identity over which they were most curious—was my religion. For me, that was not the case. While my race, class, gendered performance, and educational background rendered me quite normal in this community, my religious and sexual identities did not.

WHEN I SAID NO
Navigating Religion

The ethnographic method often includes a hidden element until you are in the field: the realization that you are going to be saying yes much more than no, and saying yes to things you might otherwise never find yourself doing. For me, this included observing a group of adults as they wandered their neighborhood in search of connection, splitting appetizers and observing adults as they silently prayed over others in the restaurant, attending women-specific luncheons, and spending every Thursday evening with a group of people far from my home, listening to their realities and worldviews. While so much of this research relied on me saying "yes," there were moments when I said no, either to myself or to them.

While boundary-work was a recurring theme in my research, I also had to navigate specific boundaries as a researcher and as a human being, overlapping categories, of course, but identities not always treated as such. Maintaining my status as a researcher meant saying no to being more involved in church activities and not immersing myself in the community in a way that ignored the reality of my reasons for being there or intentionally led on those I was researching. And for me as a human being this meant not disclosing my sexual identity.

After my first interview with Monica, who was not a member of Disciples' Journey and therefore someone I did not know before my interview with her, she asked if I would sit with her the following weekend at Sunday services. I had never been asked this before and was taken aback. I asked her where she sat in the sanctuary, and she told me, excitedly, that she sits in the front row. She, very sweetly, wanted to introduce me to her friends so that I could interview them, too. She also offered for me to join one of her small-group meetings the next fall, a group for married couples, to meet people there. I told Monica I would follow up with her over email about meeting up again. I emailed Monica on the Saturday afternoon before the services the following morning, and said that I could meet up with her to say hello after the sermon ended. During the sermon the next day, I took my place at the back of the Sanctuary and watched Monica in the front row, part of the large group of people who stand throughout the entirety of the service with their hands raised in the air. I knew I would stand out very easily in that space, and also knew that any behavior I would engage in that would make me blend in with that group would violate my ethical beliefs around this research. I was and am not an evangelical or a believer, and, for a group of people who so strongly want others to join, I was not going to give Monica or her friends a false sense that such an endeavor was or is of interest to me. After the services ended, I met up with Monica, said hello to her friends, thanked her for the invitation to join them, and explained that it was much easier for me to sit at the back and take everything in.

There were also a couple of moments when Disciples' Journey split up as a group during their missions unit. This was because their usual meeting room was serving as a temporary shelter for survivors of domestic abuse and their children. The church was helping a local nonprofit by providing this extra space. On one of these evenings, half of the group met at a fast-food spot near the church while the other half of the group volunteered with the women and children. While I strongly believe in and support such a cause, I also felt strongly that my identity as a researcher in that space was not appropriate for two reasons. First, I did not want any of the women or children, whose lives had been upended, to feel uncomfortable, confused, or concerned about my presence as a researcher. Second, I did not want any of them to think that I supported the underlying message shared with them that evening (and relayed to me by Carrie ahead of time as she talked about their plans): sharing the word of God as comfort and the solution for their problems. While I imagine witnessing these interactions would have yielded quite illuminating data, the lives and well-being of those more marginalized must always be given priority when making these decisions in the field.

Finally, when I went out on "mini-missions" in public with Disciples' Journey, I was faced with new real-time decision-making that required me to think quickly and clearly about my position in the field. For example, I accompanied Becky as she entered a restaurant in search of a server who worked there, a man she had prayed over and talked with the week prior when we were all at the restaurant as a group. We walked into the crowded restaurant. And while Becky did not see the server, I did. He was waiting on customers on the busy, warm evening, and I did not tell Becky I saw him. She gave up the search and we left. I made the decision that, while I was there to observe evangelical life, I was not there to contribute to successful evangelizing.

Navigating Sexual Identity

To return to Pastor Jeff's comment, while Pastor Jeff assumed that showing my hand in full would mean disclosing my religious beliefs, for me such an act would mean sharing my queer identity. Before I began this fieldwork, I talked with Lynne Gerber, who has done a great deal of qualitative research on White evangelicals. In talking with Lynne, I came to the conclusion that for both the ease of my data collection and my own personal health, such a disclosure was not necessary for this work. I was also able to make this decision not to disclose my sexual identity because it was not evident or questioned due to my gender normativity. However, I also feel strongly that I not blatantly lie to those who are sharing their own stories, vulnerabilities, and thoughts with me. I decided that, if I got to know someone at Lakeview well, and they asked me about my relationship history or current relationship status, I would not lie. I was only ever explicitly asked this question once, by Frank, alone in a parking lot close to 10 PM the night after Donald Trump was elected President in 2016. As I elaborate on this moment in chapter 3, these questions were also happening in the middle of an intense political rant. Because I was alone, and because of the state of his emotional response, and what he had just said about rumors of Hillary Clinton's sexual identity, I did not feel safe answering this question. I was never in a position where I needed to think about answering it again. Sometimes, people in Disciples' Journey would joke about my assumed boyfriends and, in a few cases, make jokes about me being hit on by others. Most often, these comments came from men, not women. No woman ever asked me about my relationship status. Given the anxieties in the church about singleness and marriage, I expected more concern and attention in this area, but again, curiosity over my religious identity trumped both my gender and my sexual identity— a reality I imagine I would have not experienced if I were not White and normatively gendered. Most often, people were most curious about my religious background, research, or teaching, the latter two things topics I spoke about frequently as a way to respect their desire that I share things with them.

To hide my queer identity and queer politics, my feminism, my desires for a much more progressive world meant that there were many moments in which I was silent when I otherwise would not have been in a different context. I listened painfully to casual, benevolent, and overt displays of sexism, racism, and homophobia. Comments that would have been met with strong pushback in my classroom, my friend groups, my personal life, my family I instead met with "interesting, tell me more." This was the right decision for me and for this research, but that by no means would be the right decision for everyone in this scenario. Because of the ways in which other aspects of my identity were privileged in this space, I imagine this was an easier decision for me to make than it would have been for someone else. As a normatively gendered, feminine, White, educated woman with a Christian upbringing (however loose that religious upbringing was), I was given the benefit of the doubt and the access that would have looked quite different if I were a person of color, more butch or gender queer, or not Christian (and really, here, I mean Muslim)—if I invoked in their minds (as I did that night with Frank) any component of the imagined secular.

SEX AND INSTITUTIONAL REVIEW

Although questions of sexuality were often avoided in the church, and explicitly avoided by me as I navigated my own positionality as a researcher in this space, sex became a looming issue as I tried to obtain institutional approval of this work, and then again, once I tried to get a field site.

The Institutional Review Board (IRB) at my home institution took nine months to approve my research, and I underwent "full review" twice, an unusual event for sociologists, but perhaps less unusual for those who study sexuality, and study sexuality qualitatively (Schilt, Meadow, and Compton 2018). The IRB was concerned with my focus on small groups related to sex and sexuality, specifically sexual addiction, and wanted me to obtain permission from church leadership before I conducted any interviews in the church. I broadened the scope of my research questions and interview protocol to cover themes related to marriage more generally; and I needed to make clear that observing conversations about sexuality in these spaces would not put the church leadership or respondents at risk for civil or criminal liability. I believe there was a different understanding of a small group dedicated to "sex addiction" at play here: that is, in the church this might mean watching pornography or dealing with issues of lust, and outside the church, this may mean something more severe and, in some cases, illegal.

I fought to avoid the need for permission from church leadership for interviews. I felt and still feel strongly that such requirements can easily result in coercion among parishioners and cherry-picking of respondents from church leadership. The IRB and I found a happy medium: that the church leadership would be aware of my presence in the building, and that, as I planned to go contact small-group leaders as a starting contact when obtaining a field site, they could serve as initial gate keepers for the research. While the entirety of this process was frustrating, and at many moments felt as though I was fighting for the ethical concerns of my research participants that an IRB process is supposed to ensure, the entire ordeal was a good lesson in pushing back on institutional review, and remembering that, as is a theme throughout this book, the goals and interests of the institution may not reflect, in this case, the goals of the research or the interest of the research participants.

During the time I was waiting for final human subjects approval for this work, I made a spreadsheet of churches within reasonable driving or bus distance (note: the Seattle Metro area has an extensive transit system that spans multiple cities, so this should not be taken as an indication of the proximity of Lakeview to the city) that had the following characteristics: (1) classification as a megachurch, with over 1000 members, and (2) evidence of use of a national curricula focused on sexuality, relationships, and sexual addiction. I had purchased one of these national curricula, one of the most popular of its type, via a research grant from my university. At the start of this research, I was especially interested in doing fieldwork at a church that used this curriculum because it is so widely used, and seemed to be one of the more common ways in which the church was talking about married relationships. I was interested in the church's approach to married life, as my previous research in this area generated more questions for evangelical marital support, especially around issues related to sexuality, than it did answers (Diefendorf 2015).

I came up with a list of seven churches that fit the criteria. I added two other local megachurches to the list, as I wanted to visit a broad range of churches in the area before my field site was secured. This was important so that, by the time I had established a field site, I would have a sense of how the church compared to others in the area (based at least initially upon my observations of the content and topics of the Sunday sermons). The Pacific Northwest, along with the city I lived in, Seattle, is known for its extremes when it comes to evangelical churches (Dias 2015; Paulson 2014). The now defunct Mars Hill, for example, represented an extreme for its beliefs about gendered hierarchies and its focus on promoting a somewhat violent and patriarchal masculinity, and gained national attention for such, while another evangelical church in the area made national news for its progressive stance on gay marriage and its work to welcome the LGBTQ community into their church. I wanted to locate my research in more of the ideological center of these other churches in the area. Evangelical churches encapsulate churches with a large range of beliefs in the Pacific Northwest and in the nation (Wellman 2008), so this exercise was important to help locate this work within the vast landscape of evangelism in the United States.

I attended seven of these nine churches between September and December of 2015. I alternated which church I attended each Sunday, and at each, I took field notes at the Sunday sermons to help locate the church within the range of evangelical ideological beliefs in the Pacific Northwest so that I could make an informed and contextualized decision for my field-site selection. When I obtained IRB approval in early September 2015, I sent messages to each of the nine churches with research requests. My IRB required research approval from a church leader, broadly defined as a lead, associate, or small-group pastor. I obtained email addresses that were publicly available on the church websites, and I then sent emails to church leaders, their executive assistants, associate pastors, and leaders of small groups that were promoted online. Oftentimes, this meant I was sending research requests to multiple people within the same church at the same time.

As a researcher and nonreligious outsider to the evangelical community, I included links to press on my previous research from both secular and religious news sources in these recruitment letters. The religious news sources, such as *Christianity Today,* were most important, as they provided a review of my work and interviewed pastors who agreed with my findings. These articles helped signal that, although an outsider to the community, I have a track record of conducting respectful research on evangelical communities.

I sent out a total of 40 initial interview requests, and received six rejections and the rest were nonresponses. A bit dismayed, especially after such a long human subjects' review period, I reflected on my recruitment letter. I wondered if the language I used, which included a specific focus on sex and sexuality, might be part of the problem I was experiencing in obtaining a field site. I decided to make a simple change to my recruitment letter, and removed the words "sexual" and "sexuality" from my research questions.

There are a couple of details worthy of additional reflection in this initial recruitment process. First, evangelicals may not respond to emails asking to research and question the church about its stance on sexuality, because, as this research documents, that stance is evolving and changing, and that process is not an easy one for the church. For academics, sexuality is a broad category that covers a whole set of social arrangements around it, well beyond specific types of sexual acts. I imagine that, for those who read my initial recruitment letter, sexuality signaled its most common meaning and association of sexual acts. I was, perhaps, accidentally signaling something that I did not mean to in these initial recruitment letters. Second, although I was initially worried about the need to change the wording on this email template, this project quickly turned into a project much larger than one focused specifically on questions of sexuality within the church, so the later template ended up being a more accurate reflection of my research than the first.

I sent out 13 revised interview requests and heard back from four individuals—three men and one woman—once I changed the wording of my recruitment letter by removing the words "sex" and "sexuality." I followed up with all four individuals and conducted a couple's interview with an associate pastor and his wife at a church the following weekend. I was especially interested, however, in the church that yielded responses from both a man and a woman associate pastor. This church, Lakeview, ended up becoming my field site.

I am not very worried about a self-selection issue here. I believe this strong response was due to the number of available email addresses Lakeview provided on their website, which meant I was able to email many people involved in some capacity with the church. Part of this better response rate, too, might be due to the change in wording in my template.

Pastor Jeff, one of the male associate pastors at Lakeview Church, left me a voicemail after he had emailed me in response to my interview request. Pastor Jeff told me that a few people in the church had come up to him and told him about my email, and he wanted to speak with me on the phone before he instructed them on how to respond. Interestingly, Kimberley, the woman associate pastor from Lakeview who reached out to me over email, did not go through Pastor Jeff first, which also made me excited about the possibility of this church as a field site. I wanted to conduct research in a place where there were signs that both men and women would be open to talking to me. I also wanted to conduct fieldwork in a space where women would feel comfortable talking to me independently of the men in the church, a problem I have faced in previous work on evangelicals (see methods discussion in Diefendorf 2015), where I experienced great difficulty in interviewing women. In my previous work, men sat in on my interviews with women (their wives), and it was therefore not fully clear to me how women experienced their gendered and religious lives independent from the men in the church. I wanted to make sure that I could speak with everyone, independently, in this research.

When I returned Pastor Jeff's call, I included some deference on my part in the phone conversation. I apologized for sending so many emails that had generated questions among the leadership. After about 15 minutes of conversation, Pastor Jeff warmed to me, and he somewhat enthusiastically invited me to attend a small-group meeting two weeks later. I made sure to explain to Pastor Jeff that I was also interested in questions of sexuality within the church, as this information was no longer explicit in my recruitment letter. Pastor Jeff responded and said the small group he was thinking of was going through a self-developed curriculum series on marriage and relationships, which "might be of interest to me." This response signaled to me that Pastor Jeff understood, or was at least open, to my research aims. Pastor Jeff was the leader of this small group and told me that he would talk to the group and make sure that all members were comfortable with the idea of my attendance. Pastor Jeff said that, if and when he obtained verbal consent from the group, I could join their meeting the following week, and that we could then "take it from there." I explained over the phone that I would also need to obtain consent from everyone in the room when I attended the first meeting in person.

I obtained written consent from group members on my first visit to this small group, Disciples' Journey. Pastor Jeff had introduced me and my work the week before, so that no one attending the group that night was caught off guard or surprised by my presence, and so that individuals had time to think, individually, without the presence of the rest of the group, if they felt comfortable with the idea of my attendance there as a researcher. When new people joined the group, we went through the process again. The members of Disciples' Journey were asked to reach out to Pastor Jeff if they were concerned about my presence or had any questions. They did not. As I indicate above, this does not mean I didn't receive myriad questions and comments about my work and myself while in the field.

Pastor Jeff ended up being my main gatekeeper in this research. This might be a reflection of the gendered organization to which I was seeking entrance, but it also meant that I spent a good deal of time and energy making connections with the women in the small group to build trust and rapport with them, beginning with Kimberley and Carrie. As Kimberley had been one of the two people to respond to my email from Lakeview, I made sure to spend a good deal of time talking with her on my first evening at Disciples' Journey, and she made clear to me that she and Pastor Jeff had talked together, and that they were both welcoming me into that space.

The entire exercise of IRB and field-site finding was a reminder that both the organizations we study and the institutions we rely on to do this research are often governed by the very principles we seek to question, which means the need for creativity, compromise, and thoughtful approaches to the field.

HONORING REALITY AND HOPE

In the winter of 2020, I was preparing notes for a methods workshop I was going to give at UT Austin. I became increasingly frustrated with my workshop outline, as I realized that in listing out all of the difficult elements of this research, and the solutions or approaches to think through navigating fieldwork, I missed something important: I enjoyed this work. I wanted to end that workshop with a reminder that, at least for me, engaging in this type of research is an act of hope, and one that should not be lost. And I want to end on that note here, too.

While I was in the field, and after the 2016 presidential election, I found myself thinking about Rebecca Solnit's writing on hope in dark times. Solnit does not obfuscate the social problems of the world with bright-siding; rather, she honors both the inequalities of the world and a real belief in change as she navigates and seeks out a pathway forward. And I found that to be a necessary component that sustained me during this work.

Grief, hope, and joy can coexist. The reality of multiple truths is a tricky beast. In essay published in July 2016 for the *Guardian*, Solnit wrote,

> Social, cultural or political change does not work in predictable ways or on predictable schedules. . . . We don't know what is going to happen, or how, or when, and that very uncertainty is the space of hope.
>
> Those who doubt that these moments matter should note how terrified the authorities and elites are when they erupt. That fear signifies their recognition that popular power is real enough to overturn regimes and rewrite the social contract. And it often has. Sometimes your enemies know what your friends can't believe. Those who dismiss these moments because of their imperfections, limitations, or incompleteness need to look harder at what joy and hope shine out of them and what real changes have emerged because of them, even if not always in the most obvious or recognisable ways. (Solnit 2016)

In conducting this research, I talked and connected with people who see the world very differently from me. I felt that understanding and mapping their deep stories (Hochschild 2016a) were an important empirical endeavor. And my ability to conduct this work was also clearly related to and impacted by my identities—a White, cisgender woman with religious curiosity, not trauma. I was able to enter Lakeview and hear their stories and work to make sense of them.

In one of my first couples interviews, a young man asked me if my goal was to hurt the church. I explained no, and went over my central research questions. He immediately followed his first question by asking me my religious identity, again a reminder of the salience of my lack of a religious identity in this space. I was and am an outsider, and I do imagine that, if some from Lakeview read this work, they may feel my goal was harm. My goal was to find answers to questions, and the enduring inequalities documented in this book are not meant to cause harm but relieve it in the future.

Here is to the hope that the voices calling for change will be heard.

APPENDIX B

Participant Overview

This table provides information about the individuals whose voices and actions are represented in this book. The names in this table are pseudonyms to protect the confidentiality of research participants. When an em dash is present in the table, that indicates that I was not able to collect that data. For example, I did not know the exact ages of guest speakers at church services.

TABLE 1   DEMOGRAPHIC CHARACTERISTICS OF INTERVIEW SUBJECTS

Pseudonym	Race/Ethnicity	Gender	Age
		Parishioners	
Carrie	White	Woman	39
Kelly	White	Woman	30
Steve	White	Man	47
Elaine	White	Woman	72
Heather	White	Woman	64
Frank	White	Man	67
Katherine	White	Woman	55
Emily	Asian American	Woman	29
Will	White	Man	34
Donna	White	Woman	49
Earl	White	Man	63
Becky	Mexican American	Woman	52
Laurie	White	Woman	47
Anthony	Black	Man	60

(continued)

TABLE 1 *(continued)*

Pseudonym	Race/Ethnicity	Gender	Age
		Parishioners	
Lyndsey	White	Woman	21
Jesse	White	Man	21
Eric	White	Man	45
Henry	White	Man	31
Jess	White	Woman	38
Marjorie	White	Woman	57
Adam	White	Man	36
Riley	White	Woman	37
Raymond	White	Man	55
Joe	White	Man	52
Allison	White	Woman	24
Paula	White	Woman	51
Sally	White	Woman	48
James	White	Man	32
Monica	Mexican American	Woman	65
Nicole	White	Woman	19
Craig	Latino	Man	21
Darren	White	Man	29
Annie	White	Woman	29
Eileen	White	Woman	54
Maggie	White	Woman	36
Kevin	Asian American	Man	38
Megan	White	Woman	44
Bill	White	Man	50
Shannon	White	Woman	43
		Leadership and Guests	
Pastor Jeff	White	Man	48
Pastor Kimberley	White	Woman	41
Pastor Isaac	White	Man	38
Pastor Dave	White	Man	52
Pastor Darryl	Black	Man	63
Pastor Rachel	White	Woman	39
Pastor Amy	White	Woman	35
Mark	White	Man	—
Michael	White	Man	—
Brittany	White	Woman	—
Melissa	White	Woman	—
Stephanie	White	Woman	—
Pastor Adam	White	Man	—
Norm	White	Man	—

Notes

1. GOOD AND GODLY IN TRUMP'S AMERICA

1. GSS data may underestimate the percentage of religious "nones." See Burge 2020.

2. For a thorough overview on the ways in which debates of secularization have preoccupied sociologists of religion, see Edgell 2012.

3. FYI is a branch of the evangelical Fuller Theological Seminary, focused on providing resources for youth ministry.

4. To provide a sense of what "Pentecostals with a seat-belt on" looks like in practice, take the following excerpt from a Sunday sermon delivered in late spring 2016. While many Pentecostals are known for the practice of speaking in tongues, here are Pastor Isaac's thoughts on the subject: "It's weird for some people but unfortunately it's in our Bible so we have to deal with it. Rushing wind, fire, and speaking in languages people hadn't heard before but when interpreted by those around them they were praising God. Many Pentecostals require you to speak in tongues to prove that the Holy Spirit has come, but they don't require a rushing mighty wind or a tongue of fire." At this remark, many in the audience laughed and clapped. Pastor Isaac continued, "These are not litmus tests or proofs of the grace of God. You cannot prove to me that you are Born Again Christian, it is something we live, not something we wear on our sleeves, something that becomes religious pride."

5. Lakeview Church used the New International Version (NIV) to quote during Sunday sermons. During Disciples' Journey meetings, the group leaders would often ask people to provide different translations (from different Bibles) for the same verse, but the Pathways material all used the NIV. Although this group and church approach the Bible with a literal interpretation, Sam Perry's (2020) work reminds us that the Bible is a living and changing document, even among those who argue for its literalism. Perry suggests that qualitative

researchers note which Bible is being used in the communities in question. His work also shows how changes were made to the English Standard Version (ESV) to make it more amenable to conservative interpretations of gender theology after the perceived "feminist" revisions to the NIV in the 1990s. Given the focus on questions related to biblical interpretations of gender, and relationships between men and women, during my time at Lakeview, it is especially interesting to note that the group relied mainly on the NIV, perhaps another indication of the balance they sought throughout the "messiness" of debates related to feminism.

6. Megachurches are variable in definition. In the United States, most understand megachurches as those that report weekly attendance between 1000 and 2000 on the lower end; in South Korea, however, a megachurch is one that has a weekly attendance of 10,000 or more members (Connell 2005:316; Goh 2008). Megachurches in the United States represent a hallmark of the contemporary evangelical movement, and often distinguish themselves from older and smaller churches through dynamic speakers, contemporary worship styles that include the addition of media, live bands with electronic instruments, international networks and missions, and informality and a casual approach to the overall atmosphere and people in it, as seen, for example, through norms about church clothing attire (Goh 2008). Oftentimes, megachurches in the United States are known for attracting younger demographics and more highly educated congregants (Goh 2008). An important component of the modern megachurch is the presence of small groups and church curricula. In megachurches, small groups provide an arena through which church members can develop a sense of community (Dougherty and Whitehead 2011; Smidt 2003). Frequently, these small groups are organized around a curriculum that is produced by the group, the church, or a national organization.

7. This is an estimate from Pastor Jeff, which he gave when I asked him if the church had specific demographic information about their congregants. I roughly corroborated this number based upon my observations during fieldwork. Without concrete data, this should be taken as a rough estimate, but one that matches the overall demographic makeup of evangelicals in the state.

2. THE FEAR OF RELIGIOUS AND CULTURAL DECLINE

1. For research on the role anger can play in the rhetoric of politics and mobilization, see Bostdorff 2017.

2. Interestingly, while earning a four-year college degree had a positive effect on disaffiliation for most cohorts of evangelical Protestants born between 1920 and 1949, earning a four-year college degree had a negative effect for the 1950s and 1970s cohorts. Evangelicals were becoming more educated during this time, and this increased education was less threatening to their religious affiliations and beliefs (Schwadel 2014b).

3. I use Green et al.'s definition of the Christian Right: "a social movement located principally among evangelicals, dedicated to restoring traditional values in public policy" (1996:2).

4. Those who we now call the Fundamentalists had already started to clearly distinguish themselves, with the publication of the essays titled "The Fundamentals" published between 1910 and 1916.

5. Kevin Kruse argues that part of this engagement with the world was encouraged by those outside of the church. Specifically, Kruse argues that corporate leaders and wealthy Republican elites enlisted conservative clergymen to help them promote a free-enterprise agenda under the phrase "Freedom under God." For more on the role of religious leaders in helping shape this ideology, and the role of corporate elite in helping set the stage for the rise of the Christian Right, see Kruse 2015.

6. For a thorough overview of the ways in which US economic policy and ideology and White evangelism have intersected and fueled each other, see Marti 2020.

7. Here, a status politics model might be helpful to understand the marriage of evangelical and conservative religious beliefs. Status politics, derived from Weber's distinction between status groups and social classes, is a dual approach to stratification that recognizes that societies are driven by both economic inequalities *and* competition for public respect (Wald, Owen, and Hill 1989:2). These forms of stratification can result in different forms of public action. For example, social classes might pursue material interests through political competitions, such as elections. Status groups, on the other hand, might enroll in "symbolic cultural crusades" that tend to be more episodic and decentralized in their approach. With this framing in mind, we might think of evangelicals as operating as more of a status group leading up to the early 1990s, before seeming to converge politically into a status class, marking a drastic change in their trajectory.

8. For a discussion about potential measurement issues with this highly used statistic, see Burge and Lewis 2018.

9. Pew's Religious Landscape Survey finds that, in Washington State, evangelical Protestants report higher educational attainment, and slightly more are categorized as upper-middle class compared to the nation as a whole (Pew 2015a).

10. Indeed, the authors find that individuals not only resented their own personal social prestige, but also that of other groups and categories of people, leading them to suggest that status resentment appears to be both "corporate and referential." Respondents linked their own level of social respect with other churchgoers, hard-working people, ministers, and law-abiding people.

3. THE IMAGINED SECULAR: CONFRONTING FEMINISM, GENDER, AND FAMILY LIFE

1. The laying on of hands is a practice in which someone (usually in a position of authority within the church) lays their hands, palms down, on another person (often head or shoulders) to confer a blessing.

2. The marketing pitch of this book is "the first book written by a MAN on the critical need to advance women in the workplace. Why did a man write this book? You don't have to convince women this is a good idea, you have to engage men who still hold 85% of all leadership positions." Part of the appeal

of this book to Katherine may be the comfort that men can make certain claims for and about women, in relation to the discomfort many at Lakeview expressed about women claiming certain rights or advances for themselves as women.

3. Lakeview Church records their Sunday sermons and edits them to produce one final version, available in podcast format for those who cannot attend services in person, or who would like to revisit the message of the week. As a researcher, this was a gift. I was able to be fully present at Sunday sermons, and take notes on major themes and ideas for analysis, but I was able to operate with the comfort that, if I missed something, I would catch it when I listened to the podcast during the week, a practice I initiated early on in my fieldwork. It was in listening to the podcast that I caught Pastor Dave's murmur about Baptists.

4. A year after this interview, Seattle became the first city in the country to ban plastic straws and utensils. Evangelical and secular political projects and interests are not always separate endeavors.

5. Becky did not identify as an evangelical, or even a member of a Christian church, for a good portion of her life, either. Becky, and other evangelicals, might have more of a language and understanding for coming into relationship with Christ, and being fully accepted, regardless of their previous history than they do with joining other movements.

6. Lakeview Church is in proximity to the fairly progressive, areligious city of Seattle, located in the state of Washington, a state in which 47% of its residents say they are not religious (Balk 2018). Washington State, by this measure, is the least religious it has ever been, a fact that perhaps makes this a great place to study evangelicals. We can imagine more signaling work needs to be done here than in other communities and areas in which everyone is assumed to be religious. Washington State, in general, and Seattle in particular, as the closest major urban center to Lakeview Church, might provide a type of "religious threat" off of which the church can respond and mold itself (Campbell 2006).

7. Verses 21 to 28 from the NIV read as follows:

> [21] Submit to one another out of reverence for Christ.
>
> [22] Wives, submit yourselves to your own husbands as you do to the Lord.
>
> [23] For the husband is the head of the wife as Christ is the head of the church, his body, of which he is the Savior.
>
> [24] Now as the church submits to Christ, so also wives should submit to their husbands in everything.
>
> [25] Husbands, love your wives, just as Christ loved the church and gave himself up for her
>
> [26] to make her holy, cleansing her by the washing with water through the word,
>
> [27] and to present her to himself as a radiant church, without stain or wrinkle or any other blemish, but holy and blameless.

8. The phrase "Social Justice Warrior" gained popularity following the Gamergate controversy in 2015 and is often used on websites like Reddit and 4chan.

9. The inclusion of gender dysphoria in the DSM-5 presents a complicated issue for some members of the trans and queer communities, as its inclusion can also work to provide institutional and financial support for medical care for

some transgender people. However, as long as trans individuals are understood through a pathologizing "disease" framework, they will be met with invalidation, discrimination, and abuse. Instead, medical institutions and insurance companies should update their policies to reflect the needs of all so that a reliance on the DSM for medical coverage is no longer needed. For the best recent work on gender affirmation see Meadow 2019.

10. The #MeToo movement was started by Tarana Burke to demonstrate the widespread prevalence of sexual assault and harassment. It gained international visibility in October 2017 when actress Alyssa Milano tweeted out the hashtag and encouraged other survivors of sexual harassment and abuse to do the same. While the movement had not gained large-scale traction when Frank made these comments, I mention it to highlight the juxtaposition of his words against a national dialogue that started taking place less than a year later. Issues of sexism and gender discrimination were central to the 2016 election for many, and perhaps helped to fuel support for this movement during the first year of Trump's presidency.

11. Not asking for or recording the title of this book remains one of my bigger regrets from this fieldwork. Given the intensity of the interaction, though, I am not surprised that I did not think to ask him for the title before he threw the book back into his truck.

4. WHITE EVANGELICALS: EMOTION WORK AND RACIAL INEQUALITY

1. Pastor Darryl's comments and the audience's responses are not just the casual substance of jokes, but rather what sociologist Erving Goffman (1967) called the *symbolic material* that emerges through *rituals of race*.

2. The suburbs that Lakeview members call home are 67% White (compared to 84% in the state), and the area has experienced consistent population growth since 2015.

3. See Dowling 2014, especially for a discussion about the way Whiteness is used as a strategy to combat discrimination.

4. Exec. Order No. 13788, 82 Fed. Reg. 18837 (April 21, 2017), https://www.federalregister.gov/documents/2017/04/21/2017-08311/buy-american-and-hire-american.

5. Mark may have been referencing the paper beads made popular by organizations like Bead for Life, which support women in Uganda. But this detail probably didn't matter, as the lack of knowledge of the lives of people of color as a central theme indicates.

6. These findings, of a simultaneous reworking of both Trump and Jesus, mirror Gerber's (2011) findings around the rhetoric of "a sin is a sin" used to grapple with both fatness and homosexuality.

7. This quote is taken from Cook and Baldwin 2009.

8. The mission statement for the Facebook group reads as follows: "We specialize in spanking greedy corporate asses for the harder working classes and provide a home on the internet for the millions of Americans who want to fight the power and make our country work for the other 98% of us. Other98 is the only group out there with the kind of massive audience, bold language, and

knack for storytelling that we need to create the seismic cultural shifts we need to change the world. Join us."

9. A recent, popular example includes Schaumburg 2009.

10. Data from the National Congregations Study (Chaves 2012) and Pew Research Center's Religion and Public Life Project (2015a) find that while about eight out of 10 American congregants still attend services at a place where a single racial or ethnic group comprises at least 80% of the congregation, one out of five American congregants now worship in congregations where no single racial or ethnic group predominates.

11. For more work on White evangelicals and xenophobia—something that came up a bit less than other issues at Lakeview Church—see Marti 2020; Whitehead and Perry 2020; or Du Mez 2020.

5. SACRED SEX: MARRIAGE AND HETEROSEXUALITY

1. This tapestry metaphor is often used in evangelical spaces in conjunction with Grant Colfax Tullar's poem "The Weaver," which is often then also associated with (and sometimes misattributed to) Corrie Ten Boom, Dutch watchmaker and writer (*The Hiding Place,* 1971), who is celebrated for her work and her family's work in helping Jews escape Nazis in World War II, and honored within (and outside of) evangelical Christian spaces "as an exemplar of Christian faith in action" (www.pbs.org/wgbh/questionofgod/voices/boom.html).

2. As Amy DeRogatis illustrates in her overview of evangelical literature on sex and marriage, women are taught, fairly clearly, that when women fulfill their appropriate biblical gendered "roles," men are then able to fulfill their "roles" as evangelical men (DeRogatis 2015).

3. The verses read as follows in the NIV, but it should be noted that other versions of the Bible title this passage as "Philip and the Ethiopian Eunuch," again another example of the ways in which constructions of gender and sexuality extend to the Bible itself:

> [26] Now an angel of the Lord said to Philip, "Go south to the road—the desert road—that goes down from Jerusalem to Gaza."
>
> [27] So he started out, and on his way he met an Ethiopian eunuch, an important official in charge of all the treasury of the Kandake (which means "queen of the Ethiopians"). This man had gone to Jerusalem to worship,
>
> [28] and on his way home was sitting in his chariot reading the Book of Isaiah the prophet.
>
> [29] The Spirit told Philip, "Go to that chariot and stay near it."
>
> [30] Then Philip ran up to the chariot and heard the man reading Isaiah the prophet. "Do you understand what you are reading?" Philip asked.
>
> [31] "How can I," he said, "unless someone explains it to me?" So he invited Philip to come up and sit with him.
>
> [32] This is the passage of Scripture the eunuch was reading: "He was led like a sheep to the slaughter, and as a lamb before its shearer is silent, so he did not open his mouth.
>
> [33] In his humiliation he was deprived of justice. Who can speak of his descendants? For his life was taken from the earth."
>
> [34] The eunuch asked Philip, "Tell me, please, who is the prophet talking about, himself or someone else?"

[35] Then Philip began with that very passage of Scripture and told him the good news about Jesus.

[36] As they traveled along the road, they came to some water and the eunuch said, "Look, here is water. What can stand in the way of my being baptized?"

[37][38] And he gave orders to stop the chariot. Then both Philip and the eunuch went down into the water and Philip baptized him.

[39] When they came up out of the water, the Spirit of the Lord suddenly took Philip away, and the eunuch did not see him again, but went on his way rejoicing.

4. This is unusual language for a Sunday morning sermon, even from a guest speaker.

5. See Bernstein 2010 for the interesting overlaps between evangelical and abolitionist feminist antitrafficking campaigns.

6. Take, for example, the many ways in which American Indians and enslaved Africans were constructed by White people as sexually dangerous. The construction of American Indians as sexually dangerous allowed for the justification, on the part of White settlers, to engage in both warfare and the removal of American Indians from their land (Nagel 2003). The construction of African men and women as hypersexual allowed for the justification of the murder and violence against African men in the name of the protection of White women, and the justification of the rape of African women. This construction also contributed heavily to the justification of the slavery of both. The economic and political national project that paved the way for the formation of the United States relied directly on White superiority over American Indians and enslaved Africans. Today, we find a modern form of nation-building in the missions work by White churches across the country. For longer discussions about the reliance on racialized, sexualized, and gendered othering in nation-building, see Nagel 2003.

7. According to a survey conducted by Pew in 2014, Carrie is not at all unusual in her beliefs about creationism. The poll finds that evangelicals believe strongly in the phrase "Humans have not evolved due to natural processes" compared to the religiously unaffiliated (Pew 2015c).

8. The heading to this section is an homage to Tolman 2005.

6. WE AREN'T THE EXTREMISTS: SAME-SEX MARRIAGE AND CHANGING IDEAS OF SIN

1. A covenant marriage is a type of marriage that is legally distinct in three states in the United States in 2022. In a covenant marriage in these states, those marrying consent to premarital counseling, and in addition, consent to more limited grounds for a later divorce. At Lakeview and in the evangelical community at large, the term is being used more colloquially to invoke meanings of difference between a marriage in which God is present and how evangelicals view and understand many secular marriages. Evangelicals and many other religious groups in the United States are working to redefine and promote heterosexual marriage in times of change (Heath 2012).

2. The Barna Group "provides spiritual influencers with credible knowledge and clear thinking, enabling them to navigate a complex and changing culture," according to its website in the spring of 2020.

3. This notion of Millennials as driving change and also as the group to which the church should focus its attention was a common idea shared by the Lakeview leadership staff. However, as Pastor Dave suggested in his Sunday sermon in the opening vignette of this work, Millennials are also a group that the church does not understand.

4. Found first in Whitehead and Perry 2020, with original source Heim 2017.

5. Other research suggests that sexual addiction groups might serve as a type of "White racial project" (Winant 2004), "whereby Whites share expectations about moral, appropriate, and good behavior based on an idealized form of Whiteness" (Burke and Haltom 2020:243).

6. The statement and signers can be viewed here: https://cbmw.org/nashville-statement/.

7. Two major examples include then county clerk Kim Davis, who, in August 2015, refused to issue marriage licenses to same-sex couples, citing her personal religious objections and religious liberty as her rationale, and the Colorado baker and owner of Masterpiece Cakeshop, who refused to bake a wedding cake for a same-sex marriage celebration, which went to the Supreme Court (*Masterpiece Cakeshop, LTD, v. Colorado Civil Rights Commission,* decided in favor of Masterpiece Cakeshop in June 2018).

8. To see this article as an example of the press around Eastlake Community Church reference Dias 2015.

9. In the NIV Bible, John 15:13 reads in full as "Greater love has no one than this: to lay down one's life for one's friends."

References

Abramowitz, Alan I. 2018. *The Great Alignment: Race, Party Transformation, and the Rise of Donald Trump*. New Haven, CT: Yale University Press.

Acker, Joan. 1992. "From Sex Roles to Gendered Institutions." *Contemporary Sociology* 21 (5): 565–69.

———. 2006. "Inequality Regimes: Gender, Class, and Race in Organizations." *Gender & Society* 20 (4): 441–64.

Alcoff, Linda. 1988. "Cultural Feminism versus Post-Structuralism: The Identity Crisis in Feminist Theory." *Signs: Journal of Women in Culture and Society* 13 (3): 405–36.

Ali, Syed. 2017. "Watching the Ethnographers." *Contexts* 16 (4): 60–62.

Ammerman, Nancy. 2006. "Religious Identities in Contemporary American Life: Lessons from the NJPS." *Sociology of Religion* 67 (4): 359–64.

———. 2015. "Lived Religion." In *Emerging Trends in the Social and Behavioral Sciences*, pp. 1–8. Hoboken, NJ: Wiley.

———. 2016. "Lived Religion as an Emerging Field: An Assessment of Its Contours and Frontiers." *Nordic Journal of Religion and Society* 1 (2): 83–99.

Avishai, Orit. 2008. "'Doing Religion' in a Secular World: Women in Conservative Religions and the Question of Agency." *Gender & Society* 22 (4): 409–33.

Avishai, Orit, Lynne Gerber, and Jennifer Randles. 2013. "The Feminist Ethnographer's Dilemma: Reconciling Progressive Research Agendas with Fieldwork Realities." *Journal of Contemporary Ethnography* 42 (4): 394–426.

Avishai, Orit, and Courtney Ann Irby. 2017. "Bifurcated Conversations in Sociological Studies of Religion and Gender." *Gender & Society* 31 (5): 647–76.

Avishai, Orit, Afshan Jafar, and Rachel Rinaldo. 2015. "A Gender Lens on Religion." *Gender & Society* 29 (1): 5–25.

Badran, Margot. 2005. "Between Secular and Islamic Feminism/s: Reflections on the Middle East and Beyond." *Journal of Middle East Women's Studies* 1 (1): 6–28.

Balk, Gene. 2018. "Washingtonians Are Less Religious Than Ever, Gallup Poll Finds." *Seattle Times,* April 20, 2018.

Balmer, Randall, Kate Bowler, Anthea Butler, Maura Jane Farrelly, Wes Markofski, Robert Orsi, Jerry Z. Park, James Clark Davidson, Matthew Avery Sutton, and Grace Yukich. 2017. "Forum: Studying Religion in the Age of Trump." *Religion and American Culture: A Journal of Interpretation* 27 (1): 2–56.

Balogun, Oluwakemi M. 2012. "Cultural and Cosmopolitan: Idealized Femininity and Embodied Nationalism in Nigerian Beauty Pageants." *Gender & Society* 26 (3): 357–81.

Banks, Antoine J. 2016. "Are Group Cues Necessary? How Anger Makes Ethnocentrism among Whites a Stronger Predictor of Racial and Immigration Policy Opinions." *Political Behavior* 38 (3): 635–57.

Barron, Jessica M. 2016. "Managed Diversity: Race, Place, and an Urban Church." *Sociology of Religion* 77 (1): 18–36.

Bartkowski, John P. 2001. *Remaking the Godly Marriage: Gender Negotiation in Evangelical Families.* New Brunswick, NJ: Rutgers University Press.

———. 2004. *The Promise Keepers: Servants, Soldiers, and Godly Men.* New Brunswick, NJ: Rutgers University Press.

Bartkowski, John P., and Jen'nan Ghazal Read. 2003. "Veiled Submission: Gender, Power, and Identity among Evangelical and Muslim Women in the United States." *Qualitative Sociology* 26 (1): 71–92.

Barton, Bernadette. 2011. "My Auto/Ethnographic Dilemma: Who Owns the Story?" *Qualitative Sociology* 34 (3): 431.

———. 2012. *Pray the Gay Away: The Extraordinary Lives of Bible Belt Gays.* New York: New York University Press.

Bebbington, David W. 1989. "Religion and Society in the Nineteenth Century." *Historical Journal* 32 (4): 997–1004.

Becker, Penny Edgell. 1998. "Making Inclusive Communities: Congregations and the 'Problem' of Race." *Social Problems* 45 (4): 451–72.

Bell, Leslie. 2013. *Hard to Get: Twenty-Something Women and the Paradox of Sexual Freedom.* Berkeley: University of California Press.

Bellah, Robert N., Richard Madsen, William M. Sullivan, Ann Swidler, and Steven M. Tipton. 1985. *Habits of the Heart: Individualism and Commitment in American Life.* 1st ed., with a new preface. Berkeley: University of California Press.

Berezin, Mabel. 2017. "On the Construction Sites of History: Where Did Donald Trump Come From?" *American Journal of Cultural Sociology* 5.

Berger, Peter. 1967. *The Sacred Canopy: Elements of a Sociological Theory of Religion.* Garden City, NY: Anchor Doubleday.

Bernstein, Elizabeth. 2010. "Militarized Humanitarianism Meets Carceral Feminism: The Politics of Sex, Rights, and Freedom in Contemporary Anti-trafficking Campaigns." *Signs: Journal of Women in Culture and Society* 36 (1): 45–71.

Beyerlein, Kraig. 2004. "Specifying the Impact of Conservative Protestantism on Educational Attainment." *Journal for the Scientific Study of Religion* 43 (4): 505–18.

Beyerlein, Kraig, and Mark Chaves. 2003. "The Political Activities of Religious Congregations in the United States." *Journal for the Scientific Study of Religion* 42 (2): 229–46.

Bhambra Gurminder K. 2017. "Brexit, Trump, and 'Methodological Whiteness': On the Misrecognition of Race and Class." *British Journal of Sociology* 68 (S1): S214–32.

Bielo, James S. 2011. *Emerging Evangelicals: Faith, Modernity, and the Desire for Authenticity*. New York: New York University Press.

Birnie-Porter, Carolyn, and Mitchell Hunt. 2015. "Does Relationship Status Matter for Sexual Satisfaction? The Roles of Intimacy and Attachment Avoidance in Sexual Satisfaction across Five Types of Ongoing Sexual Relationships." *Canadian Journal of Human Sexuality* 24 (2).

Blee, Kathleen M., and Sandra McGee Deutsch. 2012. *Women of the Right: Comparisons and Interplay Across Borders*. University Park: Penn State University Press.

Bonilla-Silva, Eduardo. 1997. "Rethinking Racism: Toward A Structural Interpretation." *American Sociological Review* 62.

———. 2009. *Racism without Racists: Color-Blind Racism and the Persistence of Racial Inequality in America*. 3rd ed. Lanham: Rowman & Littlefield.

Bonilla-Silva, Eduardo, and Tyrone Forman. 2000. "'I Am Not a Racist but . . .': Mapping White College Students' Racial Ideology in the USA." *Discourse & Society* 11:50–85.

Boorstein, Michelle. 2017. "The Stunning Difference between White and Black Evangelical Voters in Alabama." *Washington Post,* December 13, 2017.

Bostdorff, Denise M. 2017. "Obama, Trump, and Reflections on the Rhetoric of Political Change." *Rhetoric and Public Affairs* 20 (4): 695–706.

Bourdieu, Pierre. 1977. "The Economics of Linguistic Exchanges." *Social Science Information* 16 (6): 645–68.

———. 1991. *Language and Symbolic Power*. Cambridge, MA: Harvard University Press.

Bracey, Glenn, and Wendy Moore. 2017. "'Race Tests': Racial Boundary Maintenance in White Evangelical Churches." *Sociological Inquiry* 87 (2): 282–302.

Brasher, Brenda E. 1998. *Godly Women: Fundamentalism and Female Power*. New Brunswick, NJ: Rutgers University Press.

Braunstein, Ruth. 2017. "Muslims as Outsiders, Enemies, and Others: The 2016 Presidential Election and the Politics of Religious Exclusion." *American Journal of Cultural Sociology* 5 (3): 355–72.

———. 2018. "A (More) Perfect Union? Religion, Politics, and Competing Stories of America." *Sociology of Religion* 79 (2): 172–95.

Bridges, Tristan, and C. J. Pascoe. 2014. "Hybrid Masculinities: New Directions in the Sociology of Men and Masculinities." *Sociology Compass* 8 (3): 246–58.

Brint, Steven, and Seth Abrutyn. 2010. "Who's Right about the Right? Comparing Competing Explanations of the Link between White Evangelicals and Conservative Politics in the United States." *Journal for the Scientific Study of Religion* 49 (2): 328–50.

Brittain, Christopher Craig. 2018. "Racketeering in Religion: Adorno and Evangelical Support for Donald Trump." *Critical Research on Religion* 6 (3): 269–88.

Bruce, Steve. 2002. *God Is Dead: Secularization in the West.* Hoboken, NJ: Wiley.

Buber, Martin. [1923] 1958. *I and Thou.* Translated by Ronald Gregor Smith. New York: Charles Scribner's Sons.

Buggs, Shantel Gabrieal, Jennifer Patrice Sims, and Rory Kramer. 2020. "Rejecting White Distraction: A Critique of the White Logic and White Methods in Academic Publishing." *Ethnic and Racial Studies* 43 (8): 1384–92.

Burge, Ryan P. 2020a. "How Many 'Nones' Are There? Explaining the Discrepancies in Survey Estimates." *Review of Religious Research* 62 (1).

———. 2020b. "How Many Nones Are There? Maybe More Than We Thought." *Religion in Public.* https://religioninpublic.blog/2020/03/09/how-many-nones-are-there-maybe-more-than-we-thought/.

Burge, Ryan P., and Andrew R. Lewis. 2018. "Measuring Evangelicals: Practical Considerations for Social Scientists." *Politics and Religion* 11 (4): 745–59.

Burke, Kelsy. 2012. "Women's Agency in Gender-Traditional Religions: A Review of Four Approaches." *Sociology Compass* 6 (2): 122–33.

———. 2014. "What Makes a Man: Gender and Sexual Boundaries on Evangelical Christian Sexuality Websites." *Sexualities* 17 (1–2): 3–22.

———. 2016. *Christians under Covers: Evangelicals and Sexual Pleasure on the Internet.* Berkeley: University of California Press.

Burke, Kelsy, and Trenton M. Haltom. 2020. "Created by God and Wired to Porn: Redemptive Masculinity and Gender Beliefs in Narratives of Religious Men's Pornography Addiction Recovery." *Gender & Society* 34 (2): 233–58.

Burke, Kelsy, and Amy Moff Hudec. 2015. "Sexual Encounters and Manhood Acts: Evangelicals, Latter-Day Saints, and Religious Masculinities." *Journal for the Scientific Study of Religion* 54 (2): 330–44.

Burke, Kelsy, and Amy McDowell. 2021. "White Women Who Lead: God, Girlfriends, and Diversity Projects in a National Evangelical Ministry." *Sociology of Race and Ethnicity* 7 (1): 86–100.

Butler, Anthea. 2021. *White Evangelical Racism: The Politics of Morality in America.* Chapel Hill: University of North Carolina Press.

Butler, Judith. 2006. *Gender Trouble: Feminism and the Subversion of Identity.* 1st ed. New York: Routledge.

Calhoun, Craig, Mark Juergensmeyer, and Jonathan VanAntwerpen. 2011. *Rethinking Secularism.* Oxford: Oxford University Press.

Callimachi, Rukmini. 2016. "Was Orlando Shooter Really Acting for ISIS? For ISIS, It's All the Same." *New York Times,* June 12, 2016.

Campbell, David E. 2006. "Religious 'Threat' in Contemporary Presidential Elections." *Journal of Politics* 68 (1): 104–15.

———, ed. 2007. *A Matter of Faith: Religion in the 2004 Presidential Election.* Washington, DC: Brookings Institution Press.

Cancian, Francesca M. 1987. *Love in America : Gender and Self-Development.* New York: Cambridge University Press.

Carpenter, Laura, and John DeLamater. 2012. *Sex for Life: From Virginity to Viagra, How Sexuality Changes throughout Our Lives.* New York: New York University Press.

Chapp, Christopher B., and Kevin Coe. 2019. "Religion in American Presidential Campaigns, 1952–2016: Applying a New Framework for Understanding Candidate Communication." *Journal for the Scientific Study of Religion* 58 (2): 398–414.

Charmaz, Kathy. 2014. *Constructing Grounded Theory.* Thousand Oaks, CA: SAGE.

Chaves, Mark. 2010. "SSSR Presidential Address Rain Dances in the Dry Season: Overcoming the Religious Congruence Fallacy." *Journal for the Scientific Study of Religion* 49 (1): 1–14.

———. 2012. "National Congregations Study." https://sites.duke.edu/ncsweb/.

Chenoweth, Erica, and Jeremy Pressman. 2017. "Analysis: This Is What We Learned by Counting the Women's Marches." *Washington Post,* February 7, 2017.

Chilson, Morgan. 2014. "Prayer in School: The Case That 'Kicked God Out of the Schools.'" *Newsmax.* www.newsmax.com/fastfeatures/prayer-in-school-case/2014/11/02/id/603389/.

Cho, Sumi, Kimberlé Williams Crenshaw, and Leslie McCall. 2013. "Toward a Field of Intersectionality Studies: Theory, Applications, and Praxis." *Signs: Journal of Women in Culture and Society* 38 (4): 785–810.

Chokshi, Niraj. 2018. "Trump Voters Driven by Fear of Losing Status, Not Economic Anxiety, Study Finds." *New York Times,* April 24, 2018.

Claassen, Ryan, and Andrew Povtak. 2010. "The Christian Right Thesis: Explaining Longitudinal Change in Participation among Evangelical Christians." *Journal of Politics* 72 (1): 2–15.

Connell, Raewyn. 1987. *Gender and Power: Society, the Person, and Sexual Politics.* Stanford: Stanford University Press.

———. 2005. *Masculinities.* 2nd ed. Berkeley: University of California Press.

———. 2006. "Glass Ceilings or Gendered Institutions? Mapping the Gender Regimes of Public Sector Worksites." *Public Administration Review* 66 (6): 837–49.

Connell, Raewyn, and James W. Messerschmidt. 2005. "Hegemonic Masculinity: Rethinking the Concept." *Gender & Society* 19 (6): 829–59.

Cook, Jerry, and Stanley C. Baldwin. 2009. *Love, Acceptance and Forgiveness: Being Christian in a Non-Christian World.* Ventura, CA: Gospel Light.

Cooper, Helene, and Thomas Gibbons-Neff. 2018. "Trump Approves New Limits on Transgender Troops in the Military." *New York Times,* March 24, 2018.

Cottom, Tressie McMillan. 2019. *Thick, and Other Essays.* Reprint ed. New York: New Press.

Cox, Daniel, and Robert Jones. n.d. "America's Changing Religious Identity." *PRRI.* www.prri.org/research/american-religious-landscape-christian-religiously-unaffiliated/.

Crenshaw, Kimberle. 1997. "Intersectionality and Identity Politics: Learning from Violence Against Women of Color." In *Reconstructing Political Theory: Feminist Perspectives,* edited by M.L. Shanley and U. Narayan, pp. 178–93. University Park: Penn State University Press.

Davis, Julie Hirschfeld. 2018. "Trump's Immigration Tweets Followed by Policy Plans to Match." *New York Times,* April 4, 2018.

Deckman, Melissa, and Erin Cassese. 2021. "Gendered Nationalism and the 2016 US Presidential Election: How Party, Class, and Beliefs about Masculinity Shaped Voting Behavior." *Politics & Gender* 17 (2): 277–300.

Delehanty, Jack, Penny Edgell, and Evan Stewart. 2019. "Christian America? Secularized Evangelical Discourse and the Boundaries of National Belonging." *Social Forces* 97 (3): 1283–306.

DeRogatis, Amy. 2015. *Saving Sex: Sexuality and Salvation in American Evangelicalism.* Oxford: Oxford University Press.

Desmond, Matthew, and Mustafa Emirbayer. 2009. "What Is Racial Domination?" *Du Bois Review: Social Science Research on Race* 6 (2): 335–55.

Dias, Elizabeth. 2015. "How Evangelicals Are Changing Their Minds on Gay Marriage." *Time,* January 15, 2015.

———. 2018. "'God Is Going to Have to Forgive Me': Young Evangelicals Speak Out." *New York Times,* November 1.

———. 2019. "Evangelical Magazine Christianity Today Calls for Trump's Removal." *New York Times,* December 19, 2019.

Diefendorf, Sarah. 2015. "After the Wedding Night: Sexual Abstinence and Masculinities over the Life Course." *Gender & Society* 29 (5): 647–69.

———. 2019. "Contemporary Evangelical Responses to Feminism and the Imagined Secular." *Signs: Journal of Women in Culture and Society* 44 (4): 1003–26.

Dillon, Michele. 1999. *Catholic Identity: Balancing Reason, Faith, and Power.* Cambridge: Cambridge University Press.

Dillon, Michele, and Paul Wink. 2007. *In the Course of a Lifetime: Tracing Religious Belief, Practice, and Change.* 1st ed. Berkeley: University of California Press.

Doane, Ashley Woody. 2017. "Beyond Color-Blindness: (Re) Theorizing Racial Ideology." *Sociological Perspectives* 60 (5): 975–91.

Domke, David, and Kevin Coe. 2008. *The God Strategy: How Religion Became a Political Weapon in America.* New York: Oxford University Press.

Dougherty, Kevin D., and Andrew L. Whitehead. 2011. "A Place to Belong: Small Group Involvement in Religious Congregations." *Sociology of Religion* 72 (1): 91–111.

Dowling, Julie. 2014. *Mexican Americans and the Question of Race.* Austin: University of Texas Press.

Du Mez, Kristin Kobes. 2020. *Jesus and John Wayne: How White Evangelicals Corrupted a Faith and Fractured a Nation.* Illustrated ed. New York: Liveright.

Dupont, Carolyn Renee. 2015. *Mississippi Praying: Southern White Congregations and the Civil Rights Movement.* New York: New York University Press.

Durbin, Sean. 2020. "From King Cyrus to Queen Esther: Christian Zionists' Discursive Construction of Donald Trump as God's Instrument." *Critical Research on Religion.*

Durkheim, Émile. 1982. *Rules of Sociological Method.* 2nd ed. New York: Free Press.

Eberstadt, Nicholas. 2016. *Men without Work: America's Invisible Crisis.* West Conshohocken, PA: Templeton Foundation Press.

Edgell, Penny. 2012. "A Cultural Sociology of Religion: New Directions." *Annual Review of Sociology* 38 (1): 247–65.

———. 2017. "An Agenda for Research on American Religion in Light of the 2016 Election." *Sociology of Religion* 78 (1): 1–8.

Edgell, Penny, Joseph Gerteis, and Douglas Hartmann. 2006. "Atheists as 'Other': Moral Boundaries and Cultural Membership in American Society." *American Sociological Review* 71 (2): 211–34.

Edgell, Penny, and Eric Tranby. 2007. "Religious Influences on Understandings of Racial Inequality in the United States." *Social Problems* 54 (2): 263–88.

Edwards, Korie L. 2008. *The Elusive Dream: The Power of Race in Interracial Churches.* New York: Oxford University Press.

———. 2016. "The Space Between: Exploring How Religious Leaders Reconcile Religion and Politics." *Journal for the Scientific Study of Religion* 55 (2): 271–87.

Effron, Daniel A. 2018. "Opinion: Why Trump Supporters Don't Mind His Lies." *New York Times,* April 30, 2018.

Emerson, Michael O., and Lenore M. Knight Johnson. 2018. "Soul of the City: The Depth of How 'Urban' Matters in the Sociology of Religion." *Sociology of Religion* 79 (1): 1–19.

Emerson, Michael O., and Christian Smith. 2001. *Divided by Faith: Evangelical Religion and the Problem of Race in America.* New York: Oxford University Press.

Emerson, Robert M., Rachel I. Fretz, and Linda L. Shaw. 2011. *Writing Ethnographic Fieldnotes.* 2nd ed. Chicago: University of Chicago Press.

Epstein, Steven. 1994. "A Queer Encounter: Sociology and the Study of Sexuality." *Sociological Theory* 12 (2): 188–202.

Erzen, Tanya. 2006. *Straight to Jesus.* Berkeley: University of California Press.

Evans, Curtis J. 2009. "White Evangelical Protestant Responses to the Civil Rights Movement." *Harvard Theological Review* 102 (2): 245–73.

Fea, John. 2018. *Believe Me: The Evangelical Road to Donald Trump.* Grand Rapids, MI: William B. Eerdmans.

Ferber, Abby L. 2012. "The Culture of Privilege: Color-Blindness, Postfeminism, and Christonormativity." *Journal of Social Issues* 68 (1): 63–77.

Fine, Michelle. 1988. "Sexuality, Schooling, and Adolescent Females: The Missing Discourse of Desire." *Harvard Educational Review* 58 (1): 29–54.

Fischer, Nancy L. 2013. "Seeing 'Straight,' Contemporary Critical Heterosexuality Studies and Sociology: An Introduction." *Sociological Quarterly* 54 (4): 501–10.

Frankenberg, Ruth. 1993. *White Women, Race Matters: The Social Construction of Whiteness.* 5th ed. Minneapolis: University Of Minnesota Press.

Freedman, Estelle B., and Barrie Thorne. 1984. "Introduction to 'The Feminist Sexuality Debates.'" *Signs: Journal of Women in Culture and Society* 10 (1): 102–5.

Gallagher, Sally K. 2003. *Evangelical Identity and Gendered Family Life.* New Brunswick, NJ: Rutgers University Press.

———. 2004a. "The Marginalization of Evangelical Feminism." *Sociology of Religion* 65 (3): 215–37.

———. 2004b. "Where Are the Antifeminist Evangelicals? Evangelical Identity, Subcultural Location, and Attitudes toward Feminism." *Gender & Society* 18 (4): 451–72.

Gallagher, Sally K., and Christian Smith. 1999. "Symbolic Traditionalism and Pragmatic Egalitarianism: Contemporary Evangelicals, Families, and Gender." *Gender & Society* 13 (2): 211–33.

Gerber, Alan S., Donald P. Green, and Ron Shachar. 2003. "Voting May Be Habit-Forming: Evidence from a Randomized Field Experiment." *American Journal of Political Science* 47 (3): 540–50.

Gerber, Lynne. 2008. "The Opposite of Gay: Nature, Creation, and Queerish Ex-Gay Experiments." *Nova Religio: The Journal of Alternative and Emergent Religions* 11 (4): 8–30.

———. 2009. "My Body Is a Testimony: Appearance, Health, and Sin in an Evangelical Weight-Loss Program." *Social Compass* 56 (3): 405–18.

———. 2010. "Class and American Religion: Historic Debates, New Perspectives." *Religion Compass* 4 (6): 388–99.

———. 2011. *Seeking the Straight and Narrow: Weight Loss and Sexual Reorientation in Evangelical America.* Chicago: University of Chicago Press.

———. 2012. "Fat Christians and Fit Elites: Negotiating Class and Status in Evangelical Christian Weight-Loss Culture." *American Quarterly* 64 (1): 61–84.

———. 2015. "Grit, Guts, and Vanilla Beans: Godly Masculinity in the Ex-Gay Movement." *Gender & Society* 29 (1): 26–50.

Gerson, Michael. 2018. "The Last Temptation." *Atlantic,* April 2018.

Giddens, Anthony. 1984. *The Construction of Society.* Cambridge: Polity.

Gilkes, Cheryl Townsend. 2010. "Still the 'Most Segregated Hour': Religion, Race, and the American Experience." In *The SAGE Handbook of Race and Ethinic Studies,* edited by Patricia Hill Collins and John Solomos, pp. 415–43. Thousand Oaks, CA: SAGE.

Glaser, Barney, and Anselm Strauss. 1967. *The Discovery of Grounded Theory: Strategies for Qualitative Research.* Chicago: Aldine.

Glass, Jennifer. 2019. "Why Aren't We Paying Attention? Religion and Politics in Everyday Life." *Sociology of Religion* 80 (1): 9–27.

Glenn, Evelyn Nakano. 2015. "Settler Colonialism as Structure: A Framework for Comparative Studies of U.S. Race and Gender Formation." *Sociology of Race and Ethnicity.*

Glenn, Evelyn Nakano, Grace Chang, and Linda Rennie Forcey. 2016. *Mothering: Ideology, Experience, and Agency.* New York: Routledge.

Goffman, Erving. 1959. *The Presentation of Self in Everyday Life.* 1st ed. New York: Anchor.

———. 1963. *Stigma: Notes on the Management of Spoiled Identity.* Reissue ed. New York: Touchstone.

———. 1967. *Interaction Ritual—Essays on Face-to-Face Behavior.* New York: Pantheon.

————. 1971. *Relations in Public: Microstudies of the Public Order.* New York: Basic Books.

Goh, Robbie B. H. 2008. "Hillsong and 'Megachurch' Practice: Semiotics, Spatial Logic and the Embodiment of Contemporary Evangelical Protestantism." *Material Religion* 4 (3): 284–304.

Gómez, Laura E. 2018. *Manifest Destinies: The Making of the Mexican American Race.* 2nd ed. New York: New York University Press.

Goodstein, Laurie. 2017. "Donald Trump Reveals Evangelical Rifts That Could Shape Politics for Years." *New York Times,* December 21, 2017.

————. 2018. "'This Is Not of God': When Anti-Trump Evangelicals Confront Their Brethren." *New York Times,* May 23, 2018.

Gorski, Philip. 2017. "Why Evangelicals Voted for Trump: A Critical Cultural Sociology." *American Journal of Cultural Sociology* 5 (3): 338–54.

Gorski, Philip, David Kyuman Kim, John Torpey, and Jonathan VanAntwerpen. 2012. *The Post-Secular in Question: Religion in Contemporary Society.* New York: New York University Press.

Green, Adam Isaiah. 2008. "The Social Organization of Desire: The Sexual Fields Approach*." *Sociological Theory* 26 (1): 25–50.

Green, Emma. 2016a. "Most American Christians Believe They're Victims of Discrimination." *Atlantic,* June 30, 2016.

————. 2016b. "There Will Be an Evangelical Reckoning over Donald Trump." *Atlantic.* www.theatlantic.com/politics/archive/2016/11/the-evangelical-reckoning-on-trump/507161/.

Green, John C. 1996. "A Look at the 'Invisible Army': Pat Robertson's 1988 Activist Corps." In *Religion and the Culture Wars: Dispatches from the Front.* Lanham, MD: Rowman & Littlefield.

————. 2007. *The Faith Factor: How Religion Influences American Elections.* Westport, CT: Praeger.

Green, John C., James L. Guth, Corwin E. Smidt, and Lyman A. Kellstedt. 1996. *Religion and the Culture Wars.* Lanham, MD: Rowman & Littlefield.

Grenz, Stanley James. 1998. *Welcoming but Not Affirming: An Evangelical Response to Homosexuality.* Louisville, KY: Westminster John Knox Press.

Griffith, R. Marie. 1997. *God's Daughters: Evangelical Women and the Power of Submission.* Berkeley: University of California Press.

Guilford, Gwynn. 2016. "Donald Trump's 'Support' of LGBT Communities in One Image." *Quartz,* October 31, 2016.

Guth, James L. 1996. "The Politics of the Christian Right." In *Religion and the Culture Wars: Dispatches from the Front.* Lanham, MD: Rowman & Littlefield.

Habermas, Jürgen. 1987. *The Theory of Communicative Action: Lifeworld and System.* 2 vols. Translated by Thomas McCarthy. Boston: Beacon.

Hagerman, Margaret A. 2018. *White Kids.* New York: New York University Press.

Hahl, Oliver, Minjae Kim, and Ezra W. Zuckerman Sivan. 2018. "The Authentic Appeal of the Lying Demagogue: Proclaiming the Deeper Truth about Political Illegitimacy." *American Sociological Review* 83 (1): 1–33.

Halberstam, Judith. 1998. *Female Masculinity.* Durham: Duke University Press.

Hall, David D., ed. 1997. *Lived Religion in America*. Princeton: Princeton University Press.

Halperin, David M., and Valerie Traub. 2009. *Gay Shame*. Chicago: University of Chicago Press.

Harding, Susan. 1991. "Representing Fundamentalism: The Problem of the Repugnant Cultural Other." *Social Research* 58 (2): 373–93.

Harley, Richard M. 1980. "Evangelicals May Not Fall into Ranks behind 'New Right.'" *Christian Science Monitor,* October 29.

Harvard University. 2018. *Janelle Ibaven, Foursquare Chaplain at Harvard*. www.youtube.com/watch?v=YvaLkLEaWkQ.

Heath, Melanie. 2003. "Soft-Boiled Masculinity: Renegotiating Gender and Racial Ideologies in the Promise Keepers Movement." *Gender & Society* 17 (3): 423–44.

———. 2012. *One Marriage under God: The Campaign to Promote Marriage in America*. New York: New York University Press.

———. 2013. "Sexual Misgivings: Producing Un/Marked Knowledge in Neoliberal Marriage Promotion Policies." *Sociological Quarterly* 54 (4): 561–83.

———. 2019. "Espousing Patriarchy: Conciliatory Masculinity and Homosocial Femininity in Religiously Conservative Families." *Gender & Society* 33 (6): 888–910.

Heim, Joe. 2017. "Excitement and Caution as Liberty University Awaits Trump's Commencement Speech." *Washington Post,* May 6, 2017.

Hills, Darrius. 2018. "Back to a White Future: White Religious Loss, Donald Trump, and the Problem of Belonging." *Black Theology* 16 (1): 38–52.

Hochschild, Arlie Russell. 1979. "Emotion Work, Feeling Rules, and Social Structure." *American Journal of Sociology* 85 (3): 551–75.

———. 2016a. *Strangers in Their Own Land*. New York: New Press.

———. 2016b. "The Ecstatic Edge of Politics: Sociology and Donald Trump." *Contemporary Sociology* 45 (6): 683–89.

hooks, bell. 1994. *Teaching to Transgress: Education as the Practice of Freedom*. New York: Routledge.

Horstman, Barry M. 2002. "Billy Graham: A Man with a Mission. (Special Section)." *Cincinnati Post (Cincinnati, OH),* June 27, 2002.

Ingersoll, Julie. 2002. *Evangelical Christian Women: War Stories in the Gender Battles*. New York: New York University Press.

Ingraham, Chrys. 1994. "The Heterosexual Imaginary: Feminist Sociology and Theories of Gender." *Sociological Theory* 12 (2): 203–19.

Inskeep, Steve. 2018. "Trump's Stance on Migrant Caravan Energizes White Evangelical Voters." *NPR Morning Edition.*

Irby, Courtney Ann. 2014a. "Dating in Light of Christ: Young Evangelicals Negotiating Gender in the Context of Religious and Secular American Culture." *Sociology of Religion* 75 (2): 260–83.

———. 2014b. "Moving beyond Agency: A Review of Gender and Intimate Relationships in Conservative Religions." *Sociology Compass* 8 (11): 1269–80.

Jackson, Stevi. 2006. "Interchanges: Gender, Sexuality and Heterosexuality: The Complexity (and Limits) of Heteronormativity." *Feminist Theory* 7 (1): 105–21.

Jamieson, Kathleen Hall, and Joseph N. Cappella. 2008. *Echo Chamber: Rush Limbaugh and the Conservative Media Establishment*. New York: Oxford University Press.

Jeffers, Gromer, Jr. 2016. "Trump Rallies in Dallas, Says U.S. Must Stop People with 'Hate in Their Hearts' from Entering Country." *Dallas News*. www.dallasnews.com/news/2016/06/17/trump-rallies-in-dallas-says-u-s-must-stop-people-with-hate-in-their-hearts-from-entering-country/.

Jenkins, Philip. 2006. *Decade of Nightmares: The End of the Sixties and the Making of Eighties America*. New York: Oxford: Oxford University Press.

Jones, Robert P. 2016. "Opinion: The Rage of White, Christian America." *New York Times,* November 10, 2016.

———. 2020. *White Too Long: The Legacy of White Supremacy in American Christianity*. Illustrated ed. New York: Simon & Schuster.

Jones, Tiffany. 2018. "Trump, Trans Students and Transnational Progress." *Sex Education* 18 (4): 479–94.

Jung, Cindy. 2016. "Trump and Christian Morals." *Harvard International Review,* December 21, 2016.

Jung, Gowoon. 2020. "Mothers and Nation in the Global Era: The Role of Evangelical Protestant Mothers in the Discursive Construction of Multicultural Korea." *International Sociology* 35 (3): 353–74.

Kandiyoti, Deniz. 1988. "Bargaining With Patriarchy." *Gender & Society* 2 (3): 274–90.

Kellstedt, Lyman A., John C. Green, James L. Guth, and Corwin E. Smidt. 1994. "Religious Voting Blocs in the 1992 Election: The Year of the Evangelical?" *Sociology of Religion* 55 (3): 307–26.

Kelly, Kimberly. 2012. "In the Name of the Mother: Renegotiating Conservative Women's Authority in the Crisis Pregnancy Center Movement." *Signs: Journal of Women in Culture and Society* 38 (1): 203–30.

Kidd, Thomas S. 2019. *Who Is an Evangelical? The History of a Movement in Crisis*. New Haven, CT: Yale University Press.

Kitzinger, Celia, Sue Wilkinson, and Rachel Perkins. 1992. "Theorizing Heterosexuality." *Feminism & Psychology* 2 (3): 293–324.

Knott, Kim. 2008. "Spatial Theory and the Study of Religion." *Religion Compass* 2 (6): 1102–16.

Knowles, Eric, and Sarah DiMuccio. 2018. "How Donald Trump Appeals to Men Secretly Insecure about Their Manhood." *Washington Post.*

Krull, Laura M. 2020. "Liberal Churches and Social Justice Movements: Analyzing the Limits of Inclusivity." *Journal for the Scientific Study of Religion* 59 (1): 84–100.

Kruse, Kevin M. 2015. *One Nation under God: How Corporate America Invented Christian America*. New York: Basic Books.

Kuipers, Giselinde. 2006. "The Social Construction of Digital Danger: Debating, Defusing and Inflating the Moral Dangers of Online Humor and Pornography in the Netherlands and the United States." *New Media & Society* 8 (3): 379–400.

Kurtzleben, Danielle. 2016. "POLL: White Evangelicals Have Warmed To Politicians Who Commit 'Immoral' Acts." *NPR.Org.* www.npr.org/2016/10

/23/498890836/poll-white-evangelicals-have-warmed-to-politicians-who-commit-immoral-acts.

Laats, Adam. 2010. "A New Kind of Protestant." In *Fundamentalism and Education in the Scopes Era,* pp. 11–21. New York: Palgrave Macmillan.

Lakoff, George. 2016. "Understanding Trump." *HuffPost.* www.huffpost.com/entry/understanding-trump_b_11144938.

Lamont, Michèle, and Marcel Fournier, eds. 1992. *Cultivating Differences: Symbolic Boundaries and the Making of Inequality.* 1st ed. Chicago: University of Chicago Press.

Layman, Geoffrey. 2001. *The Great Divide: Religious and Cultural Conflict in American Party Politics.* New York: Columbia University Press.

Lee, Deborah Jian. 2016. *Rescuing Jesus: How People of Color, Women, and Queer Christians Are Reclaiming Evangelicalism.* Reprint ed. Boston: Beacon.

Le Miere, Jason. 2018. "Majority of U.S. Muslims Now Support Gay Marriage, While White Evangelical Christians Remain Opposed." *Newsweek.* www.newsweek.com/muslim-white-evangelical-gay-marriage-907627.

Lewis, Amanda E. 2004. "'What Group?' Studying Whites and Whiteness in the Era of 'Color-Blindness.'" *Sociological Theory* 22 (4): 623–46.

Lewis, Andrew R. 2019. "The Transformation of the Christian Right's Moral Politics." *Forum* 17 (1): 25–44.

Lewis, Andrew R., and Dana Huyser De Bernardo. 2010. "Belonging without Belonging: Utilizing Evangelical Self-Identification to Analyze Political Attitudes and Preferences." *Journal for the Scientific Study of Religion* 49 (1): 112–26.

Lindsay, D. Michael. 2007. *Faith in the Halls of Power: How Evangelicals Joined the American Elite.* Oxford: Oxford University Press.

Lipka, Michael. n.d. "Millennials Increasingly Are Driving Growth of 'Nones.'" *Pew Research Center.* www.pewresearch.org/fact-tank/2015/05/12/millennials-increasingly-are-driving-growth-of-nones/.

Lipsitz, George. 1995. "The Possessive Investment in Whiteness: Racialized Social Democracy and the 'White' Problem in American Studies." *American Quarterly* 47 (3): 369–87.

———. 2011. *How Racism Takes Place.* Philadelphia: Temple University Press.

Lockerbie, Brad. 2013. "Race and Religion: Voting Behavior and Political Attitudes." *Social Science Quarterly* 94 (4): 1145–58.

Luhrmann, Tanya M. 2012. *When God Talks Back: Understanding the American Evangelical Relationship with God.* New York: Alfred A. Knopf.

Luker, Kristin. 2007. *When Sex Goes to School: Warring Views on Sex—and Sex Education—since the Sixties.* New York: W. W. Norton.

———. 2010. *Salsa Dancing into the Social Sciences: Research in an Age of Info-Glut.* Cambridge, MA: Harvard University Press.

Malka, Ariel, Yphtach Lelkes, Sanjay Srivastava, Adam B. Cohen, and Dale T. Miller. 2012. "The Association of Religiosity and Political Conservatism: The Role of Political Engagement." *Political Psychology* 33 (2): 275–99.

Marsden, George M. 2006. *Fundamentalism and American Culture.* New York: Oxford University Press.

Marti, Gerardo. 2020. *American Blindspot: Race, Class, Religion, and the Trump Presidency.* Lanham, MD: Rowman & Littlefield.

Martin, Jonathan. 2016. "Donald Trump Seizes on Orlando Shooting and Repeats Call for Temporary Ban on Muslim Migration." *New York Times,* June 12, 2016.

Martin, Patricia Yancey. 2004. "Gender as Social Institution." *Social Forces* 82 (4): 1249–73.

Masci, David. 2016. "How Income Varies among U.S. Religious Groups | Pew Research Center." www.pewresearch.org/fact-tank/2016/10/11/how-income-varies-among-u-s-religious-groups/.

Maxwell, Angie, and Todd Shields. 2019. *The Long Southern Strategy: How Chasing White Voters in the South Changed American Politics.* New York: Oxford University Press.

Mayes, Brittany, Leslie Shapiro, Chris Alcantara, David Weigel, Scott Clement, Emily Guskin, Kevin Uhrmacher, Ann Gerhart, Claudia Deane, Alana Safarpour, Jocelyn Kiley, and Ben Kirchner. 2020. "Exit Poll Results and Analysis for the 2020 Presidential Election." *Washington Post.* www .washingtonpost.com/elections/interactive/2020/exit-polls/presidential-election-exit-polls/.

McDermott, Monika L. 2009. "Religious Stereotyping and Voter Support for Evangelical Candidates." *Political Research Quarterly* 62 (2): 340–54.

McElwee, Sean, and Jason McDaniel. 2017. "Economic Anxiety Didn't Make People Vote Trump, Racism Did." *Nation,* May 8, 2017.

McFarland, Michael J., Bradley R. E. Wright, and David L. Weakliem. 2011. "Educational Attainment and Religiosity: Exploring Variations by Religious Tradition." *Sociology of Religion* 72 (2): 166–88.

McGoey, Linsey. 2012. "The Logic of Strategic Ignorance: The Logic of Strategic Ignorance." *British Journal of Sociology* 63 (3): 533–76.

McGuire, Meredith B. 2008. *Lived Religion: Faith and Practice in Everyday Life.* Oxford: Oxford University Press.

Meadow, Tey. 2019. *Trans Kids.* Berkeley: University of California Press.

Merritt, Jonathan. 2015. "What Is an 'Evangelical'?" *Atlantic.* www.theatlantic .com/politics/archive/2015/12/evangelical-christian/418236/.

Miller, Eric C. 2018. "Fear, Nostalgia and Power Drove Evangelicals to Trump: Interview with Evangelical Scholar John Fea." *Religion Dispatches.* http:// religiondispatches.org/fear-nostalgia-and-power-drove-evangelicals-to-trump-interview-with-evangelical-scholar-john-fea/.

Monson, J. Quin, and J. Baxter Oliphant. 2007. "Microtargeting and the Instrumental Mobilization of Religious Conservatives." In *A Matter of Faith: Religion in the 2004 Presidential Election,* edited by David E. Campbell, 95–119. Washington, DC: Brookings Institution Press.

Moon, Dawne. 2004. *God, Sex, and Politics: Homosexuality and Everyday Theologies.* Chicago: University of Chicago Press.

Moon, Dawne, and Theresa W. Tobin. 2018. "Sunsets and Solidarity: Overcoming Sacramental Shame in Conservative Christian Churches to Forge a Queer Vision of Love and Justice." *Hypatia* 33 (3): 451–68.

Moon, Dawne, Theresa W. Tobin, and J.E. Sumerau. 2019. "Alpha, Omega, and the Letters in Between: LGBTQI Conservative Christians Undoing Gender." *Gender and Society* 33 (4): 583–606.

Moore, Wendy Leo. 2008. *Reproducing Racism: White Space, Elite Law Schools, and Racial Inequality*. Lanham, MD: Rowman & Littlefield.

Moore, Wendy Leo, and Joyce M. Bell. 2017. "The Right to Be Racist in College: Racist Speech, White Institutional Space, and the First Amendment." *Law & Policy* 39 (2): 99–120.

Morone, James A. 2003. *Hellfire Nation: The Politics of Sin in American History*. New Haven, CT: Yale University Press.

Moslener, Sara. 2015. *Virgin Nation: Sexual Purity and American Adolescence*. New York: Oxford University Press.

Mueller, Jennifer C. 2017. "Producing Colorblindness: Everyday Mechanisms of White Ignorance." *Social Problems* 64 (2): 219–38.

———. 2020. "Racial Ideology or Racial Ignorance? An Alternative Theory of Racial Cognition." *Sociological Theory* 38 (2): 142–69.

Mutz, Diana C. 2018. "Status Threat, Not Economic Hardship, Explains the 2016 Presidential Vote." *Proceedings of the National Academy of Sciences* 115 (19): E4330–39.

Nagel, Joane. 2003. *Race, Ethnicity, and Sexuality: Intimate Intersections, Forbidden Frontiers*. New York: Oxford University Press.

Newman, Brian, and Mark Caleb Smith. 2007. "Fanning the Flames: Religious Media Consumption and American Politics." *American Politics Research* 35 (6): 846–77.

New York Times. 2016. "Christopher Andrew Leinonen." *New York Times*, June 15, 2016.

Nippert-Eng, Christena. 2015. *Watching Closely: A Guide to Ethnographic Observation*. 1st ed. New York: Oxford University Press.

Noll, Mark A. 2001. *American Evangelical Christianity: An Introduction*. Hoboken, NJ: Blackwell.

O'Brien, Jodi. 2010. "Seldom Told Tales from the Field: Guest Editor's Introduction to the Special Issue." *Journal of Contemporary Ethnography* 39 (5): 471–82.

O'Brien, John, and Eman Abdelhadi. 2020. "Re-Examining Restructuring: Racialization, Religious Conservatism, and Political Leanings in Contemporary American Life." *Social Forces* 99 (2): 474–503.

Oyakawa, Michelle. 2019. "Racial Reconciliation as a Suppressive Frame in Evangelical Multiracial Churches." *Sociology of Religion* 80 (4): 496–517.

Pachuki, Mark, Sabrina Pendergrass, and Michèle Lamont. 2007. "Boundary Processes: Recent Theoretical Developments and New Contributions." *Poetics* 35 (6): 331–51.

Pascoe, C.J. 2011. *Dude, You're a Fag: Masculinity and Sexuality in High School*. Berkeley: University of California Press.

———. 2018. "What to Do with Actual People? Thinking through a Queer Social Science Method." In *Other, Please Specify, Queer Methods in Sociology*, edited by D. Compton, T. Meadow, and K. Schilt. Berkeley: University of California Press.

Pascoe, C. J., and Sarah Diefendorf. 2019. "No Homo: Gendered Dimensions of Homophobic Epithets Online." *Sex Roles* 80 (3): 123–36.

Paulson, Michael. 2014. "Divisive Pastor Quits Post at Seattle Church." *New York Times,* October 15, 2014.

Pear, Robert. 2018. "Trump Plan Would Cut Back Health Care Protections for Transgender People." *New York Times,* April 22, 2018.

Perry, Samuel L. 2020. "The Bible as a Product of Cultural Power: The Case of Gender Ideology in the English Standard Version." *Sociology of Religion* 81 (1): 68–92.

Perry, Samuel L., and Andrew L. Whitehead. 2019. "Christian America in Black and White: Racial Identity, Religious-National Group Boundaries, and Explanations for Racial Inequality." *Sociology of Religion* 80 (3): 277–98.

Pew. 2015a. "Religious Landscape Study." *Pew Research Center's Religion & Public Life Project.* www.pewresearch.org/religion/religious-landscape-study/.

———. 2015b. "U.S. Public Becoming Less Religious." *Pew Research Center's Religion & Public Life Project.* www.pewforum.org/2015/11/03/u-s-public-becoming-less-religious/.

———. 2015c. "What U.S. Religious Groups Think about Science Issues." *Pew Research Center Science & Society.* www.pewresearch.org/science/2015/10/22/science-and-religion/.

———. 2018. "How Millennials Today Compare with Their Grandparents 50 Years Ago." *Pew Research Center.* www.pewresearch.org/fact-tank/2018/03/16/how-millennials-compare-with-their-grandparents/.

———. 2019a. "In U.S., Decline of Christianity Continues at Rapid Pace." *Pew Research Center's Religion & Public Life Project.* www.pewforum.org/2019/10/17/in-u-s-decline-of-christianity-continues-at-rapid-pace/.

———. 2019b. "Attitudes on Same-Sex Marriage." *Pew Research Center.* www.pewresearch.org/religion/fact-sheet/changing-attitudes-on-gay-marriage/.

Pope, Liston. 1957. *The Kingdom beyond Caste.* 4th printing. New York: Friendship Press.

Prothero, Stephen. 2003. *American Jesus: How the Son of God Became a National Icon.* New York: Macmillan.

Puar, Jasbir K. 2007. *Terrorist Assemblages: Homonationalism in Queer Times.* Durham, NC: Duke University Press.

Putnam, Robert D., and David E. Campbell. 2010. *American Grace: How Religion Divides and Unites Us.* New York: Simon & Schuster.

Ray, Victor. 2019. "A Theory of Racialized Organizations." *American Sociological Review* 84 (1): 26–53.

Renold, Emma. 2007. "Primary School 'Studs': (De)Constructing Young Boys' Heterosexual Masculinities." *Men and Masculinities* 9 (3): 275–97.

Rich, Adrienne. 1980. "Compulsory Heterosexuality and Lesbian Existence." *Signs* 5 (4): 631–60.

Rinaldo, Rachel, and Jeffrey Guhin. 2019. "How and Why Interviews Work: Ethnographic Interviews and Meso-Level Public Culture." *Sociological Methods & Research* 51 (1).

Risman, Barbara J. 2004. "Gender as a Social Structure: Theory Wrestling with Activism." *Gender & Society* 18 (4): 429–50.

Robertson, Campbell. 2018. "A Quiet Exodus: Why Black Worshipers Are Leaving White Evangelical Churches." *New York Times,* March 9, 2018.

Santelli, John S., Leslie M. Kantor, Stephanie A. Grilo, Ilene S. Speizer, Laura D. Lindberg, Jennifer Heitel, Amy T. Schalet, Maureen E. Lyon, Amanda J. Mason-Jones, Terry McGovern, Craig J. Heck, Jennifer Rogers, and Mary A. Ott. 2017. "Abstinence-Only-until-Marriage: An Updated Review of U.S. Policies and Programs and Their Impact." *Journal of Adolescent Health* 61 (3): 273–80.

Saperstein, Aliya, and Andrew M. Penner. 2012. "Racial Fluidity and Inequality in the United States." *American Journal of Sociology* 118 (3): 676–727.

Schaumburg, Harry. 2009. *Undefiled: Redemption from Sexual Sin, Restoration for Broken Relationships.* New ed. Chicago: Moody.

Schilt, Kristen, Tey Meadow, and D'Lane Compton. 2018. "Queer Work in a Straight Discipline." In *Other, Please Specify: Queer Methods in Sociology.* Berkeley: University of California Press.

Schilt, Kristen, and Laurel Westbrook. 2009. "Doing Gender, Doing Heteronormativity: 'Gender Normals,' Transgender People, and the Social Maintenance of Heterosexuality." *Gender & Society* 23 (4): 440–64.

———. 2015. "Bathroom Battlegrounds and Penis Panics." *Contexts* 14 (3): 26–31.

Schippers, Mimi. 2007. "Recovering the Feminine Other: Masculinity, Femininity, and Gender Hegemony." *Theory and Society* 36 (1): 85–102.

Schnabel, Landon. 2016. "Gender and Homosexuality Attitudes across Religious Groups from the 1970s to 2014: Similarity, Distinction, and Adaptation." *Social Science Research* 55:31–47.

Schnabel, Landon, and Sean Bock. 2017. "The Persistent and Exceptional Intensity of American Religion: A Response to Recent Research." *Sociological Science* 4:686–700.

———. 2018. "The Continuing Persistence of Intense Religion in the United States: Rejoinder." *Sociological Science* 5:711–21.

Scholz, Susanne. 2005. "The Christian Right's Discourse on Gender and the Bible." *Journal of Feminist Studies in Religion* 21 (1): 81–100.

Schwadel, Philip. 2011. "Age, Period, and Cohort Effects on Religious Activities and Beliefs." *Social Science Research* 40 (1): 181–92.

———. 2014a. "Are White Evangelical Protestants Lower Class? A Partial Test of Church-Sect Theory." *Social Science Research* 46:100–116.

———. 2014b. "Birth Cohort Changes in the Association between College Education and Religious Non-Affiliation." *Social Forces* 93 (2): 719–46.

Seidman, Steven. 1996. *Queer Theory/Sociology.* Malden, MA: Blackwell.

Setzler, Mark, and Alixandra B. Yanus. 2018. "Why Did Women Vote for Donald Trump?" *PS: Political Science & Politics* 51 (3): 523–27.

Shellnutt, Kate. 2017. "Princeton Student Ministry Drops Evangelical Name after 80 Years." *News & Reporting.* www.christianitytoday.com/news/2017/october/princeton-christian-fellowship-drops-evangelical-name.html.

Simas, Elizabeth N., Scott Clifford, and Justin H. Kirkland. 2020. "How Empathic Concern Fuels Political Polarization." *American Political Science Review* 114 (1): 258–69.

Smidt, Corwin E. 2003. *Religion as Social Capital: Producing the Common Good*. Waco, TX: Baylor University Press.

Smidt, Corwin, and Paul Kellstedt. 1992. "Evangelicals in the Post-Reagan Era: An Analysis of Evangelical Voters in the 1988 Presidential Election." *Journal for the Scientific Study of Religion* 31 (3): 330–38.

Smith, Christian. 1998. *American Evangelicalism: Embattled and Thriving*. Chicago: University of Chicago Press.

———. 2000. *Christian America? What Evangelicals Really Want*. Berkeley: University of California Press.

Smith, David Norman, and Eric Allen Hanley. 2018. "The Anger Games: Who Voted for Donald Trump in the 2016 Election, and Why?" *Critical Sociology* 42 (2): 195–212.

Smith, Gregory A., and Jessica Martínez. 2016. "How the Faithful Voted: A Preliminary 2016 Analysis." *Pew Research Center*. www.pewresearch.org /fact-tank/2016/11/09/how-the-faithful-voted-a-preliminary-2016-analysis/.

Smith, Gregory A., and David Masci. 2016. "Exit Polls and the Evangelical Vote: A Closer Look." *Pew Research Center*. www.pewresearch.org/fact-tank/2016 /03/14/exit-polls-and-the-evangelical-vote-a-closer-look/.

———. 2018. "5 Facts about U.S. Evangelical Protestants." *Pew Research Center*. www.pewresearch.org/fact-tank/2018/03/01/5-facts-about-u-s-evangelical-protestants/.

Smith, Lauren E., and Lee Demetrius Walker. 2013. "Belonging, Believing, and Group Behavior: Religiosity and Voting in American Presidential Elections." *Political Research Quarterly* 66 (2): 399–413.

Smith, Tom W., Michael Davern, Jeremy Freese, and Stephen L. Morgan. 2019. General Social Surveys, 1972–2018 [machine-readable data file]. Principal Investigator Tom W. Smith; Co-Principal Investigators Michael Davern, Jeremy Freese, and Stephen L. Morgan; Sponsored by National Science Foundation. edited by NORC. Chicago: NORC, 2019.

Solnit, Rebecca. 2016. "'Hope Is an Embrace of the Unknown': Rebecca Solnit on Living in Dark Times." *Guardian*, July 15 2016.

Steensland, Brian, and Philip Goff. 2013. *The New Evangelical Social Engagement*. New York: Oxford University Press.

Stein, Arlene. 2001. *The Stranger Next Door: The Story of a Small Community's Battle over Sex, Faith, and Civil Rights*. 1st ed. Boston: Beacon.

Stewart, Evan, Penny Edgell, and Jack Delehanty. 2018. "The Politics of Religious Prejudice and Tolerance for Cultural Others." *Sociological Quarterly* 59 (1): 17–39.

Strolovitch, Dara Z., Janelle S. Wong, and Andrew Proctor. 2017. "A Possessive Investment in White Heteropatriarchy? The 2016 Election and the Politics of Race, Gender, and Sexuality." *Politics, Groups, and Identities* 5 (2): 353–63.

Sullivan, Amy. 2018. "Opinion: Democrats Are Christians, Too." *New York Times*, April 1, 2018.

Sutton, Matthew Avery. 2007. *Aimee Semple McPherson and the Resurrection of Christian America*. Cambridge, MA: Harvard University Press.

Swidler, Ann. 1986. "Culture in Action: Symbols and Strategies." *American Sociological Review* 51 (2): 273–86.

Tavory, Iddo. 2014. "The Situations of Culture: Humor and the Limits of Measurability." *Theory and Society* 43 (3): 275–89.

Taylor, Verta, and Leila J. Rupp. 1993. "Women's Culture and Lesbian Feminist Activism: A Reconsideration of Cultural Feminism." *Signs: Journal of Women in Culture and Society* 19 (1): 32–61.

Thomas, Jeremy N., and Daniel V. A. Olson. 2012. "Evangelical Elites' Changing Responses to Homosexuality 1960–2009." *Sociology of Religion* 73 (3): 239–72.

Tolman, Deborah. 2005. *Dilemmas of Desire: Teenage Girls Talk about Sexuality*. Cambridge, MA: Harvard University Press.

Tranby, Eric, and Douglas Hartmann. 2008. "Critical Whiteness Theories and the Evangelical 'Race Problem': Extending Emerson and Smith's Divided by Faith." *Journal for the Scientific Study of Religion* 47 (3): 341–59.

Vecsey, George. 1980. "Militant Television Preachers Try to Weld Fundamentalist Christians' Political Power." *New York Times,* January 21, 1980.

Vescio, Theresa K., and Nathaniel E. C. Schermerhorn. 2021. "Hegemonic Masculinity Predicts 2016 and 2020 Voting and Candidate Evaluations." *Proceedings of the National Academy of Sciences* 118 (2).

Voas, David, and Mark Chaves. 2016. "Is the United States a Counterexample to the Secularization Thesis?" *American Journal of Sociology* 121 (5): 1517–56.

———. 2018. "Even Intense Religiosity Is Declining in the United States: Comment." *Sociological Science* 5:694–710.

Waggoner, Michael. 2012. "When the Court Took on Prayer and the Bible in Public Schools." *Religion & Politics*. http://religionandpolitics.org/2012/06/25/when-the-court-took-on-prayer-the-bible-and-public-schools/.

Waidzunas, Tom. 2015. *The Straight Line: How the Fringe Science of Ex-Gay Therapy Reoriented Sexuality*. Minneapolis: University of Minnesota Press.

Wald, Kenneth D., Dennis E. Owen, and Samuel S. Hill. 1989. "Evangelical Politics and Status Issues." *Journal for the Scientific Study of Religion* 28 (1): 1–16.

Waldman, Paul. 2017. "Opinion: Pence's Unwillingness to Be Alone with a Woman Is a Symptom of a Bigger Problem." *Washington Post*. www.washingtonpost.com/blogs/plum-line/wp/2017/03/30/pences-unwillingness-to-be-alone-with-a-woman-is-a-symptom-of-a-bigger-problem/.

Ward, Jane. 2008. "Dude-Sex: White Masculinities and 'Authentic' Heterosexuality among Dudes Who Have Sex with Dudes." *Sexualities* 11 (4): 414–34.

———. 2015. *Not Gay*. New York: New York University Press.

———. 2020. *The Tragedy of Heterosexuality*. New York: New York University Press.

Warner, Michael .1993. Introduction to *Fear of a Queer Planet,* edited by Michael Warner. Minneapolis: University of Minnesota Press.

Wellman, James K. 2008. *Evangelical vs. Liberal: The Clash of Christian Cultures in the Pacific Northwest*. 1st ed. New York: Oxford University Press.

White, Heather R. 2017. "Virgin Nation: Sexual Purity and American Adolescence by Sara Moslener (Review)." *Journal of the History of Sexuality* 26 (2): 334–35.

Whitehead, Andrew L. 2010. "Sacred Rites and Civil Rights: Religion's Effect on Attitudes toward Same-Sex Unions and the Perceived Cause of Homosexuality*." *Social Science Quarterly* 91 (1): 63–79.

Whitehead, Andrew L., and Samuel L. Perry. 2020. *Taking America Back for God: Christian Nationalism in the United States.* New York: Oxford University Press.

Whitehead, Andrew L., Samuel L. Perry, and Joseph O. Baker. 2018. "Make America Christian Again: Christian Nationalism and Voting for Donald Trump in the 2016 Presidential Election." *Sociology of Religion* 79 (2): 147–71.

Whitehead, Andrew L., and Samuel Stroope. 2015. "Small Groups, Contexts, and Civic Engagement: A Multilevel Analysis of United States Congregational Life Survey Data." *Social Science Research* 52:659–70.

Wilkins, Amy C. 2009. "Masculinity Dilemmas: Sexuality and Intimacy Talk among Christians and Goths." *Signs: Journal of Women in Culture and Society* 34 (2): 343–68.

Willer, Robb, Christabel L. Rogalin, Bridget Conlon, and Michael T. Wojnowicz. 2013. "Overdoing Gender: A Test of the Masculine Overcompensation Thesis." *American Journal of Sociology* 118 (4): 980–1022.

Williams, Rhys H. 1997. *Cultural Wars in American Politics: Critical Reviews of a Popular Myth.* Hawthorne, NY: Aldine De Gruyter.

Winant, Howard. 2004. *The New Politics of Race: Globalism, Difference, Justice.* Minneapolis: University of Minnesota Press.

Wingfield, Adia Harvey. 2015. "If You Don't See Race, How Can You See Racial Inequality?" *Atlantic.* www.theatlantic.com/politics/archive/2015/09/color-blindness-is-counterproductive/405037/.

Wong, Janelle. 2018. "The Evangelical Vote and Race in the 2016 Presidential Election." *Journal of Race, Ethnicity and Politics* 3 (1): 81–106.

Wood, Michael, and Michael Hughes. 1984. "The Moral Basis of Moral Reform: Status Discontent vs. Culture and Socialization as Explanations of Anti-Pornography Social Movement Adherence." *American Sociological Review* 49 (1): 86–99.

Woodberry, Robert D., and Christian S. Smith. 1998. "Fundamentalism et al: Conservative Protestants in America." *Annual Review of Sociology* 24:25–56.

Worthen, Molly. 2016. "Opinion: Who Are the Gay Evangelicals?" *New York Times,* February 27, 2016.

Wuthnow, Robert. 1988. *The Restructuring of American Religion.* Princeton: Princeton University Press.

———. 1989. *The Struggle for America's Soul: Evangelicals, Liberals, and Secularism.* Grand Rapids, MI: Wm. B. Eerdmans.

Yukich, Grace. 2010. "Boundary Work in Inclusive Religious Groups: Constructing Identity at the New York Catholic Worker." *Sociology of Religion* 71 (2): 172–96.

Index